THE
BAKER'S
Manual

FIFTH EDITION

---

150 MASTER FORMULAS
FOR BAKING

JOSEPH AMENDOLA
NICOLE REES

JOHN WILEY & SONS, INC.

Interior design by Vertigo Design, NYC
Chapter opening art by Carolyn Vibbert

This book is printed on acid-free paper. ∞

For general information on our other products and services or for technical support, please contact our Customer Care Department within the United States at (800) 762-2974, outside the United States at (317) 572-3993 or fax (317) 572-4002.

Wiley also publishes its books in a variety of electronic formats. Some content that appears in print may not be available in electronic books.

Library of Congress Cataloging-in-Publication Data

Amendola, Joseph.
    The baker's manual : 150 master formulas for baking / Joseph Amendola, Nicole Rees.—5th ed.
        p.   cm.
    Includes bibliographical references and index.
    ISBN 0-471-40525-6 (pbk. : alk. paper)
        1. Baking.   2. Cake.   3. Pastry.   4. Desserts.   I. Rees, Nicole.   II. Title.

TX763 .A275 2002
641.8'15—dc21   2002028882

Printed in the United States of America.

10 9 8 7 6 5 4 3 2 1

CONTENTS

RECIPES

CHAPTER 5 EGG-BASED COMPONENTS

CHAPTER 6 PIES, TARTS, AND OTHER FRUIT DESSERTS

CHAPTER 8 WORKING WITH SUGAR

CHAPTER 7 COOKIES

CHAPTER 9 WORKING WITH CHOCOLATE

ACKNOWLEDGMENTS

Expert baker and veteran pastry chef Lisa Bell created the bread and laminate recipes for this book. Without her dedication to introducing the complexities of artisan bread baking to beginners, this book would not have been possible. Though all the recipes in this edition have been updated to reflect current tastes, the biggest change in baking over the past twenty years has been the artisan bread movement. I am grateful for her expertise.

—Nicole Rees

PREFACE

The Baker's Manual has been completely revised to better serve pastry chefs at the beginning of the twenty-first century. In doing so, this edition addresses a wider readership than ever. Today there are many career choices for pastry professionals. Neighborhood bakeries, coffeehouses, fine restaurants and hotels, artisan bread bakeries, catering companies, corporate cafeterias, resorts, cruise lines, food companies, and specialty cake businesses are just some of the options facing culinary graduates. Today's pastry chef may be the sole pastry chef in a kitchen or work as part of a large team of bakers. He or she may be self-employed and work freelance.

To accommodate such diversity, the two biggest changes to the book are the new recipes and a different recipe format. These new recipes are less centered on European classic desserts and reflect current tastes and trends in American cuisine. Sweetness level, dark versus milk chocolate, and butter as a primary fat are examples of preferences that have changed over time. The goal of this book is to provide reliable component recipes that can be assembled into any number of desserts, casual or formal. The dual-recipe format allows enthusiastic home bakers to try a single batch of a recipe, but provides professional chefs with a scaled-up version (see Chapter 1 for details). The ingredients for a single batch are written by volume, and the larger batch by weight, which should make pastry chefs at any level comfortable.

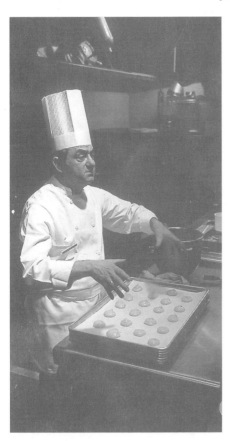

Photograph of Chef Joseph Amendola, former instructor for The Culinary Institute of America.

The Baker's Manual is a companion book to *Understanding Baking*. The latter book covers the science and theory behind pastry work, and the former provides the core recipes. Though each volume is independent of the other, they become more powerful tools when used together. Equipped with a set of reliable, basic recipes and the knowledge of how they work, each chef can tinker, experiment, and create new versions. Ultimately, these volumes encourage creativity, variety, and individuality. Enjoy!

CHAPTER 1

HOW TO USE THIS BOOK

The Baker's Manual has been revised to accommodate both home cooks and professional chefs by providing two different batch sizes for each recipe. A 5-quart capacity stand mixer will accommodate the small batch, and a 20-quart mixer fits the larger batch. The ingredient amounts for the small batch are listed first by volume, which best suits novice and home cooks. The ingredients for the larger batch are listed by weight. Professional cooks do not have time to scoop out 35 cups of flour, nor can they afford the inconsistency that measuring flour by volume creates. A scale makes measuring fast and accurate. Commercial mixer bowl sizes are generally 20, 40, 60, 80, and 120 quarts. Many bakeries purchase collars for the mixer that adapt to another bowl size—for example, so that both 40-quart and 60-quart bowls may be used on the same machine. Since you know that the second batch size is four times the first, it is a simple matter of multiplying to calculate a batch size to suit your own equipment.

The chapter on bread is written differently. Because the slightest variation in measuring can radically change the finished texture of a bread, all ingredients should be weighed, even when making a single loaf. A cup of flour can contain anywhere from 3.5 to 6 ounces of flour depending on how densely it is scooped into the cup, and even careful, consistent measuring will yield differences of $\frac{1}{2}$ ounce from cup to cup. There is no second batch size given for breads because bread-makers use what is called a baker's percentage system to change their yield (see Chapter 2). In a chef's mind, breads are not so much recipes as formulas. They contain few ingredients beyond flour, water, and yeast, so each product is thought of as a ratio of one ingredient (usually flour) to the others.

With the exception of bread and laminates, most of the recipes lack detailed discussions of ingredients and cooking methods. *Understanding Baking,* the companion volume to this book, covers those topics in great detail. Sufficient information regarding technique is included with the recipes to assure success even for those new to pastry.

CHOOSING A SCALE

Digital and balance scales are preferred by professional bakers. Spring-loaded scales are not as precise, nor do they hold up well over time. Digital and balance scales can be recalibrated to maintain accuracy. That said, there are scales to suit every need. The more weight a scale can handle, and the greater its accuracy to within a gram, the more expensive it will be. For home cooks, there are inexpensive digital scales available that will hold up to 11 pounds and be accurate to within $^1/_4$ ounce. These scales are fine to start with, and they also convert between grams and ounces.

Midsize bakeries have digital scales that handle more weight, so that chefs can place bowls onto the scale, tare the scale to zero, and scoop one ingredient after another into the bowl, taring the scale to zero after each. Often, when making cakes or cookies, a sifter is placed onto the bowl so that the dry ingredients are mixed and weighed all at once. These scales are usually accurate to within a few grams, which makes it possible to weigh small amounts of powerful ingredients like leavenings, salt, and spices. Otherwise, those ingredients should be measured by volume.

Digital scales may display weight differently. One scale may read 1 pound 12 ounces and another 1.75 pounds. The numbers are the same, but seeing ounces displayed as decimals can be confusing. The number 1.3125 looks ridiculous, but it is 1 pound 5 ounces, or 21 ounces. Such is the complexity of living with the English system, which the majority of Americans use. To make conversions easier, see the appendix for a list of decimal equivalents for fractions and decimal equivalents for ounces.

How I Measure

Everyone measures a little differently, and these differences often reveal a bias. In looking at my notes for this book, I notice that I have a bias toward a midsize bakery that employs four to eight bakers seven days a week. I also realized that much of how I measure I learned in home economics, well before I embarked on a culinary education. It was there that I first learned the difference between measuring dry and liquid ingredients.

In the back of this book is a list of volume and weight equivalents for many ingredients. I measure flours, cocoa, confectioners' sugar, and starches by the spoon-and-sweep method, which means I lightly spoon the ingredient into a measuring cup and sweep off the excess with the blade of a knife or spatula. I get 4.25 ounces of all-purpose flour per cup. If you merely dip your measuring cup into the flour, you will end up with between 5 and 5.5 ounces per cup. You can see the advantages of a scale already. Granulated sugar doesn't vary much between dipping or spooning, so I scoop it directly, but brown sugars I pack tightly into the cup.

I did not weigh the liquid ingredients; they are in fluid-ounce form. This is standard practice in small to midsize operations, except in breadmaking. Many bread bakeries have a special water system that allows the chef to instantly get a specific amount of water at a specific temperature, and the amounts are input by weight. The bread chapter lists liquid ingredients both by volume (fluid ounces) and weight (ounces).

Eggs are a special case. Some bakeries exclusively use eggs in the shell, and therefore specify a number of whole eggs, even for large batches. An equivalent number of bakeries use containers of frozen whole eggs, egg whites, and egg yolks. Large eggs are approximately 1.7 ounces out of the shell; for the larger batch I multiplied that times the number of eggs, so that the eggs may be scaled. You can easily convert back to a number of whole eggs. If the eggs are separated in the recipe, I provided the weight of the whites and yolks, respectively.

Leavenings, salt, and spices are listed by volume. In my opinion, only a scale accurate to within a gram or two is appropriate for measuring these things. The exception to this is in the bread chapter, where weights are listed for every ingredient to provide all the information necessary to use the baker's percentage system.

About Mixing

It is assumed your mixer will have a paddle, whip, and dough hook attachment. Assume that beating eggs or heavy cream requires the whip, creaming butter and sugar for batters requires the paddle, and making bread doughs requires the dough hook. Exceptions will be specified within the recipe text.

PREHEATING OVENS

Unless a recipe says to do otherwise, it is assumed you will have preheated your oven to the appropriate temperature.

THE PASTRY KITCHEN

This book has been written to accommodate the wide range of career choices for today's pastry chefs. Some chefs work in restaurants, others in bakeries, coffee shops, and catering kitchens. A smaller number venture out on their own, starting a wedding cake business, for example. With that in mind, all the recipes in this book can be made at home with good results and without expensive equipment beyond a 5-quart capacity heavy-duty stand mixer and a reliable oven. Throughout the book, however, you may notice references to specialized pieces of equipment that are commonly found in midsize bakeries. Below is a brief summary of each.

As long as an **oven** is temperature-accurate and doesn't have pronounced hot and cold spots, it is fine for bread and pastry. These basic ovens are called **conventional ovens.** Many bakeries have sets of double-doored **convection ovens.** Convection ovens have fans that circulate the hot air throughout the oven, making it cook more efficiently and evenly. As a result, convection ovens appear to bake "hotter" than other ovens. The recipes in this book have been tested in a conventional oven, so if you use them in a convection oven, decrease the heat by 25°F. The fans in most convection ovens can be turned off, which is often necessary when baking soufflés, pâte à choux, and meringue-topped pies.

Bread bakers seek out special ovens. **Deck ovens, steam injection ovens,** and **masonry ovens** make baking artisanal bread easier and more efficient. Masonry ovens radiate and hold much more heat than do other ovens, and "steam injection" means that no one has to spray the baking loaves by hand every few minutes.

I left out **cooktops** as a category because most chefs can produce fine custard and candy even off a rickety old electric range. That said,

portable cooktops can be very helpful. Long the mainstay of catering, portable cooktops give pastry chefs working in restaurants some space of their own. Modern ones, like the induction cooktop, heat only the contents in the pan. The cooktop stays cool and less heat radiates into the room.

Mixers in bakeries are usually just larger versions of the home cook's trusty KitchenAid—that is, until we get to the large industrial-size bakeries. Though the brand name Hobart dominates, any heavy-duty stand mixer is fine. Hobarts start at 20-quart capacity and go on up to 140 quarts, usually in increments of 20 quarts. You will need the three basic mixing attachments: the paddle, the whip, and the dough hook. Try to have several bowls for your mixer. Many other attachments can be purchased for a Hobart, such as a grinder.

Bread dough mixers are much more expensive than regular mixers and much more specialized. First, mixing bread in a machine requires a lot of power, and if you plan to have a large bread selection, your stand mixer may not be up to the stress. Second, specialized dough mixers have a more gentle mixing action that better mimics hand kneading. Often, the mixing bowl itself revolves. Third, a good dough mixer has a special tilting function, so you can easily pour the dough out of the bowl.

Proofers and **retarders** look like refrigerators, but they are much more sophisticated. They can be programmed to slowly increase temperature and humidity, or quickly bring the temperature down. This allows the fermentation rate of yeasted doughs to be easily and carefully controlled to maximize flavor, improve the texture of the finished product, and even save on labor. If your proofer is programmed to slowly thaw Danish dough and bring it through a rise, then you may not have to be in the kitchen at 3 A.M.

Dough sheeters are used to perfectly roll out pie dough, laminate doughs, and cookie doughs. If you make pastries and pies every day and have a small staff, a dough sheeter will save you money in the long run from all the time it takes to do turns on croissants and roll tart shells by hand. The dough passes between two rollers, which can be set to varying distances apart, and comes out smooth and even. If you have a very small space, a portable tabletop model is a possibility, but the constant rearranging can be a hassle.

If you plan to fry anything regularly, get a **deep fryer.** There is only one doughnut recipe in this book; however, one of the greatest bits of pastry wisdom to be passed around is to not fry without a dedicated fryer. It is safer, wastes less oil, is easier to control, and makes the process bearable. Ovens are hot, but frying is hotter.

Every pastry kitchen should have one **food processor**, at least a large-capacity Cuisinart or, even better, a commercial machine.

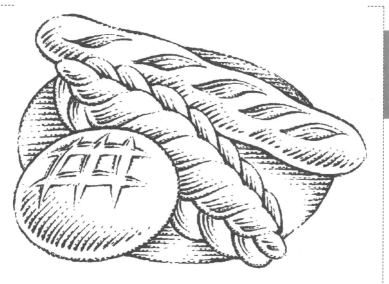

CHAPTER 2

YEAST BREADS

Risen bread is one of man's great achievements. The humble combination of wheat flour, water, and yeast is one of the simplest formulas there is, but it requires the most complex baking skills you'll ever learn. More than any other baking category, breadmaking relies on the baker's knowledge, skilled hands, and "feel" for the small corrections needed day to day to produce a consistent product.

For a period of about seventy-five years, it seemed that machines would supplant human hands entirely, but in the last ten years or so, the baking industry has witnessed a return to handcrafted breads, referred to as the artisan bread movement. Though factory-produced loaves line our store shelves today, even supermarket chains are producing breads that at least have the appearance of being handcrafted. A significant portion of the market is willing to bear the higher cost of labor and overhead incurred by artisan breadmaking.

Consequently, the following discussions of methods and the choices of recipes give an overview of this revitalization. Science, in the form of precise measurements, times, and temperatures, can eliminate much guesswork, but nothing will ever take the place of your eyes and hands in making truly great bread.

Defining Gluten

Bread relies on gluten for its unique texture. When wheat flour is mixed with water and kneaded, the glutenin and gliadin proteins present in the flour not only bond with the water but also link and crosslink with one another, forming sheets of a flexible, resilient film called gluten. Gluten traps air and gases formed by yeast, causing bread to rise. As the yeast feeds on the sugars, it produces both alcohol and carbon dioxide. The carbon dioxide is released upon contact into the air bubbles, enlarging them. In baking, the alcohol converts to gas, enlarging the bubbles even more, producing ovenspring. Flexible starch granules held in place in the gluten network also bend around the air bubbles. The gluten protein eventually cooks, releases its water into the starch, and begins to firm. This provides the structural framework for the loaf of bread. As the starch gelatinizes, it also becomes semi-rigid, giving even more support. This is the concept of breadmaking in a nutshell. What follows is the detailed version.

MEASURING INGREDIENTS

All ingredients in breadmaking should be scaled, especially flour. Cup measurements of flour differ radically from one individual to the next. Weighing the water and other liquids like milk also ensures accuracy, especially when increasing batch sizes. For this reason, liquids are measured by both cup and weight when they account for more than a few tablespoons. Remember that a liquid measured in ounces is a weight measurement, and when measured in fluid ounces (fl oz) is a volume measurement. Very small quantities of other ingredients like yeast and salt have been listed by tablespoon and teaspoon as well as weight because scales that can accurately weigh such small amounts are expensive. However, when increasing these recipes by any significant amount, multiply the weight rather than the volume. Weight is also used in the baker's percentage method discussed below. Small variations multiplied to large quantities can make a big difference in both the dough and the finished bread's texture.

BAKER'S PERCENTAGES

When making bread, bakers frequently refer to formulas rather than recipes. Most breads are simple ratios of flour, water, yeast, and salt. From day to day, bakers may vary batch sizes, increasing or decreasing the formula to produce the required number of loaves. The baker's percentage system is the easiest way for them to scale formulas up or down, determining exactly how much of each ingredient is needed. It's also a great way to fix mistakes—say, if you accidentally add too much flour to a batch of dough. The system is weight-based and either the metric (kilograms and grams) or avoirdupois (pounds and ounces) system may be used as long as the units are the same for all ingredients. Although metric may be easier in the long run, most home bakers and many bakeries still rely on pounds and ounces, so the following examples use avoirdupois weights.

In the baker's percentage system, each ingredient is expressed as a percentage of the total flour weight: thus, the flour weight is always 100 percent. If more than one flour is used, their combined weight comprises that 100 percent. In the following formula (not an actual recipe, just an example), the combined weight of the two flours is 50 pounds. Therefore, 50 is the number by which we divide each ingredient weight to determine its percentage (in relationship to the 100 percent of total flour).

40 POUNDS BREAD FLOUR = 80%

10 POUNDS WHOLE WHEAT FLOUR = 20%

33 POUNDS WATER = 66%

1 POUND SALT = 2%

.6 POUND YEAST = 1.2%

Now, this example yields only 84.6 pounds of dough. What if we wanted to make 200 loaves, each scaled at 1 pound 8 ounces? First, determine the total amount of dough needed by multiplying 200 by 1.5 (the weight of each loaf), to get 300 pounds. Then, to calculate the weight of each ingredient in the larger recipe, you add up all the percentages in the above formula. This total percentage value is 169.2. Divide this number by the desired dough weight, 300 pounds, to get .564. Round this number up to get .6. Then multiply the percentage amount for each ingredient in the above recipe by .6 to obtain the larger weight required by the larger recipe.

80% BREAD FLOUR × .6 = 48 POUNDS

20% WHOLE WHEAT FLOUR × .6 = 12 POUNDS

66% WATER × .6 = 39.60 POUNDS

2% SALT × .6 = 1.2 POUNDS

1.2% YEAST × .6 = .7 POUND

For formulas using pre-ferments (see page 33), the weight of all the flour used in the sponge must be added to the weight of the flour used in the final dough to obtain the number to use to determine percentages. For example, in the following formula, the flour weights in the pre-ferment and final dough add up to a total of 60 pounds, so

60 pounds is the 100 percent used in the baker's percentage system. Therefore, the percentages for the other ingredients below were obtained by dividing each ingredient's weight by 60.

PRE-FERMENT INGREDIENTS

15 POUNDS BREAD FLOUR = 25%

15 POUNDS WATER = 25%

.5 POUND YEAST = .83%

INGREDIENTS FOR FINAL DOUGH

33 POUNDS BREAD FLOUR = 55%

12 POUNDS WHOLE WHEAT FLOUR = 20%

24.6 POUNDS WATER = 41%

1.2 POUNDS SALT = 2%

This system is also very helpful, as mentioned above, when you make a mistake. Let's say instead of the 33 pounds of bread flour called for in the final dough above, you mistakenly added 43 pounds. This accidental increase means your divisor number would be 70 instead of 60 in determining the corrected new weights of the other ingredients in order to keep the recipe at the correct proportions. This trick thus saves you ingredients cost and labor. Making a few extra loaves is better than having to throw out everything.

To determine the percentage of pre-ferment you need in the final dough, add all the percentage figures together, to get 168.83. Divide the percentage totals for the pre-ferment, 50.83, by this number to obtain 30 percent. Divide the percentage total for the final dough by the same number to get 70 percent.

WATER AND DOUGH TEMPERATURE

Controlling water temperature is important for regulating the dough's development. Ideal dough temperature is around 78°F for straight-rise doughs and around 75°F for doughs made with pre-ferments or natural starters. Cold water (usually somewhere between 55° and 63°F) is used in pre-ferment stages (see below). In straight doughs that are mixed at a high speed for a relatively long period of time, a lot of heat is created by friction. The dough temperature increases one degree for each minute it is mixed at medium speed. A reduction in dough temperature prevents fermentation from happening too rapidly and avoids off-flavors. To achieve this end, a percentage of the formula's total water content can be added as ice or ice water.

HYDRATION

Adequately hydrated doughs have a more appealing open crumb, a chewy texture, and a longer shelf life. The hydration rate of dough can be calculated by adding the weight of the liquids, then adding the weight of the flours and grains and dividing the weight of the liquid by the weight of the dry ingredients. Ideal hydration begins around 62 percent and extends to 80 percent for really wet doughs like the Italian bread, ciabatta. If using a sponge or wild yeast starter, its liquid and dry weights must be factored in as well.

INGREDIENTS

YEAST

A number of yeast products are available today and understanding how to best utilize them is key. There is no rule of thumb for how much yeast to use, since that is determined by the fermentation time desired (for development of complex flavors) and whether the dough includes lots of sugar and fat. Yeast will multiply as long as good conditions prevail, so even a pinch will leaven several loaves—if you give them time.

The bread recipes here most frequently call for **fresh yeast** (also called baker's yeast, compressed yeast, or cake yeast) when a commercial yeast is required. Most traditional and/or artisan bakers prefer fresh yeast for several reasons. One, it is very reliable; it produces the most carbon dioxide gas per cell, giving it superior leavening capability. Two, fresh yeast is only slightly dehydrated (about 30 percent); it requires no hydration time in warm water, unlike active dry yeast. Fresh yeast works well with cool or even cold liquids, as do wild yeast leavens (starters). Three, finely crumbled fresh yeast can be incorporated directly into the dough after the autolyse period with no additional steps. Make sure the yeast is mixed in well before adding the salt, as direct contact with salt can damage the yeast cells.

Active dry yeast is dehydrated to 5 percent moisture content to improve shelf life and must be hydrated in warm water, ideally 110°F, for 5 to 10 minutes. (Very hot water should never touch yeast directly; it is killed instantly at 140°F.) The time active dry yeast requires for rehydration is called the lag time. Warm water not only increases the rate of fermentation but also prevents damage to yeast cells. Very cold water can cause the cell walls to rupture easily. This not only kills the yeast but also causes the damaged cells to release glutathione into the dough, which interrupts gluten formation.

Instant yeast (marketed under such brand names as Quick-Rise and Rapid-Rise to the home consumer), does not make dough rise faster than regular active dry yeast. Actually, instant yeast produces more gas per cell, which means *less of it* is needed to ferment a dough. Instant yeast was developed with porous cell walls that instantly absorb water, eliminating rehydration or lag time and allowing the yeast to be combined directly with the flour. However, this advance is not particularly convenient when working with recipes that require an autolyse period, a cool overall dough temperature, or a long fermentation period. If you do choose to use instant yeast in a recipe of this nature, you must combine it with a percentage of the water called for in the recipe that has been heated (to 105°F). Otherwise, the instant yeast may be starved for moisture already absorbed by the flour during the autolyse. The stress can cause its cell walls to rupture. An overall cool temperature of available liquid may also prevent the instant yeast from rehydrating. Mix in the warm yeast liquid on low speed before adding the salt at the end of the autolyse period.

Osmotolerant instant active dry yeast is employed in a few of the rich sweet dough recipes, where sugar, milk, egg, and fat are in abundance and water is not. To compensate for the sluggish performance of yeast in this environment, great amounts of yeast are usually called for in such recipes. Osmotolerant yeast does not require such bolstering, as it has been specifically selected for its optimum leavening capacities in low-moisture, high-sugar doughs. *Osmotolerant* is a big word, but the concept is very simple: Osmosis is the process of how a solution (here, water) moves through a semipermiable membrane (the cells walls of yeast). In a moisture-poor dough with added sugar, the yeast must compete with the proteins and starches in the flour and the sugar for what little water is available. This creates great osmotic pressure on the yeast cells, which have trouble maintaining moisture equilibrium. Osmotolerant describes the special yeast that can withstand (is tolerant of) the osmotic pressure.

FLOUR

Flour is the most important ingredient in bread, and the importance of choosing the right flour for the right job cannot be stressed too much. Each type of flour was developed with a specific purpose in mind. Strong flours are needed to form an elastic, good-quality gluten structure that makes great bread. Weak flours have less gluten-forming capacity and are best suited to cakes and pastry. On pages 18 and 19 is a list of basic flours used in these recipes, their relative protein contents, and their suggested uses.

SALT

Salt tightens the gluten network, which may be a hindrance to machine-mixed doughs and a blessing to doughs made with soft water. Salt slows or inhibits yeast fermentation. A fast-dissolving salt is preferred for bread doughs.

DIASTATIC MALT POWDER

A common additive, diastatic malt powder is added to flours to ensure that they are enzymatically balanced. Malt powder is literally sprouted grain that has been carefully dry-roasted (to preserve its enzymes) and ground into a powder. It is considered a dough enhancer, but malt powder primarily benefits yeast, ensuring that it has appropriate food. **Nondiastatic malt** is malt powder that is not enzymatically active. **Barley malt syrup** is a liquid form of malt powder that is slightly sweet.

TABLE 2.1 YEAST EQUIVALENTS					
Fresh (Cake or Compressed) Yeast		**Active Dry Yeast**		**Instant Active Dry Yeast**	
VOLUME	WEIGHT	VOLUME	WEIGHT	VOLUME	WEIGHT
1/4 tsp	.0275 oz	1/8 tsp	.01375 oz	pinch	.01 oz
1/2 tsp	.055 oz	1/4 tsp	.0275 oz	Generous 1/8 tsp	.021 oz
3/4 tsp	.0825 oz	3/8 tsp	.04125 oz	Generous 1/4 tsp	.03 oz
1 tsp	.11 oz	1/2 tsp	.055 oz	3/8 tsp	.04125 oz
1 1/2 tsp	1.65 oz	3/4 tsp	.0825 oz	Generous 1/2 tsp	.061875 oz
2 tsp	.22 oz	1 tsp	.11 oz	3/4 tsp	.0825 oz
2 1/2 tsp	.275 oz	1 1/4 tsp	.1375 oz	Scant 1 tsp	.10 oz
1 Tbs	.33 oz	1 1/2 tsp	.165 oz	1 1/8 tsp	.12375 oz
4 tsp	.44 oz	2 tsp	.22 oz	1 1/2 tsp	.165 oz
4 1/2 tsp	.495 oz	2 1/4 tsp	.2475 oz	1 3/4 tsp	.1856 oz
5 tsp	.55 oz	2 1/2 tsp	.275 oz	Scant 2 tsp	.2065 oz
2 Tbs	.66 oz	1 Tbs	.33 oz	2 1/4 tsp	.25 oz (.2475 exact)

This table makes substituting one type of yeast for another quick and easy. Each horizontal line of the chart represents yeast equivalents, so 2 tablespoons crumbled fresh yeast can be used instead of 2 1/4 teaspoons instant active dry yeast. Naturally, the tediously long decimals indicate that the weight is more accurate that the volume. The numbers are not shortened; if they were rounded more, then multiplying up would lead to inaccuracies.

For large scale baking, use the ratio 2:1:.075 to when converting recipes to a different type of yeast. This ratio is visible when looking at the numbers in the chart: The fresh yeast is double the amount of active dry yeast by weight, and the equivalent amount of instant yeast is 75 percent the amount of active dry yeast.

BASIC FLOURS, THEIR PROTEIN CONTENT, AND SUGGESTED USES

All-purpose flour	Available bleached or unbleached; a blend of hard spring wheat and soft winter wheat; protein content between 9 and 11 percent.
Bread flour	Available bleached or unbleached, bromated or not; hard red spring wheat; protein content between 11.5 and 13 percent; usually includes enzymatic corrective; slightly granular to the touch.
High-gluten flour	Unbleached; dark spring northern wheat; 14 percent protein content; used in combination with bread or all-purpose flours; good for highly machined doughs or in combination with grain flours lacking gluten.
Whole wheat flour	Unbleached; contains all of the wheat grain including bran, germ, and endosperm. Soft whole wheat flour is used in chemically leavened batters like muffins and pancakes; protein content is around 11 percent. Whole wheat from hard red winter wheat is used primarily in bread; protein content is around 13 percent.
Rye flours	White rye flour is milled from the center of the endosperm; cream or light-rye flour is from the next layer out of the endosperm; dark rye flour comes primarily from the outer portion of the endosperm. Various blends are available. Rye is also available as a meal, that is, ground from the whole kernel. Rye meal is available in various particle sizes, ranging from fine, to medium, to coarse. The coarse grade of rye meal is what is commonly referred to as pumpernickel flour. Rye chops are the equivalent of cracked wheat.
Patent durum or semolina flour	Fine silky grind of extremely hard cold-weather wheat; unbleached, pale yellow in character; protein content of around 12 percent; particularly good in hearth breads.
Pastry flour	Available bleached or unbleached; soft winter wheat; protein content around 9 percent.

BASIC FLOURS, THEIR PROTEIN CONTENT, AND SUGGESTED USES (Continued)

Cake flour	Always bleached and enriched; soft winter wheat, particularly from warmer growing regions; protein content around 7.5 to 8 percent; ideal for cakes, pie crusts, biscuits.
Artisanal bread flour	Unbleached; lower protein content of around 11.5 percent; performs in hearth breads much like lower protein European flours; equivalent to United States flours with higher extraction rate.
Organic flour	Always unbleached and unbromated; growing conditions are just now being standardized by the federal government; expensive, up to twice the cost of regular flour; thought by many bakers to be good for beginning naturally fermented starters owing to high content of microflora.
Wheat bran	Removed in milling, sold separately, and contains all of the cellulose in wheat that provides fiber; used extensively in health breads and in muffins.
Wheat germ	Removed in milling, toasted and sold separately; provides nutty, pleasant taste; spoils quickly, especially if not properly refrigerated.

TECHNIQUES

AUTOLYSE

In this preliminary stage, flour and water are combined (on low speed in a mixer or by hand) and left to rest for 20 to 30 minutes. This head start, so to speak, improves the dough-handling qualities throughout the breadmaking process. The flour hydrates to its fullest potential; meanwhile, gluten develops as the dough sits and enzymes within the flour begin to rearrange the unruly gluten structure into a stronger, more organized form. Any starters, intermediate sponges, commercial yeast, or salt are not added at this point—only the flour(s) and water.

TABLE 2.2 BREAD INGREDIENTS AND THEIR FUNCTIONS

Ingredients (Main Functions in Finished Product)	Binding agent	Absorbing agent	Aids keeping qualities	Backbone and structure	Affects eating qualities	Nutritional value	Affects flavor	Affects fermentation	Affects gluten	Texture and grain	Imparts crust color	Affects symmetry	Volume	Produces tenderness	Adds quality to product
Bread flour	X	X	X	X	X	X	X								
Salt							X	X	X	X					
Sugar			X		X	X	X	X	X	X	X	X		X	
Shortening			X		X	X		X		X				X	X
Milk solids			X			X	X			X	X				X
Water	X									X					
Yeast							X	X		X			X		

The leaveners would begin to acidify the dough if they were added, and the enzymes work best in a neutral environment. Salt is omitted because of its ability to tighten the dough, which prevents the flour from fully hydrating. Though the autolyse adds a step to breadmaking, the final dough comes together in less time with less mechanical kneading. In commercial bakeries where large batches of bread are mixed in large floor mixers, a reduction in mixing time and speed minimizes the risk of beating too much oxygen into the dough. Oxidization of the unsaturated fat in the flour will bleach its carotene pigments, imparting an off taste to the finished bread.

KNEADING

Home mixers and many floor-model mixers in most small to medium bakeries are planetary in action: A dough hook revolves around the bowl. Gluten is developed as the dough is turned and smacked repeatedly against the side of the bowl. These bread recipes were tested in a 5-quart KitchenAid mixer with the dough hook unless the recipe specifies otherwise. Medium speed is preferred if you want to preserve the gears of your machine. If your machine seems to be straining, just use it to perform the initial mixing phase and finish kneading by hand. Commercial mixers exist that are especially designed for bread. They knead more efficiently without heating or overworking the dough. Their action seems to mimic hand kneading more closely and doesn't tear the gluten as much. The bowl revolves around a stationary paddle and a hook.

Kneading the dough by machine is the only practical way to make bread on a large scale. Keeping the initial mix time and speed down as much as possible with an autolyse and pre-ferments means that commercially made bread on a large scale can still be absolutely authentically handcrafted. Bread recipes that use very high protein flours and have an extremely high water content can be kneaded longer at a higher speed and require a reduced fermentation time. Just keep in mind that more oxygen is being incorporated into the dough in the process; oxidation means the bread will stale faster. Timing the kneading period is a good idea, as is monitoring the temperature with an instant-read thermometer to make sure it is near 75°F. Doughs can be overmixed; once they are, there is no bringing them back. Once the gluten network is too stressed, the dough will disintegrate into a slack, watery mess.

How can you tell when the dough is sufficiently kneaded? At first it will appear shaggy and rough. As kneading continues, the dough smooths out and begins to pick up off the sides and bottom of the bowl into a single mass. It develops a bit of shine. An excellent test for gluten development is to gently work a piece of the dough between your fingers, attempting to stretch it as thin as possible—until it is almost translucent, ideally (see Figure 2.1). This is called **windowpaning** because well-developed gluten allows the dough to be stretched into a very thin, translucent membrane. If the dough rips into ropy strands, it has not been kneaded sufficiently. If forms a lumpy sheet that tears easily, it's still not there. Keep going, but watch the dough very carefully.

To avoid overmixing, **turn** the dough a couple of times during its

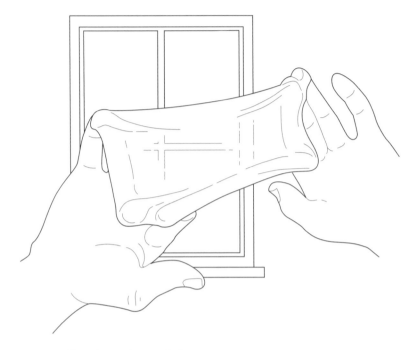

FIGURE 2.1 **Forming a gluten window.**

initial fermentation. The **turn,** misleadingly also known by the too vigorous **punch,** isn't exactly kneading, but it does continue to develop the gluten and redistributes the food supply for the yeast. When the dough has risen a while (the amount of time is variable depending on the dough), gently lift and fold the sides of the dough over onto itself. Then, flip the whole thing over.

FERMENTATION

Fermentation is equivalent to the home baker's term "first rise." The dough rises as a single piece, before being divided and shaped. This is when the yeast begin to feed and multiply. Organic acids, produced particularly by bacteria in wild yeast leavens or starters, develop that serve to condition the gluten and also impart flavor. Lactic acid is milder and contributes roundness of flavor while the more sour acetic acid provides tang. At lower temperatures, fermentation will be slow and the dough will develop more complex flavors (by-products of yeast fermentation), including an acidic or slightly sour flavor. At high temperatures, the dough ferments quickly and unpleasant flavors may be produced. Ideal fermentation temperatures range between 72° and 80°F. Doughs can be fermented most conveniently in large plastic tubs with lids.

DIVIDING AND SHAPING

Professional bakers scale the dough to ensure standard loaves, usually dividing it with a bench knife. The dough should not be stretched or torn and a minimum number of dividing cuts made. Usually after dividing, the pieces of dough are **preformed:** gently shaped, covered, and rested for a short period of time in which the gluten accommodates itself to these new demands. This procedure and the rest phase, known as **benching,** makes final shaping much easier. Plastic wrap coated with nonstick cooking spray works great to prevent just a few loaves from drying out. In bakeries the preformed loaves rest on floured boards in racks covered in plastic sheeting.

PROOFING

Professional bakers call letting the shaped bread rise the "proof." Home bakers usually term this the second rise. This rising period usually takes less time than the first, since the yeast have already multiplied. During this rise, the texture and crumb of the bread are being created. Ideal fermentation temperatures again range between 72° and 80°F. Bakeries may employ proof boxes that allow them to control both of these factors, but at home warm ovens (not on) with bowls of water work pretty well. Or, just get the room warm, keep the bread covered, and have a big pot of water steaming. Whatever methods you employ, you will need to adjust both fermenting and proofing times up or down. Generally speaking, when the dough has roughly increased $1\frac{1}{2}$ to double in size, springs back slowly when pressed, and feels nice and full of carbon dioxide gas, it's ready to be baked.

Round or oval hearth breads may be raised in floured linen-lined wicker containers (**bannetons**). Longer shapes like baguettes, batards, ficelles, and various rolls and smaller rounds may be placed in the folds of a well-floured heavy linen cloth (**couche**) in order to guide their developing shape. These same shapes, if formed with adequate care and skill, can also rise free-form on parchment-lined, cornmeal-dusted sheet pans. Loaves are usually transferred with a peel from the container directly to the oven hearth, baking stone, or tile. Perforated thin metal pans are also available for achieving a crisp crust on baguettes using conventional baking methods. Softer breads like sandwich loaves, brioche, or yeasted coffee cakes are baked in greased pans. Loaves should also be covered during almost all of the proof stage to prevent the outside of the bread from drying out. Use the same methods to cover as discussed in dividing and shaping. Sheets of heavy-duty food-grade plastic work particularly well for home bakers to cover breads rising on sheet pans or to cover couched breads that are retarded overnight in a refrigerator. Lightly spray the loaves with cooking spray before tucking the plastic around the loaves to prevent sticking.

SCORING

Scoring or slashing the bread has a functional purpose as well as an artistic one. It is usually done just before the bread goes into the oven. The slashed loaves can be exposed to the air for about 10 minutes to get the best effect. The slash allows some of the carbon dioxide gas a place to vent; otherwise, the bread will explode randomly through its skin, creating strange, uneven shapes. A razor blade or **lame** is the tool of choice. Slashes are made rapidly and smoothly at about a 45° angle, penetrating just under the surface of the loaf. This produces a lovely open, blooming cut or **grigne**. Some breads are not scored—usually those with fat or other tenderizing ingredients that impart a finer, denser crumb.

BAKING

Ovenspring—the rapid expansion of gas cells—must happen early before the crust sets for optimum volume. For this reason, hearth-style breads are baked at a very high temperature (450° to 500°F), since their dough the lacks external support of a pan and must rise and set quickly.

Irregular, elongated cells in the finished bread bear witness to good ovenspring in these breads. When bread is done, the internal temperature registers between 185° and 200°F, for enriched breads and hearth-style breads, respectively. The telltale sign is a hollow sound when the bottom of the loaf is tapped, indicating the water and starch have become a solid gel.

STEAM AND CRUST

If steam is sprayed into the oven during the early portion of the bake, the bread benefits in a number of ways. Ovenspring is maximized, since the skin on the bread is moist and flexible enough to accommodate a rapid expansion. A crackly crust develops from volatile elements precipitated out of the bread, into the steam, that make the surface of the bread crisp and brown. A number of methods exist to create these optimal humid conditions. Wet towels are used in massive masonry ovens, and many bread bakeries employ commercial ovens that can mechanically inject steam with the push of a button. In the more common bakery deck oven or in the home oven, a pressurized garden sprayer can duplicate the results. Spray the sides or bottom of the oven, not the bread (or the oven light) directly. If spraying to create steam, preheat the oven to 500°F with baking stones or masonry tiles. (Baking stones and tiles create more radiant heat that helps in producing a crisp crust.) Reduce the temperature to that specified in the recipe when the loaves actually go into the oven. This will help minimize heat loss from opening and closing the door. Unless the oven is hot enough, Maillard reactions (browning reactions between carbohydrates and proteins) and caramelization (browning of sugar) will not occur on the surface of the bread to the extent necessary for a good hearth crust. It is these reactions that give bread crust its pleasing, toasty flavor. Steam is usually created or injected only the first 10 minutes or so of the bake, usually just before the bread goes in and once or twice more. The remainder of the bake should be dry in order to develop a crisp, browned crust. All of these recipes were tested in a conventional home oven. The hearth-style breads were transferred with a peel or on the parchment paper on which they were proofed to a preheated stones in the oven, and a garden sprayer was used to create steam. Breads should be cooled immediately on wire racks in order to prevent sogginess.

TABLE 2.3 ORDINARY BREAD FAULTS AND THEIR CAUSES

Faults \ Causes	Improper mixing	Insufficient salt	Too much salt	Dough wt. too much for pan	Dough wt. too light for pan	Insufficient yeast	Too much yeast	Dough proofed too much	Dough under proofed	Dough temp. too high	Dough temp. too low	Dough too stiff	Dough too slack	Proof box too hot	Green flour	Dough chilled	Too much sugar	Insufficient sugar	Dough too young	Dough too old	Improper molding	Insufficient shortening	Oven temp. too high	Oven temp. too low	Over baked
Lack of volume	X		X		X	X			X				X			X			X	X			X		
Too much volume		X		X			X	X												X			X		
Crust color too pale											X			X				X		X					
Crust color too dark										X							X								
Crust blisters																			X	X	X		X		
Shelling of top crust		X							X			X			X										
Poor keeping qualities								X		X		X		X	X			X	X	X		X		X	
Poor texture, crumbly								X										X		X				X	
Crust too thick										X								X		X				X	X
Streaky crumb														X											
Gray crumb									X	X											X				
Lack of shred					X			X				X							X	X					
Coarse grain	X							X			X								X	X	X				
Poor taste and flavor		X					X			X	X									X					

STRAIGHT-RISE BREADS

In straight-dough or straight-rise breads, all the ingredients for the finished bread dough are combined in the initial mixing stage: flour, water, yeast, and almost always salt, along with any other additional ingredients. This is perhaps the simplest and is certainly the fastest way to make bread. Because the fermentation time is short for these breads, their flavor tends to not be especially complex. Many enriched doughs are straight-rise breads, but they have additional flavoring and tenderizing agents present. Long fermentation periods increase shelf life, so that straight-rise breads tend to stale faster unless various compensatory means are employed.

FRENCH BREAD

MAKES 3 POUNDS 6 OUNCES DOUGH OR 18 3-OUNCE ROLLS, SIX 9-OUNCE FICELLES, FOUR 13.5-OUNCE BAGUETTES, TWO 1-POUND 11 OUNCE BATARDS French bread made using the pure straight-dough method often tastes dull and bland by the end of the day. This recipe extends the fermentation time by retarding the dough overnight to increase flavor and make for an easier morning bake. To increase flavor and extend keeping qualities even further, try the pâte fermentée version (page 30). Shaping is the thing in French bread. Just keep practicing.

2 lb all-purpose or artisan (lower protein) bread flour
1 lb 5.33 oz (2²/₃ cups) cool water
.55 oz fresh yeast, crumbled (about 5 tsp)
1 tsp diastatic malt powder
.5 oz (1 Tbs) salt

In a mixer bowl, autolyse the flour and water. Add the yeast and malt powder to the dough. Knead on low speed until just combined; add the salt. Increase the speed to medium. Knead until the dough reaches windowpane stage, about

10 minutes. Ferment $1^{1}/_{2}$ hours, turning twice. Divide and preshape. Bench 10 to 15 minutes. Give the final shaping (see below for specifics). Couche. Retard overnight. Proof dough until increased by $1^{1}/_{2}$ times. Score. Peel onto oven hearth or baking stone. Bake with steam at 450°F until deeply golden, 25 to 30 minutes for baguettes.

SHAPING TECHNIQUES

FICELLE AND BAGUETTES

Gently flatten the preshaped dough into a rectangle (Figure 2.2). Fold two-thirds of the dough over upon itself, beginning with the long edge. Push back on the seam with your pinkies to stretch the "skin" of the dough. Repeat, folding the dough over from the opposite direction. Firmly flatten this seam, again pushing back so that about two-thirds of the bread is in a nice tight roll with the remaining third flattened. Fold the dough over upon itself, using the thumb of the left hand to guide and the heel of the right hand to seal firmly against the table. Straighten the dough with the seam down. Using equal pressure with both hands, gently roll the cylinder against the table while elongating. Ficelles are about 24 inches long and baguettes around 20 inches long.

BATARD

Roughly the same technique as above except that the preshaped dough begins as a round flattened into a rough oval. Fold in the same fashion, creating a hump in the middle of the cylinder. On the final fold, push more dough into the center with a guiding thumb. Roll with greater pressure toward the ends to taper into points.

BOULE

Gently flatten the preshaped round. Fold in half. Fold the half over upon itself. Situate the dough on the table with seams tucked under. Cup with your palms, pinkies against the table. Gently rotate, pressing against the table to develop and tighten the skin.

ROLLS

Same as for boule except you can round one roll in each hand (sticky bits should go against the table, hands should be lightly floured). Petit pain are formed like mini-batards. Pistolets are tight rounds with a deep crease formed in the middle with a dowel or rolling pin (see Figure 2.3, page 37).

Flatten a cylinder of dough into a rectangle.

Fold two-thirds of the dough, lengthwise, over onto itself, stretching the dough as you fold.

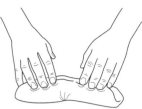

Fold the remaining one-third of the dough (the opposite edge) over the first.

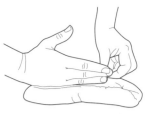

Press to seal with the side of your hand, pressing two-thirds of the dough to one side and flattening one-third.

Fold the dough over onto itself again, this time using your thumbs to flip the dough seam-side-down.

Use the heel of your hand to press the seam into the table.

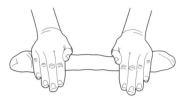

Roll and stretch the dough between your hands to elongate.

FIGURE 2.2 **Elegant baguettes and long ficelles are formed by rolling, folding, and stretching dough in a specific method.**

ALTERNATIVE FRENCH BREAD

MAKES 4 POUNDS 6 OUNCES DOUGH This alternative French bread is made with a proportion of old dough, or **pâte fermentée.** Here the old dough is a piece saved from the previous recipe. This scrap dough contains the same ingredients as the final dough, including salt and a fair amount of yeast. When the final dough is mixed, additional commercial yeast is added. The old dough should be refrigerated to prevent overfermentation. If overfermented, the old dough will become too acidic and produce alcohol. The formula can be adjusted as follows:

1 lb 8 oz (3 cups) cool water
2 lb all-purpose flour
14 oz previous day's dough
.275 oz fresh yeast, crumbled (about $2^{1}/_{2}$ tsp)
.33 oz (2 tsp) salt

In a mixer bowl, autolyse the water and flour. Add the old dough and yeast. Knead on low speed until just combined; add the salt. Mix on low speed until combined. Increase the speed to medium. Knead until the dough reaches windowpane stage, 8 minutes. Ferment 30 minutes; turn. Cut off and save in the refrigerator 14 ounce of dough for the next day's dough. Ferment the remaining dough until doubled, about $1^{1}/_{2}$ hours, turning once. Divide and preshape. Bench 10 to 15 minutes. Couche. Proof until increased $1^{1}/_{2}$ times, 3 to 4 hours. Bake as directed for French Bread.

FOCCACIA

MAKES 3 POUNDS 9 OUNCES DOUGH OR TWO HALF-SHEET FOCCACIAS OR TWO (18 INCH) ROUND PIZZAS This bread has large, airy holes with a soft interior and crisp exterior. It accommodates innumerable toppings and is great for sandwiches.

1 lb 5.33 oz (2²/₃ cups) cool water
1 lb 2 oz all-purpose flour
14 oz bread flour
.44 oz fresh yeast, crumbled (about 4 tsp)
2 oz (¹/₄ cup) olive oil
.75 oz (1 Tbs) honey
.5 oz (1 Tbs) salt
Additional olive oil for pans and drizzling
Suggested foccacia toppings: grated Parmesan cheese, coarse sea salt, dried herbs (see Note).

In a mixer bowl, autolyse the water and flour. Add the yeast, oil, and honey to the dough. Knead on low speed until just combined; add the salt. Increase the speed to medium. Knead until very smooth, shiny, and elastic, but soft dough forms, 8 to 10 minutes. The dough will clean the sides of the bowl and make a slapping noise. Ferment until doubled, about 2 hours, turning once midway. Divide. Liberally coat two half-sheet pans with olive oil. Place dough in pans; bench 15 minutes. Flip the dough so that the oiled side is facing up. Gently press the dough into the corners of the pan. Proof in a warm place until puffy, 30 minutes. Dimple the dough all over with your fingertips. Drizzle with an additional 2 to 3 tablespoons olive oil. Sprinkle with desired toppings. Cover with sprayed plastic. Proof until doubled, 1¹/₂ to 2 hours. Bake with steam at 425°F until golden and crisp, 20 to 24 minutes.

NOTE Toppings that will burn (caramelized onions, raisins, olives, etc.) should be incorporated into the dough by hand after final kneading is completed. Fresh herbs can be sprinkled on during the final few minutes of baking. A quick misting of the foccacia with water will make them stick.

PIZZA DOUGH

After scaling, preform dough into two loose rounds. Bench 15 minutes. Roll or stretch each piece of dough into an 18-inch circle. Bake at 500°F for 5 to 6 minutes. Add the toppings. Bake until the edges are crisp, blistered, and brown, 10 minutes.

PUMPERNICKEL-POTATO BREAD

MAKES 3 POUNDS DOUGH OR TWO 24-OUNCE LOAVES This pumpernickel bread is dense, chewy, moist, and slightly sweet. If possible, to prevent gumminess, let this bread dry out slightly in the oven after it's been turned off for the day.

8 oz (1 cup) hot potato cooking water
6 oz cooked, mashed potatoes (1 large baking potato, about 8 oz)
4 oz ($^1/_2$ cup) hot coffee
1.44 oz ($^1/_4$ cup) all-vegetable shortening
2.25 oz (3 Tbs) barley malt syrup or molasses
.165 oz (1$^1/_2$ tsp) instant yeast
8 oz medium rye flour
8 oz high-gluten flour
6 oz bread flour
4 oz pumpernickel flour
.47 oz (2 Tbs) cocoa powder
.5 oz (1 Tbs) salt
6 oz (1 cup) raisins (optional)
COFFEE GLAZE
1 tsp instant espresso powder
4 oz ($^1/_2$ cup) hot coffee
1 oz (2 Tbs) heavy cream

In a mixer bowl, whisk the potato water, potatoes, coffee, shortening, malt syrup, and yeast until reasonably well combined. With the mixer running on low speed, add the remaining dry ingredients by the cupful. Increase the speed to medium; knead until the dough just begins to pick up from bottom of bowl, 5 to 6 minutes. Let rise until increased 1$^1/_2$ times in size. Divide the dough into two pieces, 24 oz each. Flatten slightly and roll into loose cylinders. Cover and bench 20 minutes. Flatten into 10 by 8-inch rectangles. Sprinkle one piece with raisins, if desired. Roll up into tight cylinders starting from short end. Seal seams by pressing against table. Place seam side down on parchment-lined pans. Cover dough. Refrigerate 8 hours or overnight. Score three times on the diagonal. Proof in a humid environment until the loaves are doubled from original size, about 2 hours. Bake at 375°F for 35 minutes. Dissolve the espresso powder in the coffee; stir in the cream. Brush this coffee glaze over the loaves. Bake 5 minutes. Remove the loaves from the pans; return directly to oven racks for 4 minutes.

BREADS MADE USING PRE-FERMENTS

A **pre-ferment** is a long, preferably cool fermentation of the yeast (or wild yeast starter) with a portion of the flour and water called for in a recipe. Pre-ferments provide complex flavors akin to mild sourdough or wild yeast starters. Sometimes pre-ferments are called **sponges**. This step allows the fullest range of flavor in the wheat flour to develop, and gives time for acetic and lactic acids to form. Acetic acid, in addition to its role in flavor, acts a natural dough conditioner, greatly improving extensibility. The dough is kneaded for a shorter period of time, preventing off flavors that can occur as the dough oxidizes. A minimal amount of yeast is needed for this process, as it continues to multiply during the long wait. Pre-fermented doughs make breads with complex flavors and great moisture retention.

The following recipes employ an Italian version of a pre-ferment: the **biga**. Bigas are usually very firm doughs with only around 50 percent hydration and about 1 percent compressed yeast. Like the other pre-ferments, bigas are best fermented over a long period of time in a cool environment. Bigas tend to be more stable and keep for longer periods of time at their peak than do the more liquid pre-ferments.

BIGA

MAKES ABOUT 5 POUNDS

1 lb 14 oz (3³/₄ cups) cool water
.275 oz fresh yeast, crumbled (about 2¹/₂ tsp)
3 lb bread flour

Mix the water, yeast, and flour until combined; knead on medium speed until the dough just comes off the sides of the bowl, 2 to 3 minutes. The dough will be very stiff. Ferment at room temperature 8 to 12 hours. Refrigerate overnight before using. Biga can be held and used from refrigerator for up to three days.

WHITE SANDWICH BREAD

MAKES 2 POUNDS 14 OUNCES DOUGH OR TWO 23-OUNCE LOAVES IN 9 BY 5-INCH PANS OR TWENTY-THREE 2-OUNCE DINNER ROLLS White bread doesn't have to be insipid. A golden crust and tender crumb make this a great slicing bread for sandwiches or rolls of any sort.

10 oz bread flour
6 oz all-purpose flour
1.31 oz (3 Tbs) sugar
8 fl oz (1 cup) warm milk
4 oz butter, melted
1 lb **BIGA** (above)
.275 oz fresh yeast, crumbled (about 2¹/₂ tsp)
.33 oz (2 tsp) salt
Additional melted butter for brushing tops (optional)

In a mixer bowl, autolyse the flours, sugar, milk, and butter. Mix in the biga and yeast on low speed. Add the salt. Knead on medium speed until smooth and elastic, 8 minutes. Ferment until increased 1¹⁄₂ times, about 1 hour. Turn. Ferment until increased 1¹⁄₂ times, 45 to 60 minutes. Divide. Flatten into 10 by 8-inch rectangles. Roll up the dough into tight cylinders, starting each from short end. Seal seams by pressing dough against table. Place seam side down in greased pans. Proof until doubled, about 1¹⁄₂ hours. Bake at 350°F for 45 to 50 minutes or until golden and loaves sound hollow. Remove from pans and dry sides of loaves in oven for 5 minutes. If desired, brush the tops of the loaves with melted butter while still warm.

CINNAMON-RAISIN BREAD

Sprinkle the dough rectangle with 3.5 oz (¹⁄₂ cup) cinnamon sugar and 3 oz (¹⁄₂ cup) raisins before rolling into cylinder.

WHOLE WHEAT SANDWICH LOAF

MAKES 2 POUNDS 13 OUNCES DOUGH OR TWO 22.5-OUNCE LOAVES IN 9 BY 5-INCH PANS OR TWENTY-THREE 2-OUNCE DINNER ROLLS

8 oz bread flour
5 oz whole wheat flour
2 oz rolled oats
1.12 oz (¹⁄₄ cup) baker's dry milk powder
.25 oz (2 Tbs) wheat bran flakes
1 oz (3 Tbs) vegetable shortening or bacon fat
1.5 oz (2 Tbs) honey
1 tsp diastatic malt powder
10 oz (1¹⁄₄ cups) cool water
1 lb **BIGA** (page 34)
.275 oz fresh yeast, crumbled (about 2¹⁄₂ tsp)
.33 oz (2 tsp) salt
Melted butter for brushing tops (optional)

In a mixer bowl, autolyse the flours, oats, milk powder, wheat bran, shortening, honey, malt powder, and water. Mix in the biga and yeast on low speed. Add the salt. Knead on medium speed until smooth and elastic, 8 minutes. Ferment until increased $1^1/_2$ times, about 1 hour. Turn. Ferment until increased $1^1/_2$ times, 45 to 60 minutes. Divide. Flatten into 10 by 8-inch rectangles. Roll up into tight cylinders starting from short end. Seal seams by pressing against table. Place seam side down in greased pans. Proof until doubled, about $1^1/_2$ hours. Bake at 350°F for 45 to 50 minutes or until golden and loaves sound hollow. Remove from pans and dry out sides of loaves in oven for 5 minutes. If desired, brush the tops of the loaves with melted butter while still warm.

ITALIAN BREAD

MAKES 3 POUNDS 8 OUNCES DOUGH OR TWO 28-OUNCE BATARDS The milk powder and honey give this Italian bread the characteristic white soft interior and crackly brown exterior with just a hint of sweetness.

1 lb 5 oz bread flour
1 lb (2 cups) water
.84 oz (3 Tbs) baker's dry milk powder
1.5 oz (3 Tbs) olive oil
.80 oz (1 Tbs) honey
1 lb **BIGA** (page 34)
.0825 oz fresh yeast, crumbled (about $^3/_4$ tsp)
.66 oz (1 Tbs + 1 tsp) salt

In a mixer bowl, autolyse the flour, water, milk powder, olive oil, and honey. Mix in the biga and yeast on low speed. Add the salt. Knead on medium speed until smooth and elastic, 8 minutes. Ferment until doubled, about 2 hours, turning midway. Divide. Preshape and bench 10 minutes. Form into batards. Couche or place on parchment-lined pans sprinkled with cornmeal. Proof 45 minutes. Retard overnight or for at least 8 hours. Let warm up, 30 to 45 minutes. Bake with steam at 425°F until golden and crisp, 35 to 40 minutes.

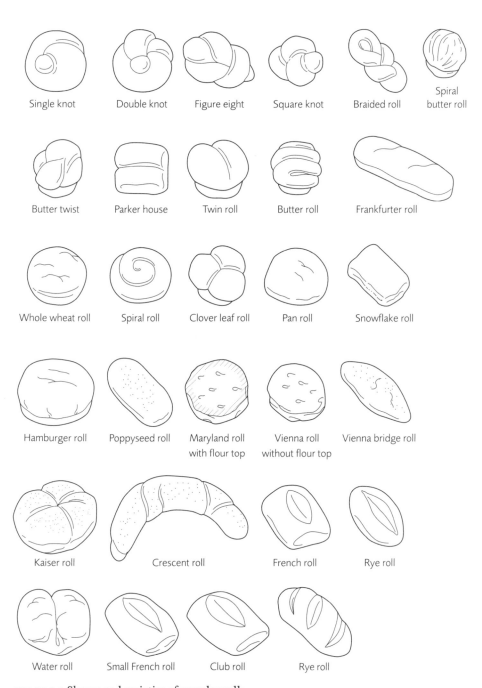

FIGURE 2.3 **Shapes and varieties of popular rolls.**

STURDY PIZZA DOUGH

For a sturdy pizza dough that can support a considerable amount of weighty toppings, divide the dough into three pieces after the first rise. Freeze two for later use. Roll or stretch the remaining dough into a 16-inch circle. Bake at 500°F for 8 to 10 minutes. Top as desired; return to oven for 8 to 10 minutes.

DRIED MUSHROOM CIABATTA

MAKES ABOUT 1 POUND 12 OUNCES DOUGH OR TWO 14-OUNCE CIABATTAS
Ciabatta dough is a sticky mess to handle, but the finished product, with its bubbly interior and chewy crust, is worth the hassle. Bake as hot as your oven allows for the first 5 minutes to achieve a truly great bread.

1 lb 8 oz (3 cups) boiling water
1 oz ($^1/_2$ cup chopped) dried mushrooms
6 oz bread flour
1 fl oz (2 Tbs) olive oil
8 oz (1 cup) water
8 oz **BIGA** (page 34)
.055 oz fresh yeast, crumbled (about $^1/_2$ tsp)
.33 oz (2 tsp) salt
2 Tbs chopped sun-dried tomatoes (optional)
2 tsp finely chopped fresh oregano (optional)

Pour the boiling water over the mushrooms; let steep 1 hour. Drain, reserving $^1/_4$ cup mushroom water. In a mixer bowl, autolyse the flour, oil, water, and reserved mushroom water for 15 minutes. Mix in the biga and yeast on low speed. Add the salt, tomatoes, and oregano. Knead on medium speed until smooth and elastic (dough will still be soft and quite sticky), about 10 minutes. Ferment until doubled, about 2$^1/_2$ hours. Heavily flour the work surface, dough, and hands. Divide, cutting and deflating the dough as little as possible, into two pieces. Gently stretch each into a slipper shape, about 12 by 9 inches. Proof on boards or parchment-lined sheet pans until doubled and puffy, $1\frac{1}{2}$ to 2 hours. Bake with steam at 425°F until golden, 35 minutes.

SEMOLINA BREAD

MAKES 1 POUND 13 OUNCES DOUGH OR ONE LARGE BATARD OR TWO MEDIUM (14-OUNCES) BOULES The semolina flour lends the interior of this loaf a golden hue and slightly nutty flavor, enhanced by the sesame seeds.

8 oz water (1 cup)
6 oz bread flour
5 oz semolina flour
.42 oz (1 Tbs plus $1\frac{1}{2}$ tsp) baker's dry milk powder
.75 oz (1 Tbs plus $1\frac{1}{2}$ tsp) olive oil
.40 oz ($1\frac{1}{2}$ tsp) honey
8 oz **BIGA** (page 34)
.0825 oz fresh yeast, crumbled (about $\frac{3}{4}$ tsp)
.33 oz (2 tsp) salt
Sesame seeds for sprinkling

In a mixer bowl, autolyse the water, flours, milk powder, oil, and honey. Mix in the biga and yeast on low speed. Add the salt. Knead on medium speed until smooth and elastic, 8 minutes. Ferment until doubled, about 2 hours, turning midway. Divide. Preshape and bench 10 minutes. Form into batards. Couche or place on parchment-lined pans sprinkled with cornmeal. Proof 45 minutes. Let rise until doubled, about 2 hours, turning once. Scale and shape into loose cylinders. Let rest 10 minutes. Form into batards. Proof 45 minutes. Retard overnight or for at least 8 hours. Let warm up, 30 to 45 minutes. Bake with steam at 425°F until golden and crisp, 35 to 40 minutes.

OTHER TYPES OF PRE-FERMENTS

Poolish or **sponge** describes a type of pre-ferment in which flour and water are combined in equal proportions into a soupy starter that begins to develop with the addition of more or less yeast depending on the desired length of fermentation. Different doughs can have different percentages of their total flour and water weight as part of the poolish, from a third to nearly all the weight. The general rule is the more liquid (thin or batterlike) a pre-ferment is, the faster the yeast will multiply. Long, cool fermentations from 3 to 15 hours with small amounts of yeast produce poolishes whose peak of optimum performance is several hours long. When fully fermented, the poolish will have risen completely, then fallen back just a bit, and the top will appear slightly wrinkled.

Chefs and **levain de pâte** are similar to pâte fermentée except that the newly mixed dough gets no additional yeast—the old dough inoculates the new dough with its yeast supply. The yeast in the piece of old dough could be either commercial or wild yeast. This term specifies that the leavening agent is a small piece of old dough, and not a starter or storage leaven. The proportion of the old dough used is greater than that in the mixed starter (pâte fermenteé and commercial yeast) discussed in the Alternative French Bread recipe on pg. 30, and the dough is fermented at room temperature. Breads made with this method closely mimic the flavors of a mild sourdough and the French *levain*.

BREADS MADE FROM WILD YEAST STARTERS

Sourdough starters, also known as **wild yeast** starters or **natural leavens,** do not contain commercial yeast. Instead, whole-grain, unbleached flour and nonchlorinated water are combined and, it is hoped, become inoculated with yeast spores and bacteria present in the grain and surrounding environment. Whole-grain flour (wheat or rye) is preferable owing to its high mineral content and enzyme activity, which encourage these organisms to thrive. Heavily chlorinated water may initially inhibit bacterial growth.

Though most bakers are familiar with the concept of developing a wild yeast starter, few realize the importance of bacteria. Flavorful sourdough breads are a collaboration between yeasts and bacteria. The bacteria provide two acids that give naturally leavened breads their distinct flavors: mild lactic acid and the more sour acetic acid. These bacteria are both lumped under the genus *Lactobacilli*. A naturally leavened dough is quite acidic with a low pH. The ratio between the acetic and lactic acids present, plus the overall pH of the dough, gives each wild yeast starter its characteristic flavor. So within this simple framework a wide range of flavor variations exist. The bacteria feed on maltose, a sugar that yeasts use as a second choice, and break it down into glucose. Bacterial fermentation results in carbon dioxide, which means that sourdough breads are leavened by the action of bacteria as well as yeast.

Wild yeast starters usually contain several yeast and bacteria strains at first, but over time a well-maintained starter will eventually have only a few dominant ones. Unless you send out your starter for microbial analysis, you won't know which species to thank.

Wild yeast starters can be thick or thin, but keep in mind that thin starters cannot be stored as long without refreshment. Thin starters run their course faster and have a tendency to develop more acid. Other than that, both are equally proficient at leavening bread doughs. The hardest part of developing the starter is having the patience to tend the sponge until it has a yeast population active enough to leaven bread. It can take a few weeks to build a powerful, flavorful wild yeast starter. Beyond that, it is simply a matter of keeping the yeast and bacteria alive by frequently discarding a portion of the old starter and refreshing it with more flour and water. Wild yeast starters stored in the refrigerator can be refreshed every few days, but at room temperature they will need to be fed daily.

Only recently refreshed starters should be stored in the refrigerator to prevent the yeast population from being depleted. Though wild yeasts don't mind cool temperatures or a fair amount of acetic acid, they do not fare well under both conditions. A refreshed starter is less acidic and provides plenty of food for a week in cold storage. The starter will require several refreshments at room temperature before it regains its previous vigor. Care should be taken to keep the starter at a moderate temperature. Warm temperatures, such as over 80°F, favor bacterial growth over yeast growth and thus alter the flavor and leavening profile of the starter.

Even with an active sponge, doughs made with wild yeast starters require a longer fermentation than those made with commercial yeast— at least eight hours. Variables such as fast or slow fermentation, hot or cold temperatures, and the viscosity of the mixture determine the flavor of the bread, since each variable affects yeast and bacterial fermentation differently. These variables apply not only to the starter but also to the intermediate and the final dough. The interaction of all these factors can be controlled to produce the desired result. Two styles of wild yeast starter are widely used: a firm, almost doughlike starter and a thin, more batterlike starter. The firm starters need less frequent feedings and are slightly more storage stabile. Batterlike starter must be kept on a tight feeding schedule and monitored for excessive acidity.

MILD FRENCH-STYLE WILD YEAST STARTER

MAKES ABOUT 8 OUNCES The French-style wild yeast starter that produces *pain au levain* is only slightly sour and possesses a deep, complex balance of flavors. The presence of both acetic and lactic acids is a necessity to achieve good flavor. Lactic acid has no special taste of its own but is needed for flavor balance. Acetic acid is primarily responsible for tangy sharpness or sourness, but on its own it will taste too vinegary and harsh. The country-style French loaf or *pain au levain* that can be produced from this starter undergoes several stages to build its dough, has a short dough fermentation, and has a long proof time.

SCHEDULE FOR MILD STARTER
DAY 1
4 oz ($^1/_2$ cup) cool water
3.5 oz pumpernickel flour
DAY 2
All of Day 1 starter (7.5 oz)
2 oz ($^1/_4$ cup) cool water
3.5 oz bread flour

DAY 3
All of Day 2 starter (13 oz)
2 oz ($^1/_4$ cup) cool water
3 oz bread flour
DAY 5
2.66 oz Day 3 starter ($^1/_3$ cup); discard remainder
2 oz ($^1/_4$ cup) cool water
3 oz bread flour
DAY 7
2 oz ($^1/_4$ cup) Day 5 starter
2 oz ($^1/_4$ cup) cool water
3 oz bread flour

This is a very firm starter in all of its stages. It can be kneaded into a ball. During the first couple of days, very little yeast activity will be observable. Gradually, however, as the yeast, and eventually the bacterial, populations increase, you will notice that the dough will be bubbly on the inside if you pull it apart. After Day 7, maintain your starter on the refreshment feeding as follows: Feed when the starter has risen to its maximum and has begun to fall. This period will become shorter and shorter as the strength of the starter increases. The eventual goal is to have a starter that can roughly triple in 8 hours. Depending on environmental conditions, this may take anywhere from two to three weeks.

REFRESHMENT FEEDING
2 oz ($^1/_4$ cup) starter
2.66 oz ($^1/_3$ cup) water
3 oz bread flour

At this point, the starter can be refrigerated and maintained by feeding once a week using the above amounts. As this starter is quite potent, smaller amounts can be refreshed for use in the specific recipes (see below). Usually, a cycle of about three refreshments gets the starter back up to speed. Any unused refreshed starter can go back into the "mother," given to friends, or simply discarded.

REFRESHED MILD STARTER
MAKES ($^1/_3$ CUP, 2.8 OZ)
1 Tbs plus 1 tsp starter
1 Tbs plus 1 tsp cool water
2 Tbs plus 2 tsp all-purpose flour

NOTE Starter can be refreshed with whole wheat flour for the Multigrain Boule (page 45).

COUNTRY FRENCH BATARD

MAKES 3 POUNDS 4 OUNCES DOUGH

OR TWO LARGE BATARDS AT 1 POUND 10 OUNCES EACH

LEVAIN
REFRESHED MILD STARTER (above)
4 oz ($^1/_2$ cup) cool water
3.5 oz bread flour
FINAL DOUGH
1 lb bread flour
8.5 oz all-purpose flour
1.25 oz whole wheat flour
1.25 oz medium rye flour
.5 oz (2 Tbs) wheat germ
.75 oz (1 Tbs) barley malt syrup
1 lb (2 cups) cool water
LEVAIN
.66 oz (1 Tbs plus 1 tsp) salt

LEVAIN Knead together ingredients for levain until smooth. Ferment at room temperature 8 hours.

FINAL DOUGH In a mixer bowl, autolyse the flours, wheat germ, barley malt syrup, and water. Mix in the fermented levain on low speed. Add the salt. Knead on medium speed until smooth and elastic, 8 to 10 minutes. Ferment until doubled, 5 to 6 hours, turning every hour for the first three hours. Divide. Preshape and bench 20 minutes. Form. Couche or place on parchment-lined pans sprinkled with cornmeal. Proof until increased $1^1/_2$ times, 3 to 4 hours. Score. Bake with steam at 450°F until deeply golden, 35 to 40 minutes.

MULTIGRAIN BOULE

MAKES ABOUT 4 POUNDS 6 OUNCES DOUGH OR THREE ROUNDS AT 1 POUND 7 OUNCES Breads that contain a significant percentage of whole wheat flour, rye flour, or other type of whole-grain flour will have less gluten-forming proteins available to create structure and height. Depending on personal taste regarding texture and nutritive qualities, the percentage of whole wheat flour in the formula can be increased, with the knowledge that the loaf will be considerably denser. Oats, millet, cornmeal, wheat bran, wheat germ, sunflower seeds, nuts—all are tasty and healthy additions. Whole grains and seeds are usually cooked or presoaked overnight to soften them. This type of recipe is usually referred to as a mixed starter: A huge percentage of the complex flavor and chewy texture comes from the use of the *levain*, while the tiny amount of commercial yeast provides a boost for the heaviness incurred by all those grains and nuts.

LEVAIN
2.8 oz ($^1/_3$ cup) **REFRESHED MILD STARTER** (page 44)
4 oz ($^1/_2$ cup) cool water
3.5 oz whole wheat flour

FINAL DOUGH
1 lb bread flour
7 oz whole wheat flour
1.75 oz dark rye or pumpernickel flour
2.75 oz ($^1/_4$ cup) barley malt syrup or molasses
.5 oz (2 Tbs) wheat germ
17 oz (2 cups) buttermilk
1 cup cooked multigrain porridge (see note)
4 oz (1 cup) toasted, chopped walnuts
2.5 oz ($^1/_2$ cup) unsalted sunflower seeds
LEVAIN
.0138 oz fresh yeast, crumbled (tiny pinch)
.5 oz (1 Tbs) salt

LEVAIN Knead ingredients for starter together until smooth. Ferment at room temperature 8 hours.

FINAL DOUGH In a mixer bowl, autolyse the flours, barley malt, wheat germ, buttermilk, porridge, walnuts, and sunflower seeds. Mix in the *levain* and yeast on low speed. Add the salt. Knead on medium speed until smooth and elastic, 8 to 10 minutes. Ferment until doubled, 4 to 5 hours, turning twice for the first two hours. Divide. Preshape and bench 20 minutes. Form. Couche or place on parchment-lined pans sprinkled with cornmeal. Proof until doubled, 3 to 4 hours. Score. Bake with steam at 425°F until deep brown, 35 to 40 minutes.

NOTE Any mixed whole-grain cereal cooked al dente will work—King Arthur Flour Company has some particularly fine blends.

BARM STARTERS

Barms are a relatively liquid type of wild yeast starter that produces a pronounced sourness in the bread. Barms are usually built into a firmer pre-ferment to develop a bit more lactic acid to round out the flavor. Sourdough starters are usually a type of barm; liquid starters tend to produce a lot of acetic acid. Acetic acid is well tolerated by the yeast associated with San Francisco sourdough. It has a tangy, even sharp flavor and very high acid level. It generally has a long, relatively cool proof since the yeasts are slowed considerably by their acidic environment. It is usually made with high-gluten flour to retain as much precious gas as possible.

SCHEDULE FOR WHITE BARM STARTER

DAY 1
8 oz (1 cup) water
.75 oz (1 Tbs) barley malt syrup
4.5 oz whole wheat flour, preferably organic stone-ground
DAY 2
All of Day 1 starter (12.5 oz)
6 oz (³/₄ cup) cool water
.375 (1¹/₂ tsp) barley malt syrup
4.75 oz bread flour
DAY 3
All of Day 2 starter (23.25 oz)
12 oz (1¹/₂ cups) cool water
9.5 oz bread flour
DAY 4
¹/₂ of Day 3 starter (11.626 oz; discard remainder)
12 oz (1¹/₂ cups) cool water
9.5 oz bread flour
DAY 5
All of Day 4 starter (33.12 oz)
12 oz (1¹/₂ cups) cool water
9.5 oz bread flour

At this point you've got about 3.4 pounds of starter that resembles pancake batter. You are beginning to develop a healthy yeast population. From this point forward, for the next three to five days, continue to develop your starter using the following formula. This will also be the formula you use to bring a refrigerated or less-than-vigorous starter back to full health.

REFRESHMENT FEEDING
7 oz STARTER
6 oz ($^3/_4$ cup) cool water
4.75 oz bread flour

The starter should now be very bubbly and active with a pleasantly sour smell. If it isn't, just be patient and keep at it for a few days. Until the point that your starter is very active, continue to let it ferment at cool room temperature (about 75°F). Once you have observed significant action, feed the starter and allow it to ferment for 4 hours at room temperature. Then, refrigerate the starter until the next feeding or when you begin to make bread. After feeding, always allow this 4-hour room temperature interlude to keep your yeast happy. Temperatures for fermentation above 80°F can permit the growth of undesirable bacteria and even molds, so monitor your starter in its early days with frequent sniffing and visual inspections. It should not ever smell like stinky cheese!

NOTE The previous formula minimizes waste, but if you intend on making lots of bread, the refreshment feedings are where you begin to scale up as needed. The ratio of feeding is 4 parts water to 3 parts flour with the aim of at least doubling the volume of your original starter. Anything less than this doesn't give the starter enough nutrients. Starters of this nature should be fed at least every two days once they are up and going. The optimum time to use the fully refreshed starter is about 24 hours after its last feeding.

SAN FRANCISCO
SOURDOUGH BREAD

MAKES 1 POUND 11 OUNCES DOUGH OR ONE LARGE BATARD OR TWO ROUNDS

Even if your *lactobacillus* is not *sanfranciscenis*, this bread will still be quite tangy and assertive. The use of an intermediate dough is sometimes referred to as a build. This firmer dough produces acids that help to blance the bread's essential tanginess. The overnight retarding helps balance the acid composition.

INTERMEDIATE BARM BUILD
10.25 oz **WHITE BARM STARTER** (page 47)
5.75 oz bread flour
FINAL DOUGH
10 oz (1$^1/_4$ cups) cool water
1 lb high-gluten flour
.375 (1$^1/_2$ tsp) barley malt syrup
INTERMEDIATE BARM BUILD
.66 oz (2 tsp) salt

BARM BUILD Stir starter and bread flour together; knead until smooth. Ferment 4 to 6 hours at room temperature. Refrigerate overnight.

FINAL DOUGH In a mixer bowl, autolyse the water, high-gluten flour, and barley malt. Mix in the barm build on low speed. Add the salt. Knead on medium speed until elastic and extensible, 8 to 10 minutes. Ferment until increased 1$^1/_2$ times, about 4 hours, turning twice during the first two hours. Divide. Preshape and bench 20 minutes. Form. Couche or place on parchment-lined pans sprinkled with cornmeal. Proof until nearly doubled, 3 to 3$^1/_2$ hours. Retard overnight. Warm up 1 hour. Score. Bake with steam at 425°F until deep brown, 40 to 45 minutes.

CHOCOLATE–SOUR CHERRY BREAD

MAKES 3 POUNDS 11 OUNCES DOUGH OR TWO ROUNDS AT 1 POUND 13.5 OUNCES EACH Deep, dark chocolate flavor is hard to come by in bread, but this one hits the mark with a combination of melted bittersweet chocolate, cocoa powder, and miniature chocolate chips.

7 oz brewed hot coffee
2 oz bittersweet chocolate, finely chopped
4 oz cool butter, in pieces
12 oz bread flour
5.5 oz (^{2}/$_3$ cup) brown sugar
2 oz (about 9 Tbs) cocoa powder
.11 oz (1 tsp) osmotolerant instant active dry yeast
1 oz (2 Tbs) hot water
8 oz **INTERMEDIATE BARM BUILD** (page 49)
.66 oz (2 tsp) salt
9 oz (1^1/$_2$ cups) miniature chocolate chips
7.5 oz (1^1/$_2$ cups) dried sour cherries, plumped in hot water, drained

In a mixer bowl, stir together the coffee, chocolate, and butter until smooth. Add the flour, brown sugar, and cocoa powder. Knead on low speed until a sticky dough forms. Let stand 25 minutes. Add the yeast to hot water. Add to dough along with the white barm build. Knead on low speed until combined. Add the salt; increase speed to medium. Knead until the dough is smooth and begins to clean the sides of the bowl, 5 to 6 minutes. Add the chips and cherries; knead until just incorporated, 1 minute. Ferment until increased 1^1/$_2$ times, giving a turn midway, 2 to 3 hours. Divide. Preshape and bench 20 minutes. Form. Couche or place on parchment-lined pans sprinkled with cornmeal. Proof 45 minutes. Retard overnight. Proof in a cool, humid environment until increased 1^1/$_2$ times, 3 to 4 hours. Bake at 350°F for 50 to 55 minutes.

RYE BREADS

Rye flour does not have enough gluten-forming proteins to make a light bread by itself. To compensate, wheat flour is added. The more wheat flour used, the lighter in texture the rye bread. Rye bread doughs containing more than 20 percent rye flour must rely on the viscosity of starches and pentosans to trap carbon dioxide gas and provide structure (instead of gluten). As the loaf of rye bread enters the oven, the gelatinized starch on the outside of the loaf forms a sort of skin that aids in gas retention.

Rye breads rely on starch for structure, but rye flour itself contains an enzyme, amylase, that destroys the structural capability of starch. This amylase is not denatured before gelatinization and is free to attack not just the initially available damaged starch but also the starch made available by gelatinization. The result is that way too much starch is converted to sugar, and the loaf flattens, sags, and becomes heavy.

Sour rye breads, made from a wild yeast leavening or a long, acid-producing fermentation, do not have this problem. The action of rye amylase is inhibited by an acidic environment, especially in conjunction with salt. Traditional rye breads are made with sour starters—the low pH slows down enzyme action and protects the starch until rye amylase is finally denatured during baking.

Rye flour is extremely hygroscopic, meaning that it will absorb moisture from the environment. For this reason rye breads have an extremely high moisture content that translates to very good keeping qualities. It also means that the baking breads take longer to set and must be thoroughly dried out in the oven.

SOUR RYE BREAD

MAKES 2 POUNDS 5 OUNCES DOUGH OR ONE LARGE BATARD OR TWO ROUNDS

INTERMEDIATE RYE BARM BUILD
10.25 oz **WHITE BARM STARTER** (page 47; see Note)
5.75 oz rye flour
FINAL DOUGH
9 oz (1 cup plus 2 Tbs) water
8 oz high-gluten flour
.375 oz (1^1/$_2$ tsp) barley malt syrup or molasses
1^1/$_2$ tsp caraway seeds
2.5 oz medium or straight-grade rye flour
1.25 oz pumpernickel flour
INTERMEDIATE RYE BARM BUILD
.0138 oz fresh yeast, crumbled (tiny pinch)
.25 oz (1^1/$_2$ tsp) salt

BARM BUILD Stir starter and rye flour together; knead until smooth. Ferment 4 to 6 hours at room temperature. Refrigerate overnight.

FINAL DOUGH In a mixer bowl, autolyse the water, high-gluten flour, barley malt, and caraway seeds. Mix in the barm build and yeast on low speed. Add the salt. Knead on medium speed until the dough is smooth and just begins to clean the sides of the bowl, 5 to 6 minutes. Ferment until doubled, about 4 hours, turning once. Divide. Preshape and bench 20 minutes. Form. Couche or place on parchment-lined pans sprinkled with cornmeal. If loaves must be moved any more than turning out of bannetons, go ahead and slash at this point. Proof in a cool, humid environment until doubled, 2 to 3 hours. Bake with steam at 425°F until deep brown, 45 to 50 minutes.

NOTE Feed the starter during a refreshment cycle with rye or whole wheat flour.

ENRICHED BREADS

Enriched breads contain tenderizing, rich ingredients like butter, sugar, and eggs. They are additionally embellished with chocolate, nuts, dried fruits, and liquor. The flour may be a mixture of bread and cake, or of pastry and bread flour depending on how much weight the dough must support. Added fat changes the texture of these breads, making them more tender and even cakelike. Since the gluten in rich doughs is interrupted by fat and sugar, these breads are often baked in pans for support. Doughs that have lots of sugar and fat, but little water, will ferment sluggishly. The more enriched a dough is, the more yeast is used. The type of yeast has an effect on fermentation as well. Osmotolerant instant dry yeast has been especially formulated for these types of doughs.

BASIC HOLIDAY
BREAD DOUGH

MAKES 3 POUNDS 6 OUNCES DOUGH Many recipes such as stollen and babka, start with this dough. **Kugelhopf** is made by baking this dough in a kugelhopf-shaped tube pan sprinkled with sliced almonds. Dried fruit is often added to kugelhopf, which is dusted with confectioners' sugar as a garnish. When baked in a ring mold and coated with rum syrup, this dough becomes a **savarin**, and when combined with raisins and baked in small cylindrical molds, it is known as **baba au rum**. Other variations of this dough are listed below.

SPONGE
4.25 oz ($^1/_2$ cup) milk
4.25 oz ($^1/_2$ cup) heavy cream
3.5 oz cake flour
.33 oz (1 Tbs) osmotolerant instant active dry yeast

FINAL DOUGH
SPONGE
3.5 oz ($^1/_2$ cup) sugar
.25 oz (1$^1/_2$ tsp) salt
6.8 oz whole eggs (4 large)
1.65 oz egg yolks (3 large)
1 lb 5 oz bread flour
8 oz unsalted butter, softened and cut into pieces

SPONGE Heat the milk and cream until hot. Combine the flour and yeast and whisk in the cream until smooth. Proof at room temperature for 45 minutes.

FINAL DOUGH Combine the sponge, sugar, and salt in a mixer bowl. Whisk the eggs and yolks together. With the paddle attachment, beat the eggs and flour into the dough alternately on low speed, ending with the flour. Beat on medium speed for 5 to 6 minutes. Reduce speed to low. Beat in the butter in pieces until just incorporated, 1 to 2 minutes.

STOLLEN

MAKES TWO 14 BY 6-INCH LOAVES

Using the Basic Holiday Bread Dough recipe, add 2 tablespoons lemon juice and 2 tablespoons lemon zest along with the eggs. After the butter has been added, flatten the dough into a rough rectangle. Sprinkle with 1$^1/_4$ cups golden raisins, 1 cup toasted sliced almonds, and 1 cup candied fruit. Roll toward the center from both short ends of the rectangle until the two rolls meet. Flatten slightly. Fold the dough over in thirds lengthwise. Ferment until increased 1$^1/_2$ times, turning once, about 1 hour. Deflate gently and retard overnight. Divide into two equal pieces. Shape into rounds; bench 15 minutes. Flatten the rounds into ovals about 12 inches long, 8 inches wide, and $^3/_4$ inch thick. Fold the long side of the oval over, not quite in half. Place on a parchment-lined sheet pan. Let rise until doubled, about 2 hours. Bake at 350°F for 40 to 45 minutes or until golden. While hot, repeatedly brush with $^1/_2$ cup melted butter and $^1/_2$ cup brandy, alternating. Dust repeatedly with confectioners' sugar.

CINNAMON-ALMOND BABKA BRAID

MAKES THREE 9 BY 5-INCH LOAVES

Prepare the Basic Holiday Bread Dough recipe (page 53). Ferment until increased 1$\frac{1}{2}$ times, turning once, about 1 hour. Deflate the dough gently and refrigerate overnight. Divide the dough in three equal pieces. Gently roll each piece into a loose cylinder. Rest 15 minutes. Flatten each cylinder into a rectangle about 12 by 8 inches. Cut each rectangle lengthwise into three strips. Pipe a line of cinnamon-almond filling (recipe follows) down the center of each strip. Fold the edges of the strip over the filling; press seam shut. For each loaf, braid together three strips, pressing ends together. Place braids in three buttered 9 by 5-inch loaf pans, tucking the ends of the braids underneath to make nice, tall loaves. Proof until doubled, about 2 hours. Bake at 350°F for 30 minutes. Cool in pans 10 minutes. Remove; brush liberally with melted butter. Roll in cinnamon-sugar to coat.

CINNAMON-ALMOND FILLING

1 lb almond paste (about 2 cups, packed)
12 oz unsalted butter, at room temperature
8 oz (1 cup plus 2 tbs) sugar
.08 oz ($\frac{1}{2}$ tsp) salt
1.10 oz egg yolks (2 large)
4 oz (1 cup) pastry crumbs, graham cracker crumbs, or flour
2 Tbs ground cinnamon

Beat (with paddle) the almond paste, butter, sugar, and salt until smooth. Beat in egg yolks. Beat in crumbs and cinnamon. Refrigerate.

HOT CROSS BUNS

MAKES 18 BUNS

Using the Basic Holiday Bread Dough recipe (page 53), add 2 tablespoons orange juice and 2 tablespoons orange zest along with the eggs. Add 3 tablespoons cinnamon, $1^1/_2$ teaspoons cloves, and $^3/_4$ teaspoon nutmeg with the flour. After the butter has been added, flatten the dough into a rough rectangle on a floured surface. Sprinkle with $2^1/_2$ cups currants. Roll toward the center jellyroll style from both short ends of the rectangle until the two rolls meet. Flatten slightly. Fold the dough over in thirds lengthwise—the business letter fold. Ferment until increased $1^1/_2$ times, turning once, about 1 hour. Deflate the dough gently and refrigerate overnight. Divide into 18 pieces (about 2.75 ounces per bun). Roll against the table to form tight rounds. Place in two buttered 9-inch square pans in rows of three. Proof until doubled, about 1 hour. Brush with egg wash. Bake at 350°F for 16 to 18 minutes or until golden. Add orange juice to confectioners' sugar to make a glaze of piping consistency. Pipe icing cross over each bun.

RICH SWEET DOUGH

MAKES 3 POUNDS 6 OUNCES DOUGH By varying this basic dough slightly, and experimenting with different fillings and shapes, you can create a number of appealing and diverse products, from breakfast pastries to coffee cakes to doughnuts.

1 lb 13 oz all-purpose flour
2.33 oz ($^1/_3$ cup) sugar
.50 oz ($4^1/_2$ tsp) osmotolerant instant active dry yeast
8.5 oz (1 cup) warm milk
6 oz ($^3/_4$ cup) hot water
1.7 oz egg (1 large)
.55 egg yolk (1 large)
1 tsp vanilla extract
.25 oz ($1^1/_2$ tsp) salt

In a mixer bowl, combine the flour and sugar. Combine the yeast, milk, and water. With mixer running on low speed, add the yeast mixture, egg, egg yolk, vanilla, and salt, one after another. Increase the speed to medium; knead until the dough cleans the sides of the bowl and is smooth and elastic, 5 to 6 minutes. Ferment until tripled in volume, 45 minutes to 1 hour. Turn. Ferment until doubled, 30 to 40 minutes. Divide and shape as desired.

STICKY BUNS

MAKES 6 DOZEN BUNS SIZED FOR STANDARD MUFFIN TINS

TOPPING
2 lb 3 oz (5 cups) sugar
1 lb (1$^1/_3$ cups) dark corn syrup
2 oz ($^1/_4$ cup) lemon juice
.05 oz (1 Tbs) vanilla extract
.08 oz ($^1/_2$ tsp) salt
BUNS
One recipe **RICH SWEET DOUGH,** ready for shaping (page 57)
2 cups **PRUNE FILLING** (page 267)
1 lb 4 oz (5 cups) pecan halves

TOPPING Whisk all ingredients for topping together until smooth. Keep in refrigerator until ready to use.

BUNS Divide the dough in half. Roll each half into rectangle 32 inches long
and 8 inches wide. Spread with prune filling to within $^1/_4$ inch of edges. Roll up
jellyroll style, beginning with long edges. Cut each roll across into 36 (1-inch)
slices. Heavily butter the muffin cups. Divide the topping among the muffin
cups. Sprinkle each with a heaping tablespoon of pecans. Top with a slice
of dough, cut side up. Proof until doubled, about 45 minutes. Bake at 350°F for
25 minutes. Invert the muffin pans onto sheet pans immediately to release the
caramel and pecans.

CINNAMON ROLLS

MAKES 3 DOZEN LARGE (5-INCH) CINNAMON ROLLS

One recipe **RICH SWEET DOUGH** (page 57)
12 oz unsalted butter, melted
1 lb 8 oz (3 cups packed) brown sugar
1 oz ($^1/_4$ cup) ground cinnamon
CONFECTIONERS' SUGAR GLAZE (page 261)

Divide the dough in half. Roll each half into a rectangle 28 inches long and 8 inches wide. Brush with melted butter. Combine the brown sugar and cinnamon. Sprinkle over the dough. Roll up jellyroll style, beginning with the long edges. Cut each roll across into 18 (about 1$^1/_2$-inch) slices. Butter three half-sheet pans. Arrange 12 rolls, cut side up, per pan in rows of four by three, spacing evenly. Let rise until doubled, about 45 minutes. Bake at 350°F for 20 to 25 minutes, or until the tops are browned. Spread the tops of the warm rolls liberally with glaze.

RAISIN-PECAN CINNAMON ROLLS

Sprinkle 2 cups each raisins (12 ounces) and pecans (8 ounces) over the brown sugar filling before rolling.

RAISED DOUGHNUTS

MAKES 3 POUNDS 6 OUNCES DOUGH OR 2 DOZEN DOUGHNUTS The dough for yeast-risen doughnuts, as opposed to cake doughnuts, which are chemically leavened, is closely related to the sweet dough used for cinnamon rolls and sticky buns. This dough for doughnuts has more fat and moisture than that sweet dough, making it richer, but lighter in texture.

1 lb 13 oz all-purpose flour
4.66 oz (^{2}/$_3$ cup) sugar
.50 oz (4^1/$_2$ tsp) osmotolerant instant active dry yeast
15 oz (about 1^3/$_4$ cups) warm milk
3.4 oz eggs (2 large)
1.1 oz egg yolks (2 large)
.17 oz (1 tsp) vanilla extract
.25 oz (1^1/$_2$ tsp) salt
Vegetable oil, for frying
CONFECTIONERS' SUGAR GLAZE (page 261) or **CHOCOLATE GLAZE** (page 247)

Combine the flour and sugar in a mixer bowl. Combine the yeast and milk in another bowl. With mixer running on low speed, add the yeast mixture, eggs, egg yolks, vanilla, and salt, one after another. Increase the speed to medium; knead until the dough cleans the sides of the bowl and is smooth and elastic, 5 to 6 minutes. Ferment until tripled in volume, 45 minutes to 1 hour. Turn. Ferment until doubled, 30 to 40 minutes. On a lightly floured surface, roll out to ^{3}/$_4$-inch thickness. Cut out doughnuts. Reroll and cut out scraps. Deep-fry at 365°F until golden, about 2 minutes per side. Drain on paper towels. Glaze with confectioners' sugar glaze or chocolate glaze, or dust with either cinnamon-sugar or confectioners' sugar.

PANETTONE

MAKES 5 POUNDS DOUGH OR TWO LARGE PANETTONE This classic Italian holiday bread is rich with butter and eggs and contains an astonishingly large amount of sugar for a yeasted dough. To achieve its great texture (and great keeping qualities), a mixed starter is used in this formula: the simple sponge utilizes osmotolerant yeast and the final dough adds a bit of firm sourdough to help overcome the heaviness and dryness that are common problems. Beating in the sugar at the end of the mix also seems to help; the gluten structure has become relatively well developed and can now accommodate the extra sugar.

SPONGE
2.66 oz ($^1/_3$ cup) hot water
.11 oz (1 tsp) osmotolerant instant active dry yeast
1.75 oz ($^1/_4$ cup) sugar
1.7 oz egg (1 large)
4.5 oz bread flour

FINAL DOUGH
4 oz ($^1/_2$ cup) brandy
1 lb (about 3 cups) candied orange and/or lemon peel
SPONGE
4 oz **INTERMEDIATE BARM BUILD** (page 49)
6.8 oz eggs (4 large)
1.65 oz egg yolks (3 large)
1.5 oz (2 Tbs) honey
.25 oz (1$^1/_2$ tsp) almond extract
.25 oz (1$^1/_2$ tsp) salt
1 lb 2 oz bread flour
5.25 oz ($^3/_4$ cup) sugar
12 oz cold unsalted butter, softened

SPONGE Combine hot water and yeast for sponge. Stir in sugar and egg. Stir in bread flour until well combined. Ferment in warm place for 1 hour.

FINAL DOUGH Heat brandy and pour over candied peel. Let stand while preparing dough.

In a mixer bowl, combine all of the sponge and the white barm build. Whisk together the eggs, yolks, honey, almond extract, and salt. With mixer fitted with paddle, running on medium speed, add the egg mixture and flour alternately, very slowly—about $1/4$ cup at a time. When all of the flour and liquid are incorporated, beat on high speed for 2 minutes. Reduce the speed to low and beat in the sugar slowly. Add the butter in pieces. Increase the speed to high; beat for 5 minutes.

Place dough on floured surface. Pat out into a rough rectangle. Sprinkle with an even layer of candied peel. Roll up jellyroll style. Flatten slightly. Fold and roll over upon itself in thirds. Ferment until doubled, about $1^{1}/_{2}$ hours, turning once. Divide dough in half. Form into rounds. Place in buttered panettone molds or clean No. 10 cans. Retard overnight. Proof in a warm, humid environment until nearly tripled, about $1^{1}/_{2}$ to 3 hours. Bake at 350°F until tops are browned and tester comes out clean, 50 minutes to 1 hour.

BRIOCHE

MAKES 3 POUNDS 4 OUNCES DOUGH OR TWO 8½-INCH CLASSIC FLUTED BRIOCHE ROUNDS, TWO 8 BY 4-INCH LOAVES, OR TWELVE 3½-INCH ROLLS
The richer the dough, the more difficult it is to handle. Brioche, for example, may have anywhere from a 1:2 ratio of butter to flour up to equal weights of each, making it delicious and tender when baked but horribly sticky as a dough. Just be patient, refrigerate as directed, and resist the evil urge to add more flour.

SPONGE
3 oz (6 Tbs) water
2 oz (about ¼ cup) milk
.11 oz (1 tsp) instant yeast
.15 oz (1 tsp) sugar
4 oz bread flour

DOUGH
SPONGE
12 oz eggs (about 8 large)
1.75 oz (¼ cup) sugar
.33 oz (2 tsp) salt
11 oz bread flour
4 oz cake flour

BUTTER MIXTURE
1 lb cold unsalted butter, cut into 1-inch pieces
1 oz bread flour

SPONGE Whisk together all the ingredients for the sponge until smooth. Cover and let rise in a warm place until bubbly and nearly doubled, about 45 minutes.

DOUGH In a mixer bowl, whisk the sponge, eggs, sugar, and salt until combined. With mixer running on low speed, add the flours, ½ cup at a time. When the dough comes together, increase the speed to medium. Knead 3 minutes; set aside.

BUTTER MIXTURE Beat the flour and butter with paddle until malleable, but still cold and firm. Add the reserved dough to the butter; beat on medium speed until butter is mostly incorporated, 3 to 4 minutes. Refrigerate overnight. Gently deflate the dough when ready to shape.

FOR CLASSIC BRIOCHE WITH TOPKNOTS Divide the dough in half (27 ounces each). Set aside a 4-ounce piece from each larger piece. Gently shape the larger pieces into rounds. Place the rounds in buttered brioche molds. With fingers, poke a hole in the center of the rounds. Shape the smaller pieces into rounds. Roll against the table to elongate one end. Insert the long end of each small piece into the holes in the larger pieces.

FOR LOAVES Divide the dough in half (27 ounces each). Knead each half briefly, four or five turns, on a lightly floured surface. Form into cylinders with slightly tapered ends. Place in buttered loaf pans.

FOR ROLLS Knead the dough briefly on a floured surface. Divide the dough into 12 (4$^1/_2$-ounce) pieces. Roll each piece into a 4-inch long cylinder. Using the side of your hand in a sawing motion, separate one-fourth of the dough from each cylinder. Place the larger pieces of dough into small fluted molds. To form topknots, with twisting motion, push the smaller pieces down into the larger pieces.

Allow the dough to double, covered, in a warm place. Preheat the oven to 425°F. Brush the tops of the brioche with egg wash. Bake 5 minutes. Reduce temperature to 375°F. Bake small brioche for 15 minutes and large brioche for 35 to 40 minutes.

CHALLAH

MAKES 1 POUND 15 OUNCES DOUGH OR ONE LARGE OR TWO SMALL (15.5-OUNCES EACH) BRAIDED LOAVES This Jewish bread is truly golden and has a light, fluffy interior. The braid is traditional, but for an even fancier look, reserve about one-fourth of the dough to make a smaller braid that is placed on top of the larger braid. For Rosh Hashanah, the Jewish New Year, challah dough is rolled into a rope that is coiled into a round to symbolize the cyclical nature of the passing seasons. For dietary reasons, challah can be prepared with oil and water (instead of milk and butter) in order to be served with the meat course.

1 lb bread flour
1.31 oz (3 Tbs) sugar
.22 oz (2 tsp) instant yeast
6 oz ($^3/_4$ cup) hot water (or 6.37 oz milk, $^3/_4$ cup)
1 oz (2 Tbs) oil or unsalted melted butter
1.65 oz egg yolks (3 large)
3.4 oz eggs (2 large)
.17 oz (1 tsp) salt
EGG WASH (page 264) for glazing

Combine the flour and sugar in a mixer bowl. Add the yeast to the hot water or milk. With mixer running on low speed, add the yeast mixture, oil or butter, yolks, whole eggs, and salt. When combined, increase the speed to medium; knead until smooth, shiny, and elastic, 6 to 8 minutes. Ferment until doubled, about 1 hour. Turn. Ferment until doubled, about 1 hour. Divide in three (or six for two smaller loaves) equal pieces; form into loose cylinders. Bench 20 minutes. Roll each cylinder into a 20-inch (12-inch for smaller loaves) rope. Braid the ropes, pinching the ends of the braid together and tucking the ends under the middle of the loaf. Place on a parchment-lined sheet pan. Let rise until doubled, 45 minutes to 1 hour. Brush heavily with egg yolk–water glaze. Bake at 375°F for 40 to 45 minutes or until golden and hollow when rapped.

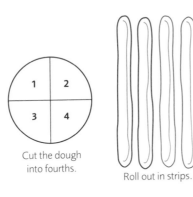

Cut the dough
into fourths.

Roll out in strips.

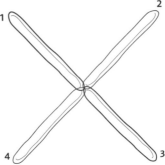

Join ends as shown. Take strip 4 in your
left hand, strip 2 in your right hand.

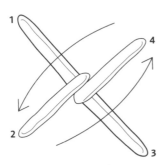

Strip 4 goes over and strip 2 goes over.

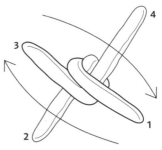

Strip 1 in your left hand goes over and
strip 3 in your right hand goes over.

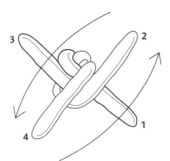

Repeat the last three steps until finished.

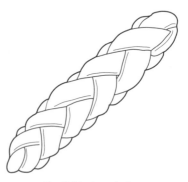

The finished product.

FIGURE 2.4 **Making a four-braided bread.**

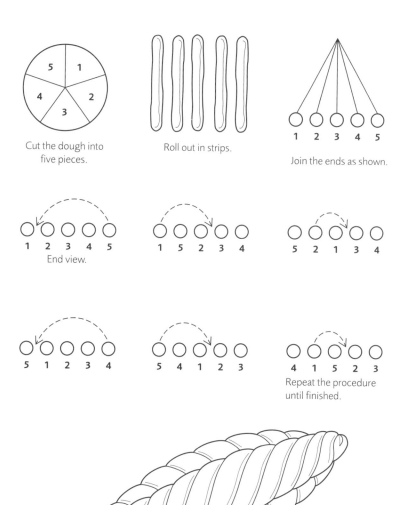

Cut the dough into
five pieces.

Roll out in strips.

1 2 3 4 5
Join the ends as shown.

1 2 3 4 5
End view.

1 5 2 3 4

5 2 1 3 4

5 1 2 3 4

5 4 1 2 3

4 1 5 2 3
Repeat the procedure
until finished.

The finished product.

FIGURE 2.5 **Making a five-braided bread.**

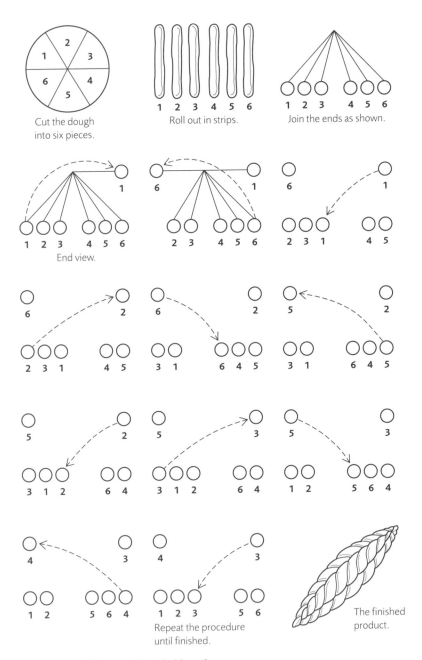

Cut the dough
into six pieces.

Roll out in strips.

Join the ends as shown.

End view.

Repeat the procedure
until finished.

The finished
product.

FIGURE 2.6 **Making a six-braided bread.**

BAGELS

Bagels get their unique texture from being poached in simmering water before baking at a relatively high temperature (425° to 475°F). Bagels are made with bread or high-protein flour and very little moisture, which makes them denser than other breads. They can be made with the straight-rise method, or they can be made with a starter. Here a poolish is used in the first recipe to improve dough extensibility and flavor (and to help increase the life of your mixer). The sourdough bagels that follow have an even more complex flavor, more chewiness, and an increased shelf life. Bagels can be topped with practically anything: poppy seeds, sesame seeds, dehydrated onion—whatever takes your fancy.

BAGELS

MAKES EIGHT LARGE (4-OUNCE) BAGELS

POOLISH
8 oz water (1 cup) water
.03 oz (generous $^1/_4$ tsp) instant yeast
4.5 oz bread flour
FINAL DOUGH
1 lb bread flour
1 Tbs (.3 oz) diastatic malt powder
.06 oz ($^1/_2$ tsp) instant yeast
4 oz ($^1/_2$ cup) hot water
POOLISH
.33 oz (2 tsp) salt

POOLISH Heat $^1/_4$ cup of the water until hot; add the yeast. Stir together the remaining $^1/_2$ cup cool water and the flour. Stir in the yeast mixture until smooth. Let rise until bubbly, doubled, and just beginning to fall, 3 to 5 hours. Refrigerate overnight.

FINAL DOUGH In a mixer bowl, combine the flour and malt powder. Combine the yeast and hot water. With mixer running on low speed, add the yeast mixture, poolish, and salt. Increase the speed to medium, and knead until smooth and elastic, 8 to 10 minutes. The dough will be quite stiff. Divide into eight 4-ounce pieces. Bench 5 minutes. Form into rounds. With a thumb, poke a hole into the center of the dough ball. Insert both thumbs and work dough into a ring shape with a $1^1/_2$-inch hole in the center. Let rise until increased by 25 percent, about $1^1/_2$ hours. (If they float, after 15 seconds in water, they are ready.) Refrigerate overnight on oiled, semonlina-dusted pans.

Bring at least 4 inches of water to a boil in a heavy pot; reduce the heat to a simmer. Poach the bagels in batches; they will sink, then bob to the surface, about 1 minute per side. Drain with a slotted spoon. Place on a freshly oiled, semolina-dusted pan at least 2 inches apart. Top as desired. Bake at 475°F for 16 to 18 minutes.

SOURDOUGH BAGELS

MAKES EIGHT LARGE (4-OUNCE) BAGELS

1 lb bread flour
1 Tbs diastatic malt powder
8 oz (1 cup) cool water
8 oz **INTERMEDIATE BARM BUILD** (page 49)
.25 oz ($1^1/_2$ tsp) salt

In a mixer bowl, autolyse the flours, malt powder, and water. Mix in the barm build on low speed. Add the salt. Knead on medium speed until smooth and elastic, 8 to 10 minutes. The dough will be quite stiff. Ferment 4 hours. Divide. Bench 5 minutes. Form into rounds. With a thumb, poke a hole into the center of each dough ball. Insert both thumbs and work dough into a ring shape with a $1^1/_2$-inch hole in the center. Proof until increased by 25 percent, 45 minutes to 1 hour. (If they float after 15 seconds in a bowl of water, they are ready.)

Retard overnight (or refrigerate) on oiled, semolina-dusted pans. Bring at least 4 inches of water to a boil in a heavy pot; reduce the heat to a simmer. Poach the bagels in batches; they will sink, then bob to the surface. Cook about 1 minute per side after they float. Drain with a slotted spoon. Place on a freshly oiled, semolina-dusted pan at least 2 inches apart. Top as desired. Bake at 475°F for 16 to 18 minutes.

SOURDOUGH EGG BAGELS

MAKES EIGHT LARGE (4-OUNCE) BAGELS

8 oz bread flour
8 oz all-purpose flour
1 Tbs diastatic malt powder
5 oz (10 Tbs) cool water
8 oz **INTERMEDIATE BARM BUILD** (page 49)
3.4 oz eggs (2 large)
.25 oz (1^1/$_2$ tsp) salt

In a mixer bowl, autolyse the flours, malt powder, and water. Mix in the barm build on low speed. Add the salt. Knead on medium speed until smooth and elastic, 8 to 10 minutes. The dough will be quite stiff. Ferment 4 hours. Divide. Bench 5 minutes. Form into rounds. With a thumb, poke a hole into the center of each dough ball. Insert both thumbs and work dough into a ring shape with a 1^1/$_2$-inch hole in the center. Proof until increased by 25 percent, 45 minutes to 1 hour. (If they float after 15 seconds in a bowl of water, they are ready.) Retard overnight (or refrigerate) on oiled, semolina-dusted pans. Bring at least 4 inches of water to a boil in a heavy pot; reduce the heat to a simmer. Poach the bagels in batches; they will sink, then bob to the surface. Cook about 1 minute per side after they float. Drain with a slotted spoon. Place on a freshly oiled, semolina-dusted pan at least 2 inches apart. Top as desired. Bake at 475°F for 16 to 18 minutes.

SOURDOUGH PUMPERNICKEL BAGELS

MAKES EIGHT LARGE (4-OUNCE) BAGELS

11 oz bread flour
5 oz pumpernickel flour
1 Tbs diastatic malt powder
8 oz (1 cup) cool water
8 oz **INTERMEDIATE BARM BUILD** (page 49)
.25 oz (1^1/$_2$) tsp. salt

In a mixer bowl, autolyse the flours, malt powder, and water. Mix in the barm build on low speed. Add the salt. Knead on medium speed until smooth and elastic, 8 to 10 minutes. The dough will be quite stiff. Ferment 4 hours. Divide. Bench 5 minutes. Form into rounds. With a thumb, poke a hole into the center of each dough ball. Insert both thumbs and work dough into a ring shape with a 1^1/$_2$-inch hole in the center. Proof until increased by 25 percent, 45 minutes to 1 hour. (If they float after 15 seconds in a bowl of water, they are ready.) Retard overnight (or refrigerate) on oiled, semolina-dusted pans. Bring at least 4 inches of water to a boil in a heavy pot; reduce the heat to a simmer. Poach the bagels in batches; they will sink, then bob to the surface. Cook about 1 minute per side after they float. Drain with a slotted spoon. Place on a freshly oiled, semolina-dusted pan at least 2 inches apart. Top as desired. Bake at 475°F for 16 to 18 minutes.

LAMINATES
(LAYERED DOUGHS)

CHAPTER 3

Laminates include **puff pastry dough, croissant dough,** and **Danish dough. Lamination** is the process of rolling and folding a piece of dough to encase a block of butter and create hundreds of stacked layers of pastry (see Figure 3.1, page 86). The ability of humble ingredients like the flour, butter, and water in classic puff pastry to rise over eight times their initial height during baking is gratifying and truly spectacular.

The method for making all laminate doughs is virtually the same. A dough, the *détrempe,* whose primary ingredients are flour, water, and salt, is wrapped around a block of cool but malleable butter, the *beurrage.* Puff pastry and Danish pastry consist of roughly equal amounts by weight of butter to flour. The **puff pastry** *détrempe* consists of flour, water, a small amount of butter, and salt. **Danish** *détrempe* is a rich, soft, yeasted dough prepared with flour, milk, eggs, sugar, a very small amount of butter, and salt. The **croissant** *détrempe* is yeasted, like the Danish *détrempe,* but is much less rich. It contains water and/or milk, flour, a bit of sugar, and salt.

Once assembled into a neat package, the resulting dough blocks— the *patons*—are then rolled and folded in a series of turns, or *tourage.* This process of lamination is the sole leavening agent of puff pastry and it is what makes yeast-risen croissants and Danish flaky instead of merely breadlike.

Surprisingly, laminates rely on a well-developed gluten structure. The repeated rolling and folding of the dough creates pockets of trapped air between the many layers, but it also coils and joins the strands of gluten to form an elastic, expansive structure. This structure must be strong enough to contain the expanding gases as the pastry bakes. In the heat of the oven, most of the fat melts into the dough, leaving air pockets behind. Steam expands the air pockets, causing the layers of dough to separate from one another and rise.

INGREDIENTS AND EQUIPMENT FOR LAMINATES

FLOUR

Hard wheat flours, which have the proteins necessary to form a strong gluten structure, are used in making laminates. The gluten allows the dough to stretch rather than break under the stress of rolling, but it also causes the dough to become resistant to rolling as it is repeatedly handled and stressed. As a result, some soft flour is incorporated into the recipes. The ratio of high-protein flour to soft changes according to the amount of time a dough is allowed to rest between turns. Rapid or quick puff pastry, for example, is given all its turns at once without resting, and therefore requires a higher amount of soft flour to accommodate the constant stretching and rolling.

FAT

Laminates may have almost equal weights of flour and fat, so naturally the fat you use affects the final texture and flavor. The fat you choose may alter the method: The ease of rolling and folding the fat into the *détrempe* is determined by that fat's melting point and plasticity.

Although butter is certainly the first choice for great-tasting pastry, it doesn't necessarily make the highest or flakiest pastry. Lard, along with hydrogenated vegetable shortenings and hard margarines designed to be rolled into laminate doughs, possess large fat crystals that contribute to flaking. Lard and shortening have a lower water content than butter, meaning that an equal amount by weight will provide more fat, and therefore create a more tender product. Unfortunately, pastry made with shortening may have a waxy aftertaste, owing to the higher melting point of the fat.

Specialized laminate shortenings, whether lard or vegetable based, remain plastic over a large temperature range, forming a thin, continuous film that separates the rolled dough layers and prevents them from merging. Unlike butter, they will neither melt into the dough before baking nor become so hard when chilled that they rupture the layers when the dough is rolled. Working with butter requires excellent technique and careful handling of the dough, to be sure, but it produces superior flavor.

Be mindful of the ambient temperature, as well as that of the components, and be as diligent as possible in sealing edges and applying even pressure during rolling. Ideally, the *détrempe* and *beurrage* will be close to the same temperature, about 60°F, to ensure even fat distribution, minimize any leakage, and prevent cold butter from tearing through the dough layers. Do not use butter softened by sitting at room temperature for laminates, as it melts when handled. Instead, beat large chunks of cold butter into a malleable state by force, either with a rolling pin or a mixer fitted with the paddle. This ensures consistent temperature throughout the block.

Usually the *détrempe* is chilled to bring it to the same temperature as the butter, but using ice water and/or very cold milk to make the *détrempe* is a faster way to achieve a cool dough. To use this shortcut with yeasted doughs, select fresh yeast, rather than a dry yeast that requires rehydration in a warm liquid.

DOUGH SHEETERS, RETARDERS, AND PROOFERS

Dough sheeters are invaluable appliances for making laminate products. The rollers of a sheeter are adjustable, able to perfectly roll a dough to the desired thickness. For laminate doughs, which start out as a thick block of dough, the rollers can be set progressively closer together after each pass of the *paton*. In addition to the obvious savings in time and labor, the even pressure applied to the dough by the rollers is hard to duplicate by hand.

The yeasted laminates—croissant and Danish—really benefit from specialized dough retarders. Retarders hold yeasted doughs slightly above normal refrigerator temperatures, allowing very slow fermentation to occur in either the *paton* or the formed product. Retarder-proofer combination models can be programmed to steadily, slowly increase the temperature and humidity for an overnight rise.

Proof boxes create a warm, humid environment, letting the dough rise uncovered and expand to maximum height. Even if you can't afford a fancy electronic model, a simple proof box can be rigged with a hotel pan filled with water set over a Sterno. Ideal proofing temperatures are between 78° and 82°F at 80 percent humidity.

PUFF PASTRIES

CLASSIC PUFF PASTRY

MAKES 2 POUNDS 11 OUNCES DOUGH Also called **pâte feuilletée**, puff pastry is the only dough that achieves its height solely through lamination. Classic puff pastry produces the highest rise of any of the laminates. It is best used in any recipe where the pastry itself must shine. Bouchées and vols-au-vents—pastry shells designed to hold fillings—require the height that can be provided only by classic puff pastry. Elaborate designs can be incised onto the pastry, creating a stunning decorative effect. Pithiviers, a French dessert of a rich almond cream baked between two circles of puff pastry, is decorated in this way. The fruit-filled turnover is another product best made with classic puff pastry.

DOUGH (*DÉTREMPE*)	LARGE BATCH
3 cups unbleached bread flour	3 lb 8 oz
$^1/_2$ cup cake flour	8 oz
$1^1/_2$ tsp salt	1 oz
$^1/_4$ cup unsalted butter, melted	8 oz
$1^1/_2$ tsp lemon juice	1 oz
$^3/_4$ cup + 2 Tbs (7 fl oz) ice water	1 lb 12 oz
BUTTER (*BEURRAGE*)	
2 cups unsalted butter, cut into 1-inch chunks	4 lb
5 Tbs unbleached bread flour	6 oz

For the dough, combine the flours and salt in a mixer bowl. Using the dough hook and with mixer on low speed, add the butter and lemon juice. Add the ice water in a slow, steady stream, scraping up mixture from the bottom. Add just enough water so that the dough comes together. Increase the speed to medium; knead until smooth and stretchy, about 45 seconds. Form into a rough rectangle; chill 1 hour. For butter mixture, fit mixer with paddle. Add the butter and flour; beat on low speed until smooth and malleable but still cool. Form butter into a block by pounding with a rolling pin on a floured surface. Divide the butter block in half. Roll each half into a 5 by 7-inch rectangle. To assemble, roll the dough into an 8 by 18-inch rectangle. Place one butter rectangle in the center of the dough. Fold over flap of dough to cover, pressing dough at edges to seal. Place the remaining butter rectangle on top of the enclosed butter. Fold the remaining flap of dough to cover, sealing with your fingers; the butter should extend fully into the corners. Roll out the dough package in the direction of the open ends of folds into a 10 by 24-inch rectangle, dusting liberally with the flour and rolling in all directions. Do not roll over the ends of the dough. Fold the dough into thirds, business-letter fashion. Refrigerate 1 hour (first turn). Rotate the dough block 90 degrees from the direction of the previous roll. Roll and repeat the 3-fold turn as before two more times (second and third turns). Refrigerate 45 minutes. Repeat the sequence, performing two more turns (fourth and fifth turns). Refrigerate at least one hour before rolling and shaping. Allow the sheet of rolled dough to rest in the refrigerator 15 minutes before cutting.

RAPID PUFF PASTRY

MAKES 2 POUNDS 6 OUNCES DOUGH Also called quick puff pastry, this pastry starts out just like pie dough. Very cold pieces of butter, flour, salt, and ice water are briefly mixed, leaving large, visible chunks of butter. The dough is given its turns immediately. The rapid dough will not rise as high as the classic, but the texture is still flaky and delicate, making it an excellent all-purpose pastry. Slightly more dense than classic puff pastry, it stands up well to savory fillings that tend to be heavy. Napoleons are much easier to cut from rapid puff pastry; when sliced, the layers tend to shatter and crumble less than with classic. Puff pastry scraps are perfect for napoleons, since the dough is docked and weighted to prevent a high rise.

		LARGE BATCH
$3^1/_3$ cups bread flour	4 lb	
$1^1/_2$ tsp salt	1 oz	
2 cups unsalted cold butter, cut into $^1/_2$-inch chunks	4 lb	
$^1/_2$ cup plus 1 Tbs (5 fl oz) ice water	1 lb 4 oz	

Combine the flour and salt in a mixer bowl. With the mixer fitted with the paddle and set on lowest speed, add the butter to the flour and salt. Add the ice water in a steady, continuous trickle; continue mixing until the dough just begins to come together. Mix until just barely combined—large pieces of butter should remain. Form into a rough block; chill at least 1 hour. (Pounding the well-floured mass into a shape on a floured surface with a rolling pin minimizes handling.) Roll out into an 8 by 20-inch rectangle. Fold the short ends of the dough inward to meet at the center. Fold the dough at the center as if you were closing a book (4-fold or book turn). Repeat for the second and third turns, rotating the dough package 90 degrees so that when the dough is rolled, the layers of the previous fold now become the short ends of the new rectangle. Refrigerate 1 hour before rolling and shaping.

Puff pastry can be refrigerated three to four days without losing quality. Freeze the assembled products, such as apple turnovers, rather than the whole *paton* for best results. Thaw filled products in the refrigerator overnight before baking. Unfilled or minimally filled products, such as palmiers or vol-au-vent shells, can be baked directly from the freezer.

For both classic and rapid puff pastry, bake small cookies (palmiers, sacristans) at 425°F, sheet-pan-sized puff pastry for napoleons at 400°F, and large filled tortas at 375°F.

YEAST-RISEN LAMINATES

Unlike making bread, the dough (*détrempe*) for croissant and Danish doughs is minimally kneaded to prevent excessive gluten formation. Plenty of gluten development will occur when the butter is rolled in and with the subsequent rolling and folding of the dough. Some bakers like to retard the yeasted *détrempe* overnight, which improves the extensibility of the gluten network and allows more turns to be done at once. This method is rumored to create the most distinct, flaky layers. Retarding or refrigerating the whole *paton* (finished dough after butter has been rolled in) overnight will also improve extensibility when rolling out the dough and reduce shrinkage.

PUFF PASTRY CLASSICS

TURNOVERS are squares of puff pastry rolled to a $^1/_4$-inch thickness. The edges are brushed with egg wash. The desired filling is placed in the middle of the square and the opposite corners are folded over to meet, forming a triangle. The edges are brushed with water and sealed with tines of a fork or back of a small knife.

NAPOLEONS are rectangular strips of puff pastry sandwiched together with a thick layer of pastry cream. They may be two or three layers high. The puff pastry dough must be well docked and weighted with another sheet pan when baked to prevent a high rise. The top layer of pastry is usually coated with a thin layer of fondant and decorated with pulled chocolate lines. Another attractive option, especially for individual portions, is to caramelize confectioners' sugar on the top layer of pastry. Assembled napoleons should be very cold before cutting; use a serrated knife and a very gentle sawing motion. Usually pastry for napoleons is rolled to fit an entire sheet pan, then sliced into rectangles after baking. Napoleons may be any flavor, like mocha or coconut-rum banana. They can be filled with fresh fruit, such as raspberries or strawberries, or with buttercream lightened with whipped cream.

VOL-AU-VENTS are patty shells for holding sweet or savory items. Roll one piece of puff pastry to a $^1/_8$-inch thickness. Cut rounds of the desired size. Roll another piece of puff pastry to a $^1/_4$-inch thickness. Cut another round of same size. Using the smaller cutter, cut out the center of the second round to form a ring. Egg wash the bottom of the ring. Carefully fit the ring onto the bottom round. Press around the edge with the back of a knife to seal. Various cases for fillings, squares and rectangles as well, can be formed in this fashion. Vol-au-vents are used frequently with savory fillings.

For both croissant and Danish dough, the *détrempe* is rolled into a square, and the *beurrage* is placed in the center of the square, cattycornered. The triangular flaps of dough are folded over the *beurrage* and pressed together to seal. The *paton* is given two 3-fold turns and one 4-fold turn, with appropriate rests between. Fewer turns are given to soft-yeasted doughs than puff pastry in order to preserve distinct visible layers.

PUFF PASTRY COOKIES

PALMIERS are crisp puff pastry cookies, usually shaped like spirals, made from rolling the dough in granulated sugar. Instead of dusting the *paton* with flour during the last two turns, use granulated sugar. To assemble, roll out the rectangle of dough to a $1/8$-inch thickness on a sugared surface. During all the folding that happens next, keep sugaring the dough. Fold over both short ends of the rectangle toward the center. Fold this fold over itself, doubling the layer. Finally, in one last fold, have the two sides almost meet in the center—about $3/8$-inch gap should exist between them. Fold in half. Freeze until very firm. Cut across into individual cookies. Space the palmiers, cut sides down, on a sheet pan. They will roughly quadruple during baking, so give them plenty of room. Flip the cookies midway through bake so that the sugar caramelizes evenly on both sides.

SACRISTAINS are puff pastry twists coated with sugar and almonds. Instead of dusting the *paton* with flour during the last two turns, use granulated sugar. To assemble, roll out the rectangle of dough to $1/8$-inch thickness on a sugared surface. Brush the rolled rectangle of dough with egg wash, then sprinkle with more sugar and sliced almonds. Flip and repeat. Cut into 1-inch strips, then across into $1 1/2$-inch rectangles. Twist. Dust with confectioners' sugar after baking.

Fresh yeast is the best choice for these laminates; it works well with cold liquids, with no need for special rehydration in warm water. The dough should be proofed in a warm (80°F), humid environment until it doubles in volume or barely holds a dent when poked. If the dough springs back to the touch, it is underproofed; if it holds a deep dent that does not offer any resistance, it is overproofed. Overproofing results in a product that collapses after baking and has an unpleasantly strong yeasty flavor. Underproofing yields a doughy, unattractive product with fused layers.

CROISSANT DOUGH

MAKES 2 POUNDS 14 OUNCES DOUGH OR 18 LARGE CROISSANTS (7 BY 5-INCH CROISSANT TRIANGLES, UNROLLED)

DOUGH (*DÉTREMPE*)		LARGE BATCH
³/₄ cup ice water	1 lb 8 oz	
³/₄ cup cold milk	1 lb 9.5 oz	
¹/₄ cup granulated sugar	7 oz	
1 oz compressed or cake yeast, crumbled	4 oz	
1 tsp salt	.67 oz	
1²/₃ cups bread flour	2 lb	
1³/₄ cups plus 2 Tbs all-purpose flour	2 lb	
BUTTER (*BEURRAGE*)		
3 Tbs all-purpose flour	3 oz	
1³/₄ cups unsalted cold butter in pieces	3 lb 8 oz	

For the *détrempe*, whisk the water, milk, sugar, yeast, and salt until well combined. Fit the mixer with the dough hook. With machine running on lowest speed, gradually add the flours. Once the dough just begins to come together, increase the speed to medium. Mix 2 minutes. Form the dough into a rough rectangle. Retard overnight. For the beurrage, with mixer on lowest speed, beat the butter and flour until malleable but still cool. Form the butter into a 5-inch square block by pounding with a rolling pin on a floured surface. To assemble the *paton*, on a well-floured surface, roll out dough (*détrempe*) into a 7-inch square. Place the butter in the center of the dough, rotated so that the corners of butter are catty-corner to the corners of the dough. Fold the triangles of dough over the butter, pressing together to seal. Pound (gently) with a rolling pin, to seal firmly and flatten package. Roll out package into a long rectangle, 9 inches wide by about 21 inches long. For the first turn, fold into thirds, business-letter style. Chill 45 minutes. For the second turn, rotate the dough package 90 degrees so that when the dough is rolled, the layers of the previous fold now become the short end of the new rectangle, about 24 by 8 inches. Fold the short ends of the dough toward the center, then fold in half (4-fold or book turn). Chill 45 minutes. Repeat sequence of first turn, ending in the business letter turn. Retard for 1 hour.

To form croissants, on a floured surface, roll dough to a $1/4$-inch thickness. Allow the dough to relax after rolling and before cutting to prevent shrinkage or warping. Cut into triangles 5 inches wide by 7 inches long (see Figure 3.2, page 87). Gently pull and stretch the triangles until nearly $1^1/2$ times longer than they began. Place a small piece of scrap dough at the top of the triangle. Fill if desired. Fold dough over scrap piece/filling. Continue, stretching out arms of croissant by rolling triangle ends against table as you roll, finishing with the point of the triangle tucked under. Proof until increased $1^1/2$ times or until a gentle poke is no longer met with springy resistance, $2^1/2$ to 3 hours at room temperature. If you have a proof box, there is no need to cover and proofing time will be considerably shorter. Brush croissants with egg wash just before baking. Bake at 375°F for about 25 minutes or until golden and crisp on ends. Transfer immediately to wire racks to cool.

CROISSANT VARIATIONS

Traditionally, chocolate croissants, or **pain au chocolat,** are squares of dough rolled around the chocolate stick or baton. **Almond croissants,** using the almond filling on page 265, is also a classic favorite; it is rolled in the traditional crescent shape. Beyond these, feel free to experiment with jam fillings or even savory preparations like ham and cheese. **Morning buns** are strips of croissant dough rolled up like a jellyroll with no filling. The roll is cut across into $1^1/2$-inch-thick pieces. The pieces proof, cut side up, in muffin tins. After baking, roll in cinnamon-sugar while warm.

DANISH DOUGH

MAKES 2 POUNDS 8 OUNCES DOUGH OR 18 LARGE INDIVIDUAL DANISH (4¹/₄-INCH SQUARES) OR TWO KRINGLES OR TEA RINGS OR ONE BRAID

DOUGH (*DÉTREMPE*)		LARGE BATCH
³/₄ cup cold milk	1 lb 9.5 oz	
¹/₄ cup granulated sugar	7 oz	
1 large egg	6.8 oz	
2 large egg yolks	4.4 oz	
1 oz compressed or cake yeast, crumbled	4 oz	
1¹/₂ Tbs unsalted butter, softened	3 oz	
³/₄ tsp salt	.5 oz	
¹/₁₆ tsp ground mace	¹/₄ tsp	
2 cups plus 2 Tbs bread flour	2 lb 8 oz	
¹/₂ cup cake flour	8 oz	
BUTTER (*BEURRAGE*)		
1³/₄ cups unsalted cold butter, in pieces	3 lb 8 oz	
2¹/₂ Tbs bread flour	3 oz	

For the *détrempe*, whisk the milk, sugar, egg, egg yolks, yeast, butter, salt, and mace in mixer bowl until well combined. Fit the mixer with the dough hook and with the machine running on lowest speed, gradually add the flours. Once the dough just begins to come together, increase the speed to medium. Mix 2 minutes. Form the *détrempe* into a rough rectangle. Retard overnight. For the *beurrage*, with mixer on lowest speed, beat the butter and flour until malleable, but still cool. Form the butter into a 5-inch square by pounding with a rolling pin on a floured surface. To assemble the *paton*, on a well-floured surface, roll out dough (*détrempe*) into a 7-inch square. Place the butter in the center of the dough, catty-corner to corners of dough. Fold the triangles of dough over the butter, pressing together to seal. Pound (gently) with the rolling pin to seal firmly and flatten the package. Roll out package into a long rectangle, 9 inches wide by about 21 inches long. For the first turn, fold into thirds, business-letter style. Chill 45 minutes. For the second turn, rotate the dough package 90 degrees so that when dough is rolled to 24 by 8 inches, the layers of the previous fold now become the short end of the new rectangle. Fold the short ends of the dough toward the center, then fold in half (4-fold or book turn). Chill 45 minutes. Repeat the sequence of the first turn, ending in business-letter turn. Retard 1 hour.

To form individual Danish, roll the dough to $1/4$-inch thickness. Allow the dough to relax after rolling and before cutting to prevent shrinkage or warping. Cut into $4^1/4$-inch squares (18 squares). Fill and finish shaping as desired. Proof until increased $1^1/2$ times or until a gentle poke is no longer met with springy resistance, $2^1/2$ to 3 hours at room temperature. If you have a proof box, there is no need cover and the proofing time will be considerably shorter. Brush with egg wash (see page 264). Bake at 375°F for 15 to 17 minutes, until golden.

INDIVIDUAL DANISH SHAPES

Cheese Danish. Dollop of Cream Cheese Filling (page 268) in the center of a square of Danish dough; wrap opposite corners folded over filling.

Pinwheels. Dollop of Lemon Curd or Frangipane (pages 146, 265) in the center of a square of Danish dough; make diagonal cuts toward the center from each corner, points folded in to form a pinwheel (see Fig. 3.3, page 89). Top with fresh or poached fruit.

Cockscomb or bear claw. Dollop of Prune Filling (page 267) or other desired filling in the center of a square of Danish dough; fold dough over to form pocket, sealing edge by brushing with water. Make $1/4$-inch-deep cuts every $1/4$ inch on edge of pocket; bend into curve, pinching ends to keep in place (see Figure 3.4, page 89).

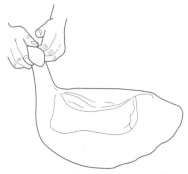

Place the butter block in the center of the rolled-out *détrempe* dough.

Fold the flaps of the *détrempe* over the butter and seal to enclose.

Roll out the paton into a long rectangle, rolling carefully and evenly so the butter does not protrude.

Fold the dough, making sure edges line up evenly.

This dough has been folded into thirds.

This dough is being folded into a four-fold turn.

FIGURE 3.1 **These are the basic steps for rolling and folding laminate doughs. Although the recipes in this chapter may vary from this format, the following illustrations provide the fundamental steps.**

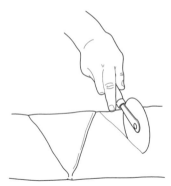

Cut the rolled dough into triangles 5 inches wide by 7 inches long.

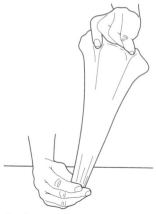

Gently pull and stretch each triangle until it is nearly 1½ times longer.

Place a small piece of scrap dough at the top edge; fold the edge over the scrap dough.

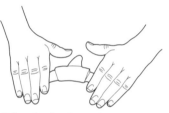

Roll up the dough, gently stretching and pulling crosswise as you roll.

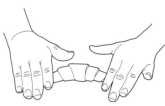

Curve the edges of the dough inward to finish shaping.

FIGURE 3.2 **Forming croissants.**

Swedish tea ring. Roll out the piece of Danish dough to a 24 by 10-inch rectangle. Spread a thin layer of Frangipane (page 265) to within $1/2$ inch of edges. (Fruit preserves may be spread over frangipane, if desired.) Roll up jellyroll style, beginning with long edge. Coil into a circle in a pan, seam side down. Brush with egg wash; sprinkle with sugar and sliced almonds. With scissors, cut the roll nearly through every 1 inch, leaving 1 inch intact to keep all the slices attached to one another. The cut slices can be fanned or arranging in alternating directions for different effects. Bake at 375°F until golden.

Kringles. Prepared in much the same fashion as tea ring, except a $1/4$-inch-thick strip of Kringle Filling (page 268) is spread down the center third (lengthwise) of the Danish dough rectangle. This filling can be sprinkled with cranberries, blueberries, and/or nuts. Fold the sides of the rectangle over the filling to cover, brushing with water to seal. Flip the strip over so that the seam side is down. Brush with egg wash. Cut vents on the diagonal in the top of the strip. Bake at 375°F until golden.

Braided Danish. A variation on either the tea ring or kringle. Spread the filling of your choice down the center third (lengthwise) of the Danish dough rectangle, leaving a 1-inch margin at top and bottom. Instead of folding over the dough, cut each side piece horizontally, about every inch or so, up to the filling to form strips. Fold the top and bottom edge of the dough over the filling to cover. Alternate strips from either side, crossing one over another to cover filling. Brush with egg wash and sprinkle with coarse sugar. Bake at 375°F until golden.

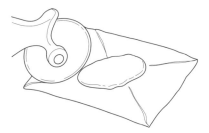

After placing filling in the square, cut the corners of the dough towards the center.

Fold one side of each triangle into the center and press to seal.

FIGURE 3.3 **Forming pinwheels from Danish dough.**

Slice off a 5-inch section of rolled and filled Danish dough. Cut halfway through the dough along one side of the roll every inch or inch and a half.

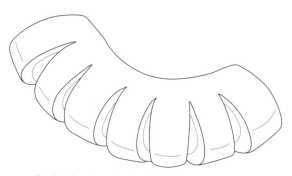

Fan the dough, so that the sliced side opens slightly.

FIGURE 3.4 **Forming bear claws or combs.**

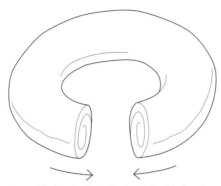

Form a filled and rolled cylinder of Danish dough
into a round by joining the ends.

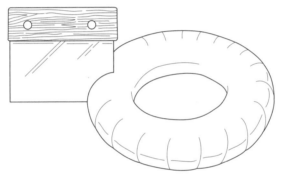

At the outer edge, slice the dough halfway towards the inside
edge, spacing each cut an inch or inch and a half from the next.

Pull each segment to fan dough.

FIGURE 3.5 **Forming a Swedish tea ring.**

Croissant and Danish dough can be frozen in *paton* form, though they fare better when frozen after being cut and shaped, either unfilled or filled and ready to bake. Yeast performance may be compromised by long-term storage in the freezer, so when freezing these doughs for more than two days, increase the amount of yeast by 10 to 25 percent. Thaw the dough completely in the refrigerator, and allow it to warm slightly at room temperature before rolling and shaping. Keep the dough well covered (sheet pans inside large garbage bags work well) during the thawing process to prevent condensation, which makes the dough soggy. Allow the dough to come to room temperature before proofing.

Rolling pastry cutters are available that cut entire rows of croissant triangles in a single pass. Adjustable pastry cutters with multiple wheels make cutting strips or squares quick and accurate.

Except for the rapid puff pastry dough, laminates require at least a 4-hour time commitment. Two-thirds of the turns must be completed in succession (about an hour apart) before the dough can be refrigerated and finished at your convenience. Large areas of extremely cold butter can tear the dough when rolled. Chilling the dough for one hour allows the gluten to relax while keeping the butter cool but pliable. Both the dough and butter should be the same temperature in order to move together as one. Once the majority of turns are completed, the butter will be thin enough to pose no threat to the dough.

Refrigerate, rather than freeze, the dough between turns. A one-hour rest in the refrigerator gives the dough time to relax while keeping the butter cool. Freezing the dough may cause the butter to become hard in some areas but soft in others. Refrigeration ensures consistent texture. If the dough seems to be rubbery and resistant to rolling, it needs to rest longer.

Wrap the *paton* in plastic before placing it in the refrigerator to prevent a dry skin from forming.

If the *beurrage* mixture becomes too soft, mound it on plastic wrap, form it into the desired shape, and chill it until workable.

If the butter comes through the dough at any point, flour heavily and chill before finishing the turn.

Brush excess flour off of the dough before folding.

To ensure an even, stable gluten structure, roll the dough in all directions. Do not roll over the ends of dough, as the pressure will push the butter out the end.

After rolling out puff pastry, lift and flap the dough gently to allow it to contract before cutting into shapes. This will prevent shrinkage. When cutting pastry for multiple-part structures, such as vol-au-vents, chill the pieces 15 to 20 minutes before assembling.

To get the most height when using scraps of dough, stack and chill them before rolling.

Cut straight down with a sharp knife to avoid compressing the layers. If the pastry is glazed on top with either egg or milk, do not glaze over the edge. The glaze can glue layers of pastry together, preventing an even rise.

Bake on parchment paper for even browning and easy transfer.

Recipes often combine double and single turns to achieve the maximum number of layers for each type of pastry, while other recipes have noticeably fewer turns. To test whether the dough can take another turn, cut off 2 inches of the dough. If you can still see distinct layers (for Rapid Puff Pastry, make sure there are visible areas of butter in the dough), try giving this portion one more turn. Then bake the test dough and a small piece from the remaining *paton* and compare them.

CHAPTER 4

CAKES

A case filled with gorgeous cakes is the primary selling point of most bakeries, but looks must be backed up with taste to ensure that customers return. Here are recipes for the basic cakes every pastry chef should know how to make, as well as information about mixing methods and other factors that affect cake structure and quality. Cakes can be frosted, filled, decorated, and garnished any which way, but it takes more than creativity to build a booming cake business—it takes good judgment. How you pair a frosting or filling with a cake has a major effect on the finished texture. The section on combining layers, fillings, and frostings will help ensure that you put your best cake forward.

INGREDIENTS AND EQUIPMENT

The functions of different ingredients in cake baking are discussed in detail in Chapter 14 of *Understanding Baking,* the companion volume to this book. At right is a chart that outlines ingredient function.

Specific mixing methods for cakes are discussed within each category, but there are general rules for producing great cakes of consistent quality.

1. Have ingredients at the appropriate temperature. This is the single most important factor in determining the final texture and height of a cake. Eggs should be around 80°F to provide maximum volume. Butter should be between 60° and 70°F to best incorporate air when creamed with the sugar. The optimum batter temperature after mixing for sponge-type cakes is 90°F and for butter-type cakes is 70°F (Pyler, p. 997).

2. Scrape the inside of the mixer bowl frequently, especially after creaming the butter and sugar, after adding the eggs, and after every addition of flour.

3. Properly grease and flour the pans for good volume and easy cake release. For certain types of sponge cakes, the bottoms of the cake pans may be greased and/or lined with paper to allow easy release, but the sides of the pans should be left ungreased to provide support.

4. Spread batter evenly into pans, smoothing with an offset spatula if necessary, to ensure even baking.

TABLE 4-1 CAKE INGREDIENTS AND THEIR FUNCTIONS

Ingredients / Main Functions in Finished Products	Binding agent	Absorbing agent	Aids keeping qualities	Nutritional value	Affects flavor	Adds sweetness	Produces tenderness	Affects symmetry	Imparts crust color	Shortness or tenderness	Color	Volume	Structure	Grain and texture	Adds quality to product	Brings out flavor
Cake flour	X	X	X	X	X								X			
Sugar			X	X	X	X	X	X	X	X	X			X		
Shortening and butter			X	X	X		X			X				X	X	
Salt					X											X
Whole eggs or yolks	X			X	X		X			X		X	X	X		
Egg whites	X											X	X	X		
Flavor and spices					X											X
Leavening agent								X				X		X		
Milk			X	X		X			X		X			X	X	X

95

5. For even baking, switch the pans from top racks to bottom at the baking mid-point. Check the accuracy of the oven regularly with a mercury thermometer.

6. Test cakes for doneness. Pound cakes, layer cakes, and quickbreads are done baking when a skewer or toothpick inserted in the center comes out with only moist crumbs clinging to it. Sponge cakes are done when their centers spring back to the touch.

Pan grease is made for the specific purpose of greasing cake and cookie pans. Though melted butter tastes best, it burns more easily and has a short shelf life. To make pan grease, beat 3 cups shortening with 3 cups all-purpose flour until fluffy. Then slowly beat in $^3/_4$ cup plus 2 tablespoons soybean oil. Alternatively, a top-quality spray pan release is available through distributers to commercial bakeries.

CHANGING THE PAN SIZE

In the appendix is a listing of the volume capacities of common baking pans, which will help you select a different pan shape or size than called for in a recipe. The baking times will change and sometimes the actual recipe may need to be adjusted.

Generally, to bake cupcakes instead of cake layers, you need only increase the oven temperature or decrease the cooking time. But baking a devil's food cake batter in a tube pan may not work: The batter contains a lot of liquid, and in a pan with limited surface area the baking time will increase, drying out the sides. The cake may even collapse. To convert this recipe, use less liquid and more fat and egg.

Baking cake layers in sheet pans rather than several round pans may require a decrease in leavening (since the cake batter has more surface area and needs to rise less) and a decrease in baking time. Pan extenders can be purchased to fit full and half sheet pans, allowing you to bake taller cakes in those pans. Pan extenders also prevent the sides of the cake from overbrowning.

Novelty cakes, cakes that are sculpted to look like an object, may require that the batter be baked in large Pyrex bowls or measuring cups for spherical and conical shapes. The white cake and devil's food cake batter are perfect for such cakes, but bolstering their structure by adding an additional egg is helpful.

COMBINING CAKE LAYERS, FILLINGS, AND FROSTINGS

There are several considerations when pairing cake layers with fillings and frostings. One is serving temperature. Buttercream and butter-rich layer cakes are hard when chilled because butter is hard when cold, and these desserts must sit at room temperature for a while before being served. Mousse fillings are a staple of European cakes, or *gateaux,* where they are paired with a sponge-type cake that remains soft when cold. Genoise, the classic cake for European *gateaux,* contains a small amount of butter, but it remains soft when cold owing to its high egg content. Flourless chocolate tortes, or any cake containing a high amount of cocoa butter, will also be hard when cold. These cakes do not taste or feel fudgy unless they are allowed to come to room temperature.

For catering chefs, the hot summer months may mean reinforcing fillings with additional gelatin, or making ganache fillings thicker than normal. All of these considerations go into menu planning.

SPONGE CAKES

Sponge cakes are leavened primarily by beating air into eggs. They typically have a high proportion of eggs to flour. High egg protein and very little flour causes sponge cakes to be flexible and springy.

Good egg foams are essential to sponge cakes. Use room-temperature eggs for maximum volume. If sugar will be beaten into the eggs, warm the eggs to help dissolve the sugar crystals. Whole eggs are beaten to the ribbon stage—when they become pale, thick, and a ribbon of egg foam dropped from the whip remains on the surface of the foam below. The sugar should not be added until this late stage, and even then it should be added very slowly, with the mixer running, to prevent volume loss and to give the sugar time to dissolve.

Grease-free utensils are required to achieve the greatest volume of egg-white foam. Cream of tartar, an acid, is often added to prevent overwhipping and to give stability. Sugar, too, will add stability and should be added after the soft peak stage. Beating the egg whites at medium to medium-high speed results in better cake volume. Though it is faster to whip the whites at high speed, a slightly lower speed creates a greater number of air bubbles, which are smaller and more consistent in size. Care must be taken not to overbeat egg whites. Once they have reached the soft peak stage, watch the whites closely. Though most recipes call for folding stiffly beaten egg whites into the batter, it is better to err on the side of caution: Overbeaten whites look grainy and dry, rather than shiny, and have lost much of their leavening ability.

GENOISE

THREE 6-INCH ROUND CAKE LAYERS Genoise is the cake used in classic French *gateaux*. It is richer and tastier than ordinary sponge cake because of the addition of melted butter; otherwise, it closely resembles biscuit in formula. Genoise, a relatively dry cake, is brushed with a flavored sugar soaking syrup to keep it moist. It is the preferred cake for buttercream and mousse fillings. The eggs are warmed and beaten whole, rather than separated, in the classic method for genoise. Melted butter is quickly folded into the batter at the end which minimizes deflation of the batter. The amount of butter can be varied slightly with no ill effects.

		LARGE BATCH
7 large eggs	2 lb 5.67 oz	
2 large egg yolks	4.4 oz	
1¼ cups granulated sugar	2 lb 3 oz	
1½ cups all-purpose flour	1 lb 9.5 oz	
¼ cup cornstarch	5.33 oz	
¼ tsp salt	1 tsp	
6 Tbs to ½ cup clarified browned butter	12 oz to 1 lb	
1½ tsp vanilla extract	2 Tbs	

Butter three 6 by 3-inch round cake pans; line the bottoms with parchment. Butter and flour the parchment. Whisk the eggs, yolks, and sugar together in a bowl. Place bowl inside a larger bowl filled with hot water or over a burner on a low heat. Stir until sugar is dissolved and eggs are warm. Beat the eggs until pale, thick, and a ribbon of batter dropped from the whip remains on the surface. Transfer to a wide bowl. Sift the flour, cornstarch, and salt together. Resift over the egg mixture and gently fold in. Fold in the butter and vanilla. Divide batter evenly among the prepared pans; bake at 350°F for 25 to 30 minutes.

NUT GENOISE

Follow the recipe above, reducing the flour to $^3/_4$ cup (large batch: 12.75 oz). Grind 1 cup (large batch: 20 oz) toasted hazelnuts or almonds with $^1/_4$ cup (large batch: 7 oz) of the sugar. Stir the nut mixture into the sifted flour mixture; do not resift or the nuts will be strained out. Use only 6 tablespoons (large batch: 12 oz) browned butter.

CHOCOLATE GENOISE

		LARGE BATCH
7 large eggs	2 lb 5.67 oz	
2 large egg yolks	4.4 oz	
1$^1/_3$ cups granulated sugar	2 lb 5.33 oz	
$^3/_4$ cup all-purpose flour	12.75 oz	
$^3/_4$ cup unsweetened Dutch-processed cocoa powder	11.25 oz	
$^1/_4$ tsp salt	1 tsp	
6 Tbs to $^1/_2$ cup clarified browned butter	12 oz to 1 lb	
1$^1/_2$ tsp vanilla extract	2 Tbs	

Follow mixing directions for plain genoise, sifting the cocoa with the flour and salt.

BISCUIT

MAKES ONE FULL SHEET PAN OF THIN BISCUIT, OR ONE 1¼-INCH-HIGH HALF SHEET PAN Biscuit, also known as plain sponge cake, is similar to genoise except that it has no added butter or fat. It comes in three different styles: Plain biscuit is simply a layer or sheet cake; *biscuit à la cuillère,* known as **ladyfingers,** is piped; *biscuit à roulade,* sometimes called jellyroll cake, is a flexible sponge cake that can be filled and rolled. The main difference among these cakes is the amount of flour they contain.

The mixing method for biscuit differs from genoise. First, there is no warming of the eggs and sugar over a heat source. Second, the eggs are separated and beaten in two steps before being folded together. Egg yolks become very thick when whipped and resist folding; to make this step easy and lessen the deflation of the egg foam, these recipes call for one whole egg to be beaten with the yolks.

	LARGE BATCH
6 large eggs, separated	1 lb 11.6 oz whites, 13.2 oz yolks
1¼ cups granulated sugar	2 lb 3 oz
2 large egg yolks	4.4 oz
1 large egg	6.8 oz
1½ tsp vanilla extract	2 Tbs
1¾ cups cake flour	1 lb 12 oz
¼ tsp salt	1 tsp

Grease a full sheet pan, line the bottom with parchment, grease the parchment, and dust the inside of the pan with flour. Whip the six egg whites to soft peaks. With the mixer running at medium speed, add ¾ cup of the sugar (large batch: 1 lb 5 oz), a tablespoon at a time. Transfer to a large, wide bowl. In the mixer bowl, beat the eight egg yolks and whole egg to the ribbon stage. With the mixer running at medium speed, add the remaining ½ cup sugar (large batch: 14 oz), a tablespoon at a time. Beat in the vanilla. Scrape the yolk mixture into the bowl with the beaten whites; begin to fold them together. Sift the flour and salt over the mixture and finish folding the batter together. Spread evenly into the prepared pan; bake at 400°F for 7 to 10 minutes. (The batter may also be baked in round pans; fill the pans no more than half full.) Like genoise, plain sponge cake benefits from being brushed with a flavorful simple syrup.

BISCUIT À LA CUILLÈRE (LADYFINGERS)

MAKES 6 DOZEN LADYFINGERS

6 large eggs, separated	1 lb 11.6 oz whites, 13.2 oz yolks	
1 large egg	6.8 oz	
¹/₂ plus ¹/₃ cup granulated sugar	1 lb 7.3 oz	**LARGE BATCH**
1 tsp vanilla extract	4 tsp	
1 cup cake flour	1 lb	
¹/₄ tsp salt	1 tsp	
Confectioners' sugar for dusting		

Grease and flour a half sheet pan or line with parchment. Whip the six separated egg whites to soft peaks. With the mixer running at medium speed, add the ¹/₂ cup sugar (large batch: 14 oz), a tablespoon at a time. Transfer to a large, wide bowl. In the mixer bowl, beat the six egg yolks and whole egg to the ribbon stage. With the mixer running at medium speed, add the remaining ¹/₃ cup sugar (large batch: 9.3 oz), a tablespoon at a time. Beat in the vanilla. Scrape the yolk mixture into the bowl with the whites; begin to fold them together. Sift the flour and salt over the eggs; finish folding batter together. Place the batter in a large pastry bag fitted with a ¹/₂-inch plain tip. For ladyfingers, pipe 4-inch-long tubes, spacing them 2 inches apart. Or pipe diagonally across the entire surface of the pan to cut sheets of ladyfingers to fit the bottom of molds for charlottes and bavarians. Dust the batter with confectioners' sugar before baking. Bake at 400°F for 5 to 7 minutes.

BISCUIT À ROULADE (JELLYROLL)

MAKES ONE HALF SHEET PAN This recipe makes a fluffy jellyroll cake that is 1 inch thick. For a thinner layer, use a larger pan or reduce the recipe by a third (roughly 5 whole eggs, no yolks, $^3/_4$ cup sugar, and $^1/_2$ cup flour).

		LARGE BATCH
6 large eggs, separated	1 lb 11.6 oz whites, 13.2 oz yolks	
1$^1/_4$ cups granulated sugar	2 lb 3 oz	
2 large egg yolks	4.4 oz	
1 large egg	6.8 oz	
1$^1/_2$ tsp vanilla extract	2 Tbs	
$^3/_4$ cup cake flour	12 oz	
$^1/_4$ tsp salt	1 tsp	
Confectioners' sugar, for dusting		

Grease and flour a half sheet pan; line the bottom with parchment. Butter and flour the parchment. Whip the six separated egg whites to soft peaks. With the mixer running at medium speed, add $^3/_4$ cup of the sugar (large batch: 1 lb 5 oz), a tablespoon at a time. Transfer to a large, wide bowl. In the mixer bowl, beat the eight egg yolks and whole egg to the ribbon stage. With the mixer running at medium speed, add the remaining $^1/_2$ cup sugar (large batch: 14 oz), a tablespoon at a time. Beat in the vanilla. Scrape the yolk mixture into the bowl with the beaten whites; begin to fold them together. Sift the flour and salt over the eggs, finish folding batter together. Spread batter evenly in the prepared pan. Bake at 425°F for 10 to 12 minutes. Immediately loosen cake from sides of pan. Dust with confectioners' sugar, top with parchment, and invert onto a cooling rack. Remove the parchment liner from the bottom of the cake. Dust with confectioners' sugar. Top with parchment and roll up the cake, beginning with long side. Place a tea towel over the cake and let cool. Fill and reroll cake.

ANGEL FOOD CAKE

MAKES ONE 10-INCH TUBE CAKE Angel food cake is regarded as somehow tricky and difficult, but the truth is that it hardly ever falls if the egg whites have been properly beaten. This means that the egg whites must be at room temperature, if not actually warm, to dissolve the sugar. The sugar is added very slowly to give it time to dissolve and stabilize the egg whites. Naturally, if the egg whites are beaten past the soft peak stage before the sugar is added, the cake will not be successful. There is no easy way to tell if the cake is done: Yes, the cake will spring back to the touch, but inserting a skewer into the cake to test for doneness is unreliable. Time is the primary factor: An undercooked or overcooked angel food cake is prone to collapse.

	LARGE BATCH
1 cup cake flour	1 lb
1²/₃ cups superfine sugar	2 lb 14.65 oz
12 large egg whites	3 lb 7.2 oz
2 Tbs water	¹/₂ cup
1¹/₂ tsp cream of tartar	2 Tbs
¹/₄ tsp salt	1 tsp
1 tsp vanilla extract	4 tsp

Sift the flour with ²/₃ cup of the sugar (large batch: 1 lb 2.65 oz). In a mixer bowl, whip the egg whites and water until frothy. Add the cream of tartar and salt; continue to whip to soft peaks. Reduce the mixer speed to medium. With the mixer running, add the remaining 1 cup sugar (large batch: 1 lb 12 oz) a tablespoon at a time. Increase the mixer speed to high and whip 1 minute more, until the meringue is shiny and forms stiff peaks when the whip is pulled away. Beat in the vanilla. Transfer the whites to a large, wide bowl. Sift the flour mixture again, directly over the meringue; fold into the whites gently and quickly. Spread the mixture in a 10-inch ungreased tube pan with removable bottom. Run a knife through the center of the batter to deflate any air pockets, or rap pan on counter. Bake at 375°F in the lower third of the oven for 30 to 35 minutes. Cool cake upside down by placing the center of the inverted pan over the neck of a glass bottle, such as a wine bottle. (If the pan has "legs," simply invert the pan on the counter.) It is necessary to cool the cake upside down to prevent collapse, as the egg protein structure is still soft when hot from the oven.

CHOCOLATE ANGEL FOOD CAKE

For chocolate-flavored angel food cake, eliminate the water from the egg whites. Instead, dissolve 3 tablespoons (large batch: 2.5 oz) unsweetened cocoa powder in 3 tablespoons (large batch: $^3/_4$ cup) boiling water, and add this mixture at the end, after the flour. Also, reduce the flour in the recipe by 2 tablespoons (large batch: 2 oz), for a total of $^3/_4$ cup plus 2 tablespoons (large batch: 14 oz).

LEMON ANGEL FOOD CAKE

Replace the water in the recipe with lemon juice, and fold in 2 to 3 teaspoons (large batch: 2 Tbs plus 2 tsp to 4 Tbs) grated lemon zest after the flour.

CHIFFON CAKE

MAKES TWO 9-INCH ROUND CAKE LAYERS Chiffon cake is a twentieth-century American version of the sponge cake, which came to us from Europe. Created in the early part of the century by Californian Harry Baker, chiffon cake has the richness of genoise but the lightness of sponge cake. Though originally baked in a tube pan, chiffon cake layers are perfect for filled cakes, such as Boston cream pie, black forest cake (use the chocolate version below), or any cake that will be filled with a rich mousse or buttercream. Since chiffon cakes use oil instead of butter, they are soft even when eaten straight from the refrigerator. This recipe uses the original chiffon mixing method, but the sugar can be beaten with the egg whites for a more resilient egg foam, or the eggs can be beaten whole and folded into the dry ingredients. The oil can be increased to $^1/_3$ cup for a richer cake.

1 cup cake flour	1 lb
²/₃ cup granulated sugar	1 lb 2.67 oz
1 tsp baking powder	4 tsp
¹/₄ tsp salt	1 tsp
4 large eggs, separated	1 lb 2.4 oz whites, 8.8 oz yolks
¹/₄ cup vegetable oil	1 cup
¹/₄ cup milk	1 cup
¹/₂ tsp vanilla extract	2 tsp

LARGE BATCH

Grease and flour bottoms only of two 9 by 2-inch round cake pans. Whisk the cake flour, sugar, baking powder, and salt together in a large bowl until well combined. Whisk in the yolks, oil, milk, and vanilla until smooth. Beat the egg whites almost to the stiff peak stage; fold the whites into the yolk mixture in two additions. Divide the batter evenly between the prepared pans. Bake at 350°F for 20 to 25 minutes. Let the cake cool 3 minutes, or until it falls below the top edge of the pan, and then invert the cake until cool. If the cake feels as if it will fall out of the pan, let it cool right side up.

CHOCOLATE CHIFFON CAKE

Follow the recipe above, reducing the flour to ²/₃ cup (large batch: 10.67 oz), and adding ¹/₃ cup (large batch: 5 oz) Dutch-processed cocoa. Coffee may be substituted for the milk.

HOT MILK SPONGE CAKE

MAKES TWO 9-INCH ROUND CAKE LAYERS Hot milk sponge cake is more flavorful than plain chiffon cake, but also more dense. It will stand up to rich fillings and resists sogginess when filled with sweetened berries and whipped
cream for a layered strawberry shortcake. The best aspect of this recipe is its
versatility. It can easily be flavored—with coconut milk and a touch of coconut
extract replacing the milk, for example. Strained fruit purées, like raspberry, or
citrus juice can replace half the milk in the recipe. The butter can be adjusted to
make the cake richer or lighter.

		LARGE BATCH
1³/₄ cups cake flour	1 lb 12 oz	
1¹/₂ tsp baking power	2 Tbs	
¹/₂ tsp salt	2 tsp	
4 large eggs	1 lb 11.2 oz	
1¹/₃ cups granulated sugar	2 lb 5.33 oz	
1 cup milk	1 qt	
4 to 6 Tbs butter, melted	8 to 12 oz	
1 tsp vanilla extract	2 tsp	

Grease and flour two 9 by 2-inch round cake pans. Sift the flour, baking powder, and salt together. In a mixer bowl, whip the eggs until frothy and slightly
thickened. Slowly add the sugar to the running mixer, about a tablespoon at a
time. Meanwhile, in a small saucepan or in a microwave-safe bowl, heat the milk
and butter to almost a boil; stir in the vanilla. At low speed, add the flour all at
once to the egg mixture. Increase the mixer speed to medium-low and slowly
pour the hot milk down the side of the bowl. The batter will be thin. Divide the
batter between the prepared pans. Bake at 350°F for 20 to 22 minutes.

BUTTER CAKES

There are three main mixing methods for butter- and shortening-
based cakes. The most familiar is the **creaming method,** whereby the

fat and sugar are beaten together until they form a light, fluffy mass. Though many batters contain additional leaveners, the creaming of the butter and sugar establishes the foundation for raising the batter. The sharp edges of the sugar crystals create small pockets of air in the fat as they are beaten together. Butter must be soft enough to beat, but cool enough not to melt—around 65°F is ideal. If the butter begins to melt, it will not be effective at trapping air. Shortening already has small air bubbles in it, about 12 percent by weight, and they are very finely dispersed. This gives shortening an edge over butter at aerating. Shortening is all fat, unlike butter, which is 4 to 8 percent water. Shortening has a greater temperature range for creaming than butter; it has a higher melting point and is softer when cold. As a fat, it performs better than butter, but the flavor of butter is associated with fine baking. Margarines have varying amounts of water—more variable than butter—and do not possess its sweet flavor. Some margarines are available that have a very low water content and behave more like shortening in baked goods.

The eggs are beaten into the creamed butter and sugar next, usually in small increments to ensure even absorption. If the eggs are not the same temperature as the creamed butter, the batter may look curdled. The last step in the creaming method is to add the sifted dry ingredients and any additional liquids, usually starting and ending with the dry ingredients. A portion of flour is added first so that it may be coated with fat particles. This helps minimize gluten formation when the liquid is added to the mixer. Adding the liquid ingredients too fast can result in a curdled-looking batter, as the fat-in-water emulsion inverts to a water-in-fat one. When the remaining flour is added, the batter will smooth out. The creaming method aerates better than the other methods, but the volume difference between creamed batters and those mixed with the high-ratio method is relatively small.

The **high-ratio method,** also known as the **two-stage method,** came about with the advent of chlorinated cake flour and modern shortenings in the 1930s. Bleaching soft flour with chlorine gas created cake flours that tolerated higher levels of liquid. Improved shortenings dispersed the fat and air pockets better in batters, creating tender cakes. Cakes made with these two ingredients came to be known as high-ratio cakes because they absorbed a higher amount of moisture.

Today, the high-ratio mixing method is used for batters whose sugar exceeds the weight of the flour. Pound cakes and yellow or white layer cakes are candidates for this method, but very thin batters such as for devil's food cake are not. Though either butter or shortening can be used, cake flour is essential for success.

Liquid ingredients, such as milk, eggs, and vanilla extract, are combined separately. For large batches, where it is inconvenient to combine them, only the eggs have to be lightly beaten until homogenous. Dry ingredients are combined at low speed in a mixer, which replaces the repeated sifting used in other methods. The shortening or softened butter is added next and is cut into the flour by the beaters. After the flour begins to be coated with the fat, just enough liquid is added to the running mixer (low speed) to disperse the fat. If the eggs have not been mixed with the other liquids, they are added first. This step also aerates the batter. The rest is added slowly, creating a homogenous batter, then beaten at a higher speed until fluffy. This method yields a more velvety and tender-crumbed cake than other methods.

For cake recipes using a liquid fat such as melted butter or oil, there is another mixing method, called the **one-stage** or **dump method**. All the dry ingredients are mixed in a bowl, and all the liquid ingredients, including the oil or melted butter, are combined separately. The liquid ingredients are "dumped" into the dry ingredients and mixed only until they are evenly dispersed to minimize gluten formation. Some recipes call for all the ingredients to be added to the mixer at once and combined, but this creates a tougher cake since it requires more mixing to combine all the ingredients evenly. Clearly the one-stage method is faster than the others, but it does pose the threat of developing too much gluten. The best way to minimize gluten formation is to add the oil or melted fat to the flour first. By coating the flour with the fat, the liquid is prevented from being immediately absorbed by the flour to create gluten. This method can be used for muffins, quickbreads, and oil-based devil's food cakes. Still, muffins made by creaming are taller and more tender than ones made by the one-stage method; some volume and texture are sacrificed for the sake of speed.

Many other hybrid mixing methods exist. Some carrot cake recipes, for example, start by beating the oil, sugar, and eggs together, despite the fact that more emulsification than aeration occurs. A better alternative would be to beat the eggs with the sugar first, then add the rest of the ingredients. Many old-fashioned recipes for cakes use the creaming method, but then beat the egg whites separately and fold them in last.

POUND CAKE

MAKES ONE BUNDT CAKE Pound cake got its name from its original formula: a pound of butter, a pound of sugar, a pound of eggs, and a pound of flour. Modern tastes dictate that pound cakes be a little less dense and more moist, reflected in the recipe below. Pound cakes last just under a week at room temperature, and six months if frozen. They are usually served plain, as an accompaniment to tea or with fruit and whipped cream, but a thin confectioners' sugar glaze flavored with liquor, citrus, or ginger adds a flavorful touch. Some chefs like to brush the tops of pound cakes with a flavored sugar syrup while still warm for added moisture. This is a versatile recipe; you can turn it into a chocolate-chip, coconut, blueberry or gingered-orange cake—the possibilities are endless.

	LARGE BATCH
3 cups cake flour	3 lb
2 tsp baking powder	2 Tbs plus 2 tsp
1/2 tsp salt	2 tsp
1 1/2 cups unsalted butter	3 lb
1 2/3 cups granulated sugar	2 lb 14.67 oz
5 large eggs	2 lb 2 oz
1 tsp vanilla extract	4 tsp
1/2 cup milk	2 cups

Grease and flour a 12-cup Bundt pan. Sift together the cake flour, baking powder, and salt. In a mixer bowl, beat the butter and sugar until light and fluffy. One at time, beat in the eggs. Beat in the vanilla. Alternately add the flour mixture and the milk, starting and finishing with the flour mixture. Pour into a prepared pan. Bake at 350°F for 55 to 65 minutes.

LEMON POUND CAKE

Follow the recipe for pound cake above, adding 2 tablespoons (large batch $^1/_2$ cup) lemon juice, 1 tablespoon (large batch $^1/_4$ cup) grated lemon zest, and $^1/_4$ cup (large batch 1 cup) poppy seeds to the batter.

CHOCOLATE POUND CAKE

MAKES TWO 8 BY 4-INCH LOAVES OR ONE BUNDT CAKE This is an unusually dark, chocolaty cake retaining all the properties of a pound cake, such as beautiful slices and slightly springy crumb, without scrimping on chocolate flavor. I don't think it's possible to make this recipe more chocolaty, except to add mini-chocolate chips or chopped semisweet chocolate to the batter. Though pound cakes were originally keeping cakes, this recipe is best served within the week it is made, but it can be frozen for six months.

	LARGE BATCH
2 cups cake flour	2 lb
1 cup unsweetened Dutch-processed cocoa powder	15 oz
2 tsp baking powder	2 Tbs plus 2 tsp
$^3/_4$ tsp salt	1 Tbs
$1^1/_2$ cups unsalted butter	3 lb
$2^2/_3$ cups granulated sugar	4 lb 10.67 oz
4 large eggs	1 lb 11.2 oz
1 tsp vanilla extract	4 tsp
1 cup sour cream	1 qt
1 cup mini semisweet chocolate chips or finely chopped chocolate (optional)	1 lb 8 oz

Grease and flour two 8 by 4-inch loaf pans, or a 12-cup Bundt pan. Sift the cake flour, cocoa powder, baking powder, and salt together. In a mixer bowl, beat the butter and sugar until light and fluffy. One at time, beat in the eggs. Beat in the vanilla. On low speed, beat in half the dry ingredients, then the sour cream, then the remaining dry ingredients. Fold in the chocolate, if desired. Divide the batter between the prepared pans. Bake at 350°F for 45 to 50 minutes for loaves, 55 to 65 minutes for a Bundt cake.

WHITE CAKE

MAKES TWO 9-INCH ROUND CAKE LAYERS These recipes for white and yellow cake offer the best of everything to bakers: They are surprisingly buttery, rich, and ultra-moist and tender without being too sweet. On the other hand, they can still be handled without falling apart when assembled into layer cakes, wedding cakes, and novelty cakes. Because novelty cakes require cutting and sculpting, and take more time to assemble and decorate, many chefs overlook the importance of good cake in favor of a good-looking cake. This recipe delivers a flavorful cake that customers will rave about. Once crumb-coated with buttercream and wrapped in plastic, the cake will stay moist for five or six days. Naturally, the unadorned layers can be frozen for months. With no adjustments, this recipe can be baked in rounds, cupcakes, sheet pans, and heatproof bowls. If you plan to bake in a bowl with over 2-quart capacity, add an additional egg to give the batter more structure. (This also makes a tighter crumb which is easier to slice and frost.) Large bowl cakes should be baked at 325°F.

	LARGE BATCH
3 cups cake flour	3 lb
1 Tbs baking powder	1/4 cup
1/2 tsp salt	2 tsp
1 cup plus 2 Tbs unsalted butter	2 lb 4 oz
1 1/2 cups granulated sugar	2 lb 10 oz
6 large egg whites	1 lb 11.6 oz
1 tsp vanilla extract	4 tsp
1 1/4 cups milk	5 cups

Grease and flour two 9 by 2-inch round cake pans. Sift together the cake flour, baking powder, and salt. In a mixer bowl, beat the butter and sugar until light and fluffy. With the mixer running, slowly add the egg whites and vanilla. Alternately add the flour mixture and milk, starting and finishing with the flour mixture. Pour into the prepared pans. Bake at 350°F, about 25 to 30 minutes.

YELLOW CAKE

Follow the recipe for white cake, substituting 2 whole large eggs (large batch: 13.6 oz) and 4 large egg yolks (large batch: 8.8 oz) for the egg whites.

DEVIL'S FOOD CAKE

MAKES THREE 9-INCH ROUND CAKE LAYERS Super-fudgy and moist, this is a very tender cake. If you plan to split the cake layers or make any kind of a novelty cake, you must add a fourth egg to the batter. Chocolate cake appears to be a high-ratio cake because it has more sugar than flour by weight, but it must be mixed using the creaming method. Below is an alternate cake made with oil, which stays tender even when served cold but is every bit as chocolaty. Once crumb-coated with buttercream and wrapped in plastic, the cake will stay moist for five or six days. Naturally, the unadorned layers can be frozen for months. Large bowl cakes should be baked at 325°F.

	LARGE BATCH
2 cups all-purpose flour	2 lb 2 oz
1 cup unsweetened Dutch-processed cocoa powder	15 oz
1 Tbs baking powder	1/4 cup
3/4 tsp salt	1 Tbs
1 cup unsalted butter	2 lb
2 cups granulated sugar	3 lb 8 oz
3 to 4 large eggs	1 lb 4.4 oz to 1 lb 11.2 oz
1 tsp vanilla extract	4 tsp
1 1/4 cups strong coffee or water	5 cups
1 cup milk	1 qt

Grease and flour three 9 by 2-inch round cake pans. Sift together the flour, co-coa, baking powder, and salt. In a mixer bowl, beat the butter and sugar until light and fluffy. With the mixer running, add the eggs, one at a time. Beat in the vanilla. Alternately add the flour mixture and coffee and milk, starting and fin-ishing with the flour mixture. Divide the batter evenly among the prepared pans. Bake at 350°F, about 25 to 30 minutes.

ALTERNATE DEVIL'S FOOD CAKE

MAKES ONE 10-INCH ROUND CAKE LAYER

		LARGE BATCH
1$^1/_2$ cups all-purpose flour	1 lb 9.5 oz	
$^2/_3$ cup unsweetened natural cocoa powder	10 oz	
1$^1/_2$ tsp baking powder	2 Tbs	
$^1/_2$ tsp baking soda	2 tsp	
$^1/_2$ tsp salt	2 tsp	
1$^1/_2$ cups granulated sugar	1 lb 10 oz	
2 large eggs	13.6 oz	
1 tsp vanilla extract	4 tsp	
$^1/_3$ cup milk	1$^1/_3$ cups	
$^1/_2$ cup vegetable oil	2 cups	
1 cup boiling water or hot coffee	1 qt	

Grease and flour a 10 by 2$^1/_2$-inch round cake pan. Instead of using the cream-ing method, place all the sifted dry ingredients in the mixer bowl, including the sugar. In another bowl, whisk the eggs, vanilla, and milk together. With the mixer running, pour the oil into the bowl. Pour in the egg mixture and then the hot water. Mix only until the ingredients are smooth—remember that there is no protective coating of fat on the flour from the creaming process to minimize gluten formation. Pour the batter into the prepared pan. Bake at 350°F for 35 minutes.

LEMON CAKE

MAKES TWO 9-INCH ROUND CAKE LAYERS This is a tart cake with a fragile, delicate crumb. The acidity of the batter contributes to the cake's tenderness. Note that the basic formula follows a classic recipe known as the 1-2-3-4 cake: 1 cup fat, 2 cups sugar, 3 cups flour, and 4 eggs. These cakes usually have 1 cup milk, but here half the liquid is lemon juice.

	LARGE BATCH
3 cups cake flour	3 lb
1 Tbs plus $^1/_2$ tsp baking powder	$^1/_4$ cup plus 2 tsp
$^1/_2$ tsp salt	2 tsp
1 cup unsalted butter	2 lb
1 Tbs grated lemon zest	$^1/_4$ cup
2 cups granulated sugar	3 lb 8 oz
4 large eggs	1 lb 11.2 oz
$^1/_2$ cup milk	2 cups
$^1/_2$ cup fresh lemon juice	2 cups

Grease and flour two 9 by 2-inch round cake pans. Sift together the flour, baking powder, and salt. In a mixer bowl, beat the butter and lemon zest until fluffy. Cream the butter with the sugar. One at a time, beat in the eggs. Alternately add the flour mixture and the milk and lemon juice, beginning and ending with the flour. Divide the batter evenly between the prepared pans. Bake at 350°F for 35 to 40 minutes.

CREAM CHEESE COFFEE CAKE

MAKES ONE BUNDT CAKE This is technically a pound cake, but it is the perfect cake for people who want something not too sweet to go with a morning cup of coffee. It is unusually moist and dense, and can be adjusted to suit any flavor combination, like cherry-almond or lemon-blueberry.

		LARGE BATCH
3 cups cake flour	3 lb	
1 tsp baking powder	4 tsp	
½ tsp salt	2 tsp	
¼ tsp baking soda	1 tsp	
1 cup unsalted butter	2 lb	
One 8-oz package cream cheese	2 lb	
1⅓ cups granulated sugar	2 lb 5.3 oz	
5 large eggs	2 lb 2 oz	
1½ tsp vanilla extract	2 Tbs	
BROWN SUGAR STREUSEL (about 1½ cups; optional; page 274)	6 cups	

Grease and flour a 12-cup Bundt pan. Sift together the flour, baking powder, salt, and baking soda. In a mixer bowl, cream the butter, cream cheese, and sugar together until light and fluffy. One at a time, beat in the eggs. Beat in the vanilla. Gradually beat in the flour mixture. Spread the batter into the prepared pan, arranging the streusel between layers of batter and sprinkling more streusel on top. Bake at 350°F for 50 to 55 minutes.

SOUR CREAM CRUMB CAKE

MAKES ONE 9 BY 13-INCH CAKE This cake is rich and melt-in-your mouth tender. The addition of tart fruit, like cranberries, is the perfect foil for the sweetness of the crumb topping, but many prefer their "crumb buns" plain. If you choose a different fruit, use fresh, not frozen. Frozen cranberries are unique in their ability to have the same affect on cakes whether fresh or frozen. This recipe uses brown streusel, but white streusel is also common.

		LARGE BATCH
2$^1/_2$ cups cake flour	2 lb 8 oz	
1$^1/_2$ tsp baking powder	2 Tbs	
$^3/_4$ tsp baking soda	1 Tbs	
$^1/_2$ tsp salt	2 tsp	
1 cup unsalted butter	2 lb	
1$^1/_2$ cups granulated sugar	2 lb 10 oz	
3 large eggs	1 lb 4.4 oz	
1$^1/_2$ tsp vanilla extract	2 Tbs	
1 cup sour cream	1 qt	
3 cups frozen cranberries	3 lb	
BROWN SUGAR STREUSEL (about 1$^1/_4$ cups; page 274)	5 cups	

Grease and flour a 9 by 13-inch baking pan. Sift together the flour, baking powder, baking soda, and salt. In a mixer bowl, cream the butter and sugar together until light and fluffy. One at a time, beat in the eggs. Beat in the vanilla. Alternately beat in the flour mixture and sour cream, starting and ending with the flour. Spread half the batter into the prepared pan. Place the cranberries over the batter, and spread the remaining batter on top. Sprinkle the streusel over the top. Bake at 350°F for 1 hour.

FRUITCAKE

MAKES TWO 9 BY 5-INCH LOAVES OR EIGHT MINI LOAVES Using less candied fruit makes this recipe more appealing to American palettes—that and a generous amount of fine liquor. Adjustments can be made to suit your taste; crystallized ginger or candied pineapple are interesting variations. Fruitcake really does age well—up to three months. It must be made a week ahead to let the flavors mellow, and during this time the cakes are brushed daily with bourbon or rum. Fruitcakes that are not brushed with liquor do not fare well.

		LARGE BATCH
1¹⁄₂ cups chopped candied cherries	2 lb 1 oz	
1¹⁄₂ cups dried tart cherries or cranberries	1 lb 14 oz	
1¹⁄₂ cups dates, chopped	1 lb 11 oz	
1¹⁄₂ cups figs or prunes, chopped	2 lb 4 oz	
1 cup golden raisins	1 lb 8 oz	
1 cup dried apricots, chopped	1 lb 2 oz	
2 cups rum, bourbon, or brandy, or any combination	2 qt	
6 large eggs	2 lb 8.8 oz	
2 large egg yolks	4.4 oz	
¹⁄₂ cup orange juice	2 cups	
2 tsp grated orange zest	2 Tbs plus 2 tsp	
3¹⁄₄ cups all-purpose flour	3 lb 7.25 oz	
1³⁄₄ cups granulated sugar	3 lb 1 oz	
1 Tbs ground ginger	¹⁄₄ cup	
1¹⁄₂ tsp ground cinnamon	2 Tbs	
¹⁄₄ tsp ground cloves	1 tsp	
2 tsp baking powder	2 Tbs plus 2 tsp	
¹⁄₂ tsp salt	2 tsp	
1¹⁄₂ cups unsalted butter	3 lb	
2 cups sliced natural almonds, toasted and finely chopped	1 lb 8 oz	
Bourbon, rum, or brandy for additional brushing		

Grease and flour two 9 by 5-inch loaf pans or eight 2-cup capacity mini loaf pans. The day before making the cakes, place the dried fruit and liquor in a large saucepan. Cover the pan; bring the liquid to a simmer. Turn off the heat and pour the mixture into a large bowl. Cover the bowl with plastic and let it sit overnight, stirring occasionally. The fruit should soak up all the liquid.

In a liquid measuring cup, whisk together the eggs, yolks, orange juice, and zest; set aside. Place the flour, sugar, spices, leavening, and salt in a mixer bowl. With the mixer running at low speed, toss the softened butter into the bowl, 1 tablespoon at a time. Slowly pour in half the egg mixture. Increase the speed to medium; slowly pour in the remaining egg mixture. Beat 1 minute. Fold in the soaked fruit and nuts. Divide the batter among the prepared pans. Decorate the tops of the cakes with extra candied cherry halves and sliced or slivered almonds—in flower shapes, for example. Bake small cakes at 325°F for 40 to 45 minutes, larger ones at 300°F for approximately $1\frac{1}{2}$ hours. Brush the cakes with liquor while still warm. When cool, remove from pans. Clean the pans and line with plastic wrap. Return the cakes to the pans; cover with plastic. Brush the cakes daily with liquor for one week.

MISCELLANEOUS CAKES

CARROT CAKE

MAKES THREE 9-INCH CAKE LAYERS This is a classic version of carrot cake. Ginger or pineapple are welcome flavor additions. Cream Cheese Frosting (page 258) is traditionally used to frost carrot cake.

		LARGE BATCH
2 cups all-purpose flour	2 lb 2 oz	
1 tsp baking soda	4 tsp	
1 tsp baking powder	4 tsp	
1 tsp ground cinnamon	4 tsp	
1/2 tsp salt	2 tsp	
1/4 tsp ground cloves	1 tsp	
1 cup granulated sugar	1 lb 12 oz	
1/2 cup packed dark brown sugar	1 lb	
4 large eggs	1 lb 11.2 oz	
1 1/4 cups vegetable oil	5 cups	
1 tsp grated orange zest	4 tsp	
4 medium carrots (1 1/3 lb), peeled and shredded (about 4 cups)	5 lb 5.33 oz	
1 cup chopped walnuts, toasted	1 lb	

Grease and flour three 9 by 2-inch round cake pans. Sift the flour, baking soda, baking powder, cinnamon, salt, and cloves together. In a mixer bowl, combine the sugar and 1 egg until smooth. One at a time, beat in the remaining eggs until the sugar begins to dissolve. Beat in the oil and orange zest. Fold in the carrots, then the walnuts. Divide the batter among the prepared pans. Bake at 350°F for 20 to 25 minutes.

FLOURLESS CHOCOLATE ROULADE

MAKES ONE 10¹/₂ BY 15¹/₂-INCH CAKE LAYER Unlike a sponge cake, this flourless roulade is moist and fudgy and not the least bit difficult to roll. Where buttercream is the ideal filling for a rolled sponge cake, here a light mousse or white chocolate whipped cream is necessary to complement the richness of the "cake." The filled cake will keep two to three days depending on the stability of the filling.

		LARGE BATCH
4 ounces bittersweet chocolate, chopped	1 lb	
2 ounces unsweetened chocolate, chopped	8 oz	
1 whole large egg	6.8 oz	
5 large eggs, separated	11 oz yolks and 1 lb 7 oz whites	
1¹/₄ cups superfine sugar	2 lb 3 oz	
2 tablespoons brandy, bourbon, rum, or cooled espresso	¹/₂ cup	
Pinch of salt	¹/₂ tsp	

Grease a 10¹/₂ by 15¹/₂-inch jellyroll pan. Line the bottom of the pan with parchment paper, leaving a short overhang on two sides for easy cake removal. Grease the parchment paper. Melt the chocolates together. Beat the whole egg and 5 egg yolks at high speed until thick and pale, about 4 minutes. With the mixer running, slowly beat in ³/₄ cup sugar (large batch: 1 lb 5 oz), a tablespoon at a time. Beat in the melted chocolates just until combined. Beat in the liquor or espresso.

In another bowl, beat the egg whites at medium-high speed until foamy; add the salt. Beat to soft peak stage. Reduce the speed to medium; with the mixer running, slowly add the remaining ¹/₂ cup sugar (large batch: 14 oz) to the egg whites, a tablespoon at a time. Increase the mixer speed to high and beat until the whites are stiff, another 30 seconds to a minute. Gently but quickly fold the egg whites into the chocolate mixture in three additions. Pour the batter into the pan, smoothing gently with a spatula. Bake at 350°F for 15 minutes, or until a toothpick inserted in the center of the cake comes out clean.

Run a knife around the sides of the cake. Cover the cake with a sheet of parchment paper; place a dishtowel over the parchment to soften the top crust. Cool the cake completely. When you are ready to fill the cake, invert it onto a rack, peel off the parchment, and invert it again onto a piece of fresh parchment paper. Fill the side that was the top crust. The cake will hold between 3 and 4 cups of mousse or white chocolate whipped cream. Using the parchment paper as a guide, roll the cake lengthwise at tight as possible. Wrap in plastic and refrigerate before frosting, glazing, or dusting with confectioners' sugar.

ALMOST FLOURLESS CHOCOLATE TORTE

MAKES ONE 8-INCH CAKE Less dense than a truly flourless cake, this torte is more like a fudgy brownie. In fact, you'll notice that only the addition of an egg and the absence of baking powder make the brownies on page 225 different from this recipe, leaving the mixing method here to give this cake a more sophisticated texture: The eggs are beaten to ribbon stage and the torte is baked in a water bath. A thin glaze of ganache is the only adornment necessary. It will keep for a week in the refrigerator and for up to six months frozen (unglazed). To enjoy the luscious, creamy texture, be sure to serve the torte at room temperature—remember that chocolate and butter become hard when refrigerated.

		LARGE BATCH
1 cup unsalted butter	2 lb	
10 oz bittersweet chocolate, chopped	2 lb 8 oz	
2 Tbs brandy, rum, bourbon, or espresso	$^1/_2$ cup	
3 large eggs	1 lb 4.4 oz	
$^3/_4$ cup granulated sugar	1 lb 5 oz	
$^1/_2$ cup all-purpose flour	8.5 oz	
1 tsp baking powder	4 tsp	
$^1/_4$ tsp salt	1 tsp	

Grease an 8 by 3-inch round cake pan; line the bottom of the pan with parchment paper. Grease the parchment paper; dust the pan with flour. Melt the butter with the chocolate. Stir in the liquor or coffee. Beat the eggs at high speed until pale and very thick, about 4 minutes. With the mixer running, slowly add the sugar a tablespoon at a time. This should take a few minutes. Reduce the speed to medium and beat in the chocolate mixture. On low speed, beat in the flour, baking powder, and salt just until combined. Spread the batter into the pan. Bake the cake at 350°F in a water bath for 35 minutes. There is no visual clue for doneness. Remove the pan from the water bath. Cool cake in the pan, then loosen and invert onto an 8-inch cardboard round. Cool the cake completely before glazing or garnishing.

CHOCOLATE TORTE FOR PASSOVER

MAKES ONE 8-INCH CAKE This is simply a variation of the recipe above. Toasted ground hazelnuts can be added for flavor, though purists prefer the smooth texture of chocolate alone. Like the torte above, this torte is typically enrobed in chocolate ganache. It will keep for a week in the refrigerator and for up to six months frozen (unglazed). Because this torte is hard and dense when cold, let it sit at room temperature for 30 minutes before serving.

	LARGE BATCH
1 cup unsalted butter	2 lb
10 oz bittersweet chocolate, chopped	2 lb 8 oz
2 Tbs kosher brandy	1/2 cup
3 large eggs	1 lb 4.4 oz
3/4 cup granulated sugar	1 lb 5 oz
1/2 cup matzo cake meal or finely ground matzo meal	8 oz
1/4 tsp salt	1 tsp

Grease an 8 by 3-inch round cake pan; line the bottom of the pan with parchment paper. Grease the parchment paper; dust the pan with matzo meal. Melt the butter with the chocolate. Stir in the brandy. Beat the eggs at high speed until pale and very thick, about 4 minutes. With the mixer running, slowly add the

BUCHE DE NÖEL (yule log) is a roulade or jellyroll cake that is filled, rolled, and cut to resemble a fallen log. It is frosted with chocolate buttercream or ganache, typically roughened with the tines of a fork to look like bark. The cake may be any flavor, and the filling is usually buttercream or a firm mousse. Mushroom-shaped meringues commonly garnish this cake.

BLACK FOREST CAKE consists of layers of Chocolate Genoise or Chiffon Cake (pages 99, 104) filled with whipped cream and a kirsch-spiked Sour Cherry Filling (page 270). The cake is frosted with kirsch-laced whipped cream. Kirsch is a clear *eau-de-vie* distilled from cherry pits and juice. Pipe a ring of buttercream at the outer edge of each layer to form a barrier to hold in the cherry filling. Once the layers are assembled and chilled, the whole cake can be covered with stabilized (page 275) or, even better, white chocolate whipped cream.

BOSTON CREAM PIE is a cake, not a pie, composed of two layers of yellow sponge or chiffon cake split and filled with vanilla pastry cream. It is topped with chocolate glaze, and the sides are left unadorned.

DOBOS TORTE is composed of nine thin layers of plain genoise or sponge cake. Chocolate buttercream is spread between each layer and used to coat the entire cake. The final layer, which is finished separately, is glazed with light amber caramel that hardens upon cooling. This final layer is sliced into twelve wedges that are arranged decoratively on top of the torte.

SACHERTORTE is formed with chocolate genoise (or chiffon) layers that are split and filled with apricot preserves. The torte is glazed with ganache and served with rosettes of whipped cream.

sugar a tablespoon at a time. This should take a few minutes. Reduce the speed to medium and beat in the chocolate mixture, matzo cake meal, and salt just until combined. Spread the batter into the pan. Bake the cake at 350°F in a water bath for 35 minutes. There is no visual clue for doneness; timing is everything. Remove the pan from the water bath. Cool the cake in the pan, then loosen from pan and invert onto an 8-inch cardboard round. Cool the cake completely before glazing or garnishing.

QUICKBREADS, MUFFINS, BISCUITS, AND SCONES

Muffins, quickbreads, biscuits, scones, and shortcakes are not really breads. They are less rich, less tender and less sweet than cakes and taste best with a pat of butter. These items are ephemeral; with the exception of quick breads, they do not keep well. Waffles and pancakes fall into this section, which could also be named "things to make for breakfast."

GINGERBREAD

MAKES ONE BUNDT CAKE Coffee gives this gingerbread depth. Flat beer, usually stout, is another common ingredient in gingerbread, and it may be used here instead of the coffee. While a plain confectioners' sugar glaze is the standard garnish, adding instant espresso powder to it is delicious. The cake keeps for three days, but brushing it with a flavored simple syrup or thinned confectioners' sugar glaze while it is still warm will keep it moist longer.

		LARGE BATCH
3^1/$_3$ cups all-purpose flour	3 lb 8.67 oz	
1 Tbs plus 1 tsp ground ginger	1.33 oz	
2 tsp baking powder	2 Tbs plus 2 tsp	
1^1/$_2$ tsp ground cinnamon	2 Tbs	
^{3}/$_4$ tsp baking soda	1 Tbs	
^{3}/$_4$ tsp salt	1 Tbs	
^{1}/$_8$ to ^{1}/$_4$ tsp ground cloves	^{1}/$_2$ to 1 tsp	
1^1/$_2$ cups unsalted butter	3 lb	
1^1/$_2$ cups granulated sugar	2 lb 10 oz	
4 large eggs	1 lb 11.2 oz	
1 cup dark molasses	1 qt	
^{3}/$_4$ cup strong hot coffee	3 cups	

Grease and flour a 12-cup Bundt pan. Sift the flour, ginger, baking powder, cinnamon, baking soda, salt, and cloves together. In a mixer bowl, cream the butter with the sugar. One at a time, beat in the eggs. Beat in the molasses, half the flour, the coffee, and the remaining flour mixture. Pour into the prepared pan. Bake at 350°F for 55 to 65 minutes.

ZUCCHINI BREAD

MAKES TWO 9 BY 5-INCH LOAVES

		LARGE BATCH
3 medium zucchini (1 lb), shredded, about 4 cups	4 lb	
$^3/_4$ tsp plus $^1/_8$ tsp salt	1 Tbs plus $^1/_2$ tsp	
$^3/_4$ cup granulated sugar	1 lb 5 oz	
$^3/_4$ cup packed light brown sugar	1 lb 8 oz	
4 large eggs	1 lb 11.2 oz	
$^3/_4$ cup vegetable oil	3 cups	
2 Tbs lemon juice	$^1/_2$ cup	
1 tsp vanilla extract	4 tsp	
3 cups all-purpose flour	3 lb 3 oz	
1 Tbs baking powder	$^1/_4$ cup	
$^1/_2$ tsp baking soda	2 tsp	
2 tsp grated lemon zest	2 Tbs plus 2 tsp	
1 tsp ground cinnamon or allspice	4 tsp	
1 cup chopped walnuts, toasted	1 lb	

Grease and flour two 9 by 5-inch loaf pans. Place the zucchini in a colander. Sprinkle $^1/_8$ teaspoon salt (large batch: $^1/_2$ tsp) over the shredded zucchini; let stand 15 minutes. Squeeze the zucchini of excess liquid; you should have 2 cups zucchini. In a mixer bowl, beat the sugars with eggs until the sugar partially dissolves. Beat in the oil, lemon juice, and vanilla. Stir in the zucchini. Sift the dry ingredients; combine with the batter. Fold in walnuts. Divide batter between pans. Bake at 350°F for 40 to 45 minutes.

APPLE CAKE

MAKES TWO 8-INCH SQUARE OR TWO 9-INCH ROUND CAKE LAYERS

		LARGE BATCH
3 cups all-purpose flour	3 lb 3 oz	
1^1/$_2$ tsp ground cinnamon	2 Tbs	
1^1/$_2$ tsp baking powder	2 Tbs	
1 tsp salt	4 tsp	
^{1}/$_2$ tsp baking soda	2 tsp	
^{1}/$_4$ tsp ground cloves	1 tsp	
^{1}/$_4$ tsp ground nutmeg	1 tsp	
1 cup granulated sugar	1 lb 12 oz	
1 cup packed light brown sugar	2 lb	
5 large eggs	2 lb 2 oz	
1^1/$_2$ cups vegetable oil	6 cups	
3 tart apples (1^1/$_2$ lb), peeled and cut into ^{1}/$_4$- to ^{1}/$_2$-inch dice, about 3 cups	6 lb	
1 cup chopped walnuts, toasted (optional)	1 lb	

Grease and flour two 8-inch square or two 9-inch round cake pans. Sift the flour, cinnamon, baking powder, salt, baking soda, cloves, and nutmeg together. In a mixer bowl, beat the sugars and eggs until the sugar granules begin to dissolve. Beat in the oil. Gently stir in the flour mixture. When the flour is almost incorporated, fold in the apples and nuts. Pour into the preapred pans and bake at 350°F for 25 to 30 minutes.

PUMPKIN BREAD

MAKES ONE BUNDT CAKE OR TWO 8 BY 4-INCH LOAVES This basic recipe is very moist and keeps almost a week at room temperature or several months frozen. Toasted nuts and even chocolate chips are nice additions.

		LARGE BATCH
3 cups all-purpose flour	3 lb 3 oz	
2 tsp baking powder	2 Tbs plus 2 tsp	
2 tsp ground ginger	2 Tbs plus 2 tsp	
1 tsp baking soda	4 tsp	
1 tsp ground cinnamon	4 tsp	
$^1/_2$ tsp salt	2 tsp	
$^1/_8$ tsp ground nutmeg	$^1/_2$ tsp	
$^1/_8$ tsp ground cloves	$^1/_2$ tsp	
$1^3/_4$ cups (15 oz) solid pack pumpkin	3 lb 12 oz	
$1^1/_2$ cups granulated sugar	2 lb 10 oz	
1 cup vegetable oil	1 qt	
4 large eggs	1 lb 11.2 oz	
2 Tbs dark molasses	$^1/_2$ cup	

Grease and flour a 12-cup Bundt pan or two 8 by 4-inch loaf pans. Sift together the flour, baking powder, ginger, baking soda, cinnamon, salt, nutmeg, and cloves. In a large bowl, whisk the pumpkin, sugar, oil, eggs, and molasses together. Gently stir in the dry ingredients. Divide the batter evenly between the prepared pans. Bake at 350°F for 50 to 60 minutes.

CRANBERRY-ORANGE BREAD

MAKES ONE 9 BY 5-INCH LOAF

		LARGE BATCH
1¹/₂ cups all-purpose flour	1 lb 9.5 oz	
¹/₂ cup cake flour	8 oz	
2 tsp baking powder	2 Tbs plus 2 tsp	
1 tsp orange zest	4 tsp	
¹/₂ salt	2 tsp	
¹/₄ tsp baking soda	1 tsp	
¹/₂ cup sour cream	2 cups	
¹/₄ cup fresh orange juice	1 cup	
6 Tbs unsalted butter	12 oz	
²/₃ cup granulated sugar	1 lb 2.67 oz	
2 large eggs	13.6 oz	
1 cup fresh cranberries, coarsely chopped (see Note)	1 lb	

Grease and flour a 9 by 5-inch loaf pan. Whisk the flours, baking powder, orange zest, salt, and soda together in a bowl. In another container, combine the sour cream and orange juice. In a mixer bowl, cream the butter and sugar together until light and fluffy. One at a time, beat in the eggs. Alternately beat in the flour mixture and sour cream, beginning and ending with the flour. Just before the last of the flour is fully incorporated, fold in the cranberries. Spread the batter into the prepared pan; bake at 350°F for 45 to 50 minutes.

NOTE
Frozen cranberries may be used; however, they should be at least partially thawed and blotted.

BANANA NUT BREAD

MAKES ONE 9 BY 5-INCH LOAF

		LARGE BATCH
2^1/$_2$ cups all-purpose flour	2 lb 2.25 oz	
2 tsp baking powder	2 Tbs plus 2 tsp	
^{1}/$_2$ tsp salt	2 tsp	
^{1}/$_4$ tsp baking soda	1 tsp	
^{1}/$_2$ cup unsalted butter	1 lb	
1 cup granulated sugar	1 lb 12 oz	
2 large eggs	13.6 oz	
1^1/$_3$ cups (1 lb) mashed ripe bananas (about 2 large)	4 lb	
1 tsp vanilla extract	4 tsp	
^{1}/$_2$ cup buttermilk	2 cups	
1 cup chopped toasted walnuts or pecans	1 lb	

Grease and flour a 9 by 5-inch loaf pan. Whisk the flour, baking powder, salt, and soda together in a bowl. In a mixer bowl, cream the butter and sugar together until light and fluffy. One at a time, beat in the eggs. Beat in the bananas and vanilla. Alternately beat in the flour mixture and buttermilk, beginning and ending with the flour. Just before the last of the flour is fully incorporated, fold in the walnuts. Spread the batter into the prepared pan; bake at 350°F for 45 to 50 minutes.

CORNBREAD OR MUFFINS

MAKES ONE 8-INCH ROUND BREAD OR 8 MUFFINS This recipe is for plain corn-bread, not too cakey, not too dry. I usually stir in 1 cup shredded cheddar cheese, 1 minced jalapeño, or even chopped fresh corn kernels. Sausage and herb cornbread is good, too. If you like your cornbread richer and more cakey, add a tablespoon or two more oil or butter, or use half-and-half instead of milk. The better quality your cornmeal, the better corn flavor you'll get. The most sublime cornbread is baked in a cast-iron cornstick pan or an 8-inch round cast-iron skillet that has been preheated in a 425°F oven. Bacon drippings (or clari-fied butter) are drizzled into the pan just before the batter goes in. The oven temperature is reduced to 350°F after the pans are returned to the oven. Turn the finished cornbread onto a rack immediately after baking and you have a golden crisp, almost fried crust. But alas, this method is impractical for large-scale operation.

	LARGE BATCH
1 cup all-purpose flour	1 lb 1 oz
1/3 cup cake flour	5.33 oz
2/3 cup yellow cornmeal	13.33 oz
3 Tbs granulated sugar	5.25 oz
2 tsp baking powder	2 Tbs plus 2 tsp
1/4 tsp baking soda	1 tsp
1/4 tsp salt	1 tsp
1 cup milk	1 qt
1/3 cup vegetable oil or 6 Tbs melted butter	1 1/3 cups or 12 oz
1 large egg	6.8 oz

Grease and flour an 8-inch round cake pan or eight standard muffin cups. In a medium bowl, whisk the flours, cornmeal, sugar, baking powder, baking soda, and salt together. Stir in any desired herbs, cheese, or other flavorings. In an-other bowl, whisk the milk, oil, and egg together. Pour the liquid into the flour mixture, quickly and gently stirring just until combined. Spread the batter into the prepared pan. Bake at 375°F for 20 to 25 minutes for the 8-inch round, 15 to 18 minutes for muffins.

BRAN MUFFINS

MAKES 12 MUFFINS

2 cups bran cereal, such as Kellogg's All-Bran	1 lb 4 oz	**LARGE BATCH**
1³/₄ cups buttermilk	7 cups	
¹/₃ cup raisins	8 oz	
¹/₃ cup vegetable oil	1¹/₃ cups	
¹/₄ cup maple syrup	1 cup	
1 large egg	6.8 oz	
¹/₄ cup packed light brown sugar	8 oz	
1¹/₄ cups all-purpose flour	1 lb 5.25 oz	
2 tsp baking powder	2 Tbs plus 2 tsp	
1 tsp baking soda	4 tsp	
¹/₄ tsp salt	1 tsp	

Grease and flour 12 standard muffin cups. Combine the bran cereal, buttermilk, and raisins in a large bowl; let stand 10 minutes. Whisk in the oil, maple syrup, egg, and brown sugar. Sift the dry ingredients over the mixture and gently stir until combined. Divide the batter evenly among the prepared muffin cups. Bake at 425°F for 18 to 20 minutes.

OAT MUFFINS

Follow the directions for bran muffins, substituting old-fashioned rolled oats (large batch: 1 lb 12 oz) for the bran cereal, decreasing the buttermilk to 1¹/₂ cups (large batch: 6 cups), and adding 1 egg (large batch: 4 eggs). The salt will need to be increased to ³/₄ teaspoon. Dried apple or chopped toasted pecans may be added to the batter instead of raisins.

BERRY MUFFINS

MAKES 12 STANDARD OR 8 LARGE MUFFINS This muffin recipe can be used as a base for many flavor variations. Like all true muffins, they are not overly cakey and are best served the day they are made. Like most muffin and quickbread recipes, these muffins can be made using the one-bowl "dump" mixing method if melted butter is used, but for muffins with tall peaks, use the creaming method.

		LARGE BATCH
2¹/₂ cups all-purpose flour	2 lb 10.5 oz	
2 tsp baking powder	2 Tbs plus 2 tsp	
2 tsp grated lemon zest	2 Tbs plus 2 tsp	
¹/₂ tsp baking soda	2 tsp	
¹/₂ tsp salt	2 tsp	
¹/₂ cup unsalted butter	1 lb	
²/₃ cup granulated sugar	1 lb 2.67 oz	
2 large eggs	13.6 oz	
1 tsp vanilla	4 tsp	
1¹/₄ cups buttermilk	5 cups	
1¹/₂ cups fresh blueberries	6 cups	

Grease and flour 12 standard or eight 6-ounce muffin cups. Whisk the flour, baking powder, lemon zest, soda, and salt together in a bowl. In a mixer bowl, cream the butter and sugar together until light and fluffy. One at a time, beat in the eggs. Beat in the vanilla. Alternately beat in the flour mixture and buttermilk, beginning and ending with the flour. Just before the last of the flour is fully incorporated, fold in the blueberries. Divide the batter among the muffin cups. Bake at 425°F for 12 to 15 minutes.

IRISH SODA BREAD

MAKES ONE 10-INCH ROUND LOAF

		LARGE BATCH
1 cup old-fashioned rolled oats	14 oz	
1³/₄ cups buttermilk	7 cups	
1 large egg	6.8 oz	
3 cups all-purpose flour	3 lb 3 oz	
3 Tbs granulated or light brown sugar	5.25 oz granulated or 6 oz light brown sugar	
1¹/₂ tsp baking soda	2 Tbs	
1 tsp salt	4 tsp	
6 Tbs cold butter, cut into ¹/₂-inch dice	12 oz	
³/₄ cup currants	1 lb 2 oz	

Combine the oats and 1 cup buttermilk in a bowl; let stand 10 minutes. Whisk the remaining buttermilk with the egg. Place the flour, brown sugar, baking soda, and salt in a mixer bowl. With the mixer running at low speed, slowly toss the diced butter into the bowl. When the butter pieces have been reduced to ¹/₈-inch pieces, add the oat mixture and just enough of the egg mixture to form a stiff dough. Add the currants at the end of the mixing process, or knead them in by hand. The dough should be kneaded briefly on a floured surface until it is smooth and then formed into a ball. With a floured knife, slash a cross into the dough about ¹/₂ inch deep. Bake on a parchment-lined baking sheet at 400°F for 40 minutes, or until the bottom of the loaf sounds hollow when tapped and a knife inserted into the top comes out clean.

BUTTERMILK BISCUITS

MAKES 8 TO 12 BISCUITS The key to tall, flaky biscuits is giving the dough a few turns, as you would puff pastry or croissants, without developing too much gluten. Dust the round cutter with flour after cutting out each biscuit to prevent the layers from sticking to one another, and let the cut-outs rest in the refrigerator for 20 minutes before baking for the highest, most even rise. The dough can be made and held overnight, but biscuits are at their best for only a couple of hours after they come out of the oven.

		LARGE BATCH
2 cups all-purpose flour	2 lb 2 oz	
1 cup cake flour	1 lb	
1 Tbs baking powder	$^1/_4$ cup	
$^3/_4$ tsp salt	1 Tbs	
$^1/_2$ tsp baking soda	2 tsp	
$^1/_2$ cup cold unsalted butter	1 lb	
$^1/_4$ cup cold shortening	5.75 oz	
$1^1/_4$ cups cold buttermilk	5 cups	

Whisk all the dry ingredients together in a medium bowl. Using a pastry blender or box grater, cut in the butter until pea-size clumps form. For large batches, use the paddle attachment to cut in the fat. Cut the shortening into the flour as well. While tossing the flour mixture with a fork, gradually pour enough buttermilk into the bowl to form a shaggy dough when pressed. Reserve any remaining buttermilk. Form the dough into a disk with your hands, adding buttermilk if necessary. On a floured surface, pat the dough into a $^1/_2$-inch-thick rectangle; fold the dough in half. Repeat. Roll the dough into a 1-inch-thick rectangle. With a floured 2- to 3-inch round cutter, cut out biscuits; place on parchment-lined baking sheets. Reroll scraps. Refrigerate dough 20 minutes. Brush the tops of the rounds with reserved buttermilk. Bake at 425°F for 14 to 16 minutes, or until golden.

CREAM SCONES

MAKES 8 TO 12 SCONES Scones are a richer version of biscuits, and more cakey because of the egg. Giving the dough a few turns will add layers to the scones, but not as much as for biscuits.

		LARGE BATCH
2 cups all-purpose flour	2 lb 2 oz	
3 Tbs granulated sugar	5.25 oz	
2 tsp baking powder	2 Tbs plus 2 tsp	
$^1/_4$ tsp salt	1 tsp	
6 Tbs cold unsalted butter	12 oz	
$^1/_3$ cup currants (optional)	8 oz	
$^1/_3$ cup heavy cream	1$^1/_3$ cups	
1 large egg	6.8 oz	
1 tsp vanilla extract	4 tsp	

Whisk all the dry ingredients together in a medium bowl. Using a pastry blender or box grater, cut the butter into the flour until pea-size clumps form. Stir in the currants, if using. In another bowl, whisk together the cream, egg, and vanilla. While tossing the flour mixture with a fork, gradually pour enough liquid into the bowl to form a dough when pressed. Reserve remaining liquid. Form the dough into a disk with your hands, adding cream if necessary. On a floured surface, pat the dough into a $^1/_2$-inch-thick rectangle; fold dough in half. Repeat. Roll dough into a 1-inch-thick rectangle. With a floured 2- to 3-inch round cutter, cut out biscuits; place on parchment-lined baking sheets. Reroll scraps. Alternately, form dough into a round disk 1$^1/_2$ to 1$^3/_4$ inches high; cut into eight wedges with a floured knife. Refrigerate dough 20 minutes. Brush tops of dough with any remaining cream mixture, using additional cream if necessary. For shiny tops, brush the biscuits with beaten egg instead of cream. Bake at 425°F for 14 to 16 minutes, or until golden.

CREAM SHORTCAKES

Follow the recipe for scones, using $^1/_4$ cup sugar (large batch: 7 oz) instead of 3 tablespoons, omitting the currants, and sprinkling the tops of the cream-brushed dough with sugar before baking.

WAFFLES AND PANCAKES

MAKES EIGHT 4-INCH SQUARE BELGIAN WAFFLES OR SIXTEEN 4-INCH PAN-CAKES Without a single change, this recipe can be used for waffles or pancakes. The batter will keep for up to three days in the refrigerator; just cover the surface directly with plastic wrap to prevent discoloration. Waffles freeze beautifully and can go directly into the oven to be retoasted. For buckwheat cakes, replace $^1/_4$ cup to $^1/_2$ cup of the cake flour with buckwheat flour.

	LARGE BATCH
$1^1/_2$ cups all-purpose flour	1 lb 9.5 oz
$^3/_4$ cup cake flour	12 oz
2 tsp baking powder	2 Tbs plus 2 tsp
$^1/_2$ tsp baking soda	2 tsp
$^1/_2$ tsp salt	2 tsp
2 cups buttermilk	2 qt
6 Tbs. unsalted butter, melted	12 oz
2 large eggs	13.6 oz
2 large egg yolks	4.4 oz
3 Tbs granulated sugar	5.25 oz
1 tsp vanilla extract	4 tsp

Sift the flours, baking powder, baking soda, and salt into a medium bowl. In another bowl, whisk together the buttermilk, butter, eggs, egg yolks, sugar, and vanilla. Pour the buttermilk mixture into the flour mixture and gently stir just until combined. Let batter stand 5 to 10 minutes before using. Cook two to four minutes on a hot, greased griddle, turning once, or in a preheated waffle iron. For thinner pancakes, use additional buttermilk. Keep in mind that pancakes can be kept warm until served, but waffles quickly lose their crunchy edge and should be placed on a rack in the oven until served.

WHOLE-GRAIN WAFFLES OR PANCAKES

MAKES EIGHT 4-INCH SQUARE BELGIAN WAFFLES OR SIXTEEN 4-INCH PANCAKES

		LARGE BATCH
1 cup all-purpose flour	1 lb 1 oz	
1/3 cup oat flour	6 oz	
1/3 cup whole wheat pastry flour	6 oz	
1/3 cup cake flour	5.33 oz	
1/4 cup toasted wheat germ	4 oz	
2 tsp baking powder	2 Tbs plus 2 tsp	
1/2 tsp baking soda	2 tsp	
2 cups buttermilk	2 qt	
1/2 cup unsalted butter, melted, or 1/3 cup vegetable oil	1 lb or 1 1/3 cups	
3 large eggs	1 lb 4.4 oz	
3 Tbs granulated sugar	5.25 oz	
1 tsp vanilla extract	4 tsp	

Follow the mixing directions for regular waffles and pancakes.

CREPES

MAKES 18 TO 30 CREPES Crepes are essentially very thin, eggy pancakes. The classic dessert, crepes Suzette, is folded crepes with an orange-butter sauce. A touch of Grand Marnier is added to flambé the crepes immediately before serving. Today, many chefs prefer to design their own crepes, filled with fruit or chocolate and accompanied by various sauces. Crepe batter may be made ahead and stored in the refrigerator, but it is easier to make all the crepes at once and warm them as needed. If the milk and eggs are not room temperature, the butter will harden and the batter will appear curdled.

		LARGE BATCH
¹/₂ cup all-purpose flour	8.5 oz	
¹/₂ cup cake flour	8 oz	
3 Tbs granulated sugar	5.25 oz	
¹/₈ tsp salt	¹/₂ tsp	
3 large eggs	1 lb 4.4 oz	
1 cup milk	1 qt	
2 Tbs unsalted butter, melted	4 oz	
Liqueur, vanilla extract, or lemon zest, for flavor (optional)		

Whisk the dry ingredients together in a bowl. Whisk in the eggs and milk until smooth, then whisk in the melted butter and flavoring of your choice. Let the batter rest 1 hour before using. Heat a skillet (6 to 8 inches, typically) over medium-high heat until hot. If necessary, brush the skillet with oil, shortening, or clarified butter to prevent sticking, wiping out excess fat. Pour just enough batter into the pan to coat the bottom of the skillet, tilting and rotating the pan to spread the batter evenly and thinly. Cook each crepe until it is golden on the underside and set on top, then loosen the sides with a spatula, flip the crepe, and briefly brown the other side.

CHAPTER 5

EGG-BASED
COMPONENTS

Flour is the pastry chef's central ingredient, and chocolate is certainly the most glamorous, but no ingredient is as versatile as the egg, as the range of dishes covered in this chapter demonstrates. The methods used to make custards, meringues, and pâte à choux have little in common, yet each of these foods owes its unique texture to the humble egg.

STIRRED CUSTARDS

Stirred custards are cooked on the stove top with frequent stirring, hence the name. The goal in making these custards is to cook them without scrambling the eggs. Egg whites cooked alone begin to set at 145°F and yolks at about 155°F. The presence of sugar and starch will raise the temperature at which the eggs are cooked; thus, the cooking temperature for stirred custards is variable. Pastry cream can be brought to a boil without curdling, but crème anglaise will scramble if boiled. Most chefs strain their stirred custards after cooking to ensure a perfectly smooth texture. After cooking the custard, place plastic wrap directly on the surface to prevent a skin from forming.

Starch-thickened custards must be brought to a boil to kill alpha amylase. This enzyme, present in egg yolks, breaks down the amylase present in starch and causes the pastry cream to thin.

CRÈME ANGLAISE

MAKES ABOUT 3 SCANT CUPS Crème Anglaise is both a rich dessert sauce and the base for ice cream. It can be used to make a decadent chocolate ganache or a buttercream. If it is not made in a bowl over simmering water, you must exercise great care to prevent the egg from scrambling from direct heat. Crème Anglaise is a barely thickened sauce that is fully cooked at 175°F, well below boiling. It keeps three days in the refrigerator.

		LARGE BATCH
2 cups heavy cream	2 qt	
2 cups whole milk	2 qt	
1 vanilla bean, split and scraped	4	
8 large egg yolks	17.6 oz	
¹/₂ cup granulated sugar	14 oz	
Pinch of salt	¹/₂ tsp	

In a medium saucepan, bring the cream, milk, and vanilla bean to a boil; remove from heat. Let the vanilla bean steep 15 to 30 minutes. Gently reheat mixture. Meanwhile, whisk the yolks, sugar, and salt together in a large bowl; slowly pour the hot cream into the yolks, whisking constantly. Return the mixture to the pan and cook over low heat, stirring constantly with a wooden spoon. The crème anglaise is done when a path drawn across a sauce-coated spoon remains clear, or the temperature reaches 175°F. Flavor as desired. Transfer to a bowl; cool over an ice water bath. Cover the surface with plastic wrap before refrigerating.

NOTE

For use as an **ice cream base,** increase the sugar to ²/₃ cup (1 lb 2.67 oz). To improve the texture of homemade ice cream, whip the egg yolks with the sugar to ribbon stage before tempering them with the hot milk and cream.

PASTRY CREAM

MAKES ABOUT 3 SCANT CUPS Pastry cream is one of the most important components of baking. It can be used to fill tarts, eclairs, and cakes; it can serve as the base for cream pie filling and pudding; and it even can be used as the base for a buttercream. Basic pastry cream should be thick enough to pipe into eclairs. Using part cream makes a smoother, richer product, but also reduces the shelf life to three days.

		LARGE BATCH
1/2 cup granulated sugar	14 oz	
1/4 cup cornstarch	5.33 oz	
1/8 tsp salt	1/2 tsp	
6 large egg yolks	13.2 oz	
2 1/2 cups milk	2 qt plus 2 cups	
1/4 vanilla bean, split and scraped	1	
2 Tbs unsalted butter	4 oz	

In a large bowl, stir together the sugar, cornstarch, and salt; whisk in the egg yolks. Bring the milk and vanilla bean to a boil over medium heat. Slowly pour the hot milk into the eggs, whisking constantly. Return the mixture to the saucepan. Cook over medium-low heat, stirring, until the mixture just reaches a boil. Strain into a bowl; stir in the butter. Cover the surface with plastic wrap and refrigerate. If needed, soften cold pastry cream by mixing briefly at medium speed.

VANILLA PUDDING

Follow the recipe above, using half-and-half instead of milk and reducing the cornstarch by half.

CREAM PIE FILLING

Follow the recipe above, substituting 1/2 cup heavy cream (large batch: 17 oz) for 1/2 cup of the milk (large batch: 17 oz).

COCONUT CREAM PIE FILLING

Follow the recipe for vanilla cream pie filling, above, stirring in 1¼ cups toasted, sweetened flaked coconut (large batch: 15 oz). For added creaminess, substitute 1¼ cups coconut milk for 1¼ cups of the whole milk (large batch: 5 cups). If coconut milk is used, there is no need to add heavy cream in the filling.

BUTTERSCOTCH PUDDING

MAKES ABOUT 3 SCANT CUPS

	LARGE BATCH
½ cup packed dark brown sugar	1 lb
2 Tbs cornstarch	2.67 oz
⅛ tsp salt	½ tsp
6 large egg yolks	13.2 oz
2 cups milk	2 qt
½ cup heavy cream	2 cups
¼ cup unsalted butter	8 oz
2 Tbs dark rum	½ cup
1 tsp vanilla extract	4 tsp

In a large bowl, stir together the brown sugar, cornstarch, and salt; whisk in the egg yolks. Bring the milk and cream to a boil over medium heat. Slowly pour the hot milk into the eggs, whisking constantly. Return the mixture to the saucepan. Cook over medium-low heat, stirring, until mixture just reaches a boil. Turn off the heat; stir in the butter, rum, and vanilla until the butter is melted and smooth. Strain into a bowl. Cover the surface with plastic wrap and refrigerate.

CHOCOLATE CREAM PIE FILLING

MAKES ENOUGH FILLING FOR ONE 9-INCH PIE

²/₃ cup granulated sugar	1 lb 2.67 oz	
3 Tbs cornstarch	4 oz	
¹/₈ tsp salt	¹/₂ tsp	
2 large eggs	13.6 oz	
2 large egg yolks	4.4 oz	
2 cups milk	2 qt	**LARGE BATCH**
1 cup heavy cream	1 qt	
2 Tbs unsweetened cocoa powder	1.88 oz	
8 oz semisweet chocolate, chopped	2 lb	
2 Tbs unsalted butter	4 oz	
1 tsp vanilla extract	4 tsp	

In a large bowl, stir together the sugar, cornstarch, and salt; whisk in the eggs and yolks. Bring the milk, cream, and cocoa powder to a boil over medium heat. Slowly pour the hot milk into the eggs, whisking constantly. Return the mixture to the saucepan. Cook over medium-low heat, stirring, until the mixture just reaches a boil. Strain into a bowl; stir in the chocolate, butter, and vanilla. Cover surface with plastic wrap and refrigerate.

CHOCOLATE PUDDING

Follow the recipe above, but reduce cornstarch to 2 Tbs (large batch: 2.67 oz) and semisweet chocolate to 6 ounces (large batch: 1 lb 8 oz).

BASIC BAVARIAN

MAKES 5 CUPS A bavarian is a flavored custard that has been stabilized with gelatin and lightened with a little whipped cream. It is poured into molds to set, and is used to make desserts such as **charlotte royal** and **charlotte russe.** Charlotte royal is a bavarian set inside a mold lined with slices of a jam-filled jelly roll cake. Charlotte russe is a bavarian set inside a mold lined with ladyfingers. Bavarian cream is vanilla flavored and softly set. When more whipped cream or whipped egg whites are added, it becomes a mousse. Flavor this bavarian any way you like—with espresso, praline paste, coconut, chocolate, or orange. It will keep four to five days.

	LARGE BATCH
2 cups **CRÈME ANGLAISE** (page 141)	2 qt
1 Tbs powdered gelatin	1/4 cup
1 1/2 Tbs water	6 Tbs
1 1/2 Tbs liquor of your choice	6 Tbs
1 1/2 cups heavy cream	6 cups

Warm the crème anglaise slightly. Sprinkle the gelatin over the water and liquor; let soften 5 minutes. Melt the gelatin gently over low heat until completely dissolved, or in the microwave for 10 to 15 seconds. Whisk into the custard. Stir the mixture over an ice water bath, or refrigerate until it begins to set. When the custard has the consistency of raw egg whites, whip the cream and fold it in. Pour into mold(s) and chill for 4 to 6 hours, until cold and set.

FRUIT BAVARIANS

Follow the recipe above, substituting 1 or more cups of sweetened fruit purée or coulis (see page 270), such as raspberry or passion fruit, for an equal portion of crème anglaise. Fresh pineapple, kiwi, mango, ginger, and papaya should not be used because they contain an enzyme that inhibits gelatin from setting. Canned versions are fine, since the enzyme is destroyed by pasteurization.

LEMON CURD

MAKES 2²/₃ CUPS Lemon curd is used to fill tarts, cakes, and lemon bars. It also may accompany fresh berries and slices of angel food, chiffon, or pound cake. Lemon curd keeps a week in the refrigerator.

4 large eggs	1 lb 11.2 oz	
6 large egg yolks	13.2 oz	**LARGE BATCH**
1 cup granulated sugar	1 lb 12 oz	
1 cup lemon juice	1 qt	
1 Tbs grated lemon zest	¹/₄ cup	
6 Tbs unsalted butter	12 oz	
Pinch of salt	¹/₂ tsp	

Whisk all the ingredients together in a medium saucepan over medium heat. Cook, stirring constantly, just until mixture comes to a boil. Strain into a bowl. Cover the surface with plastic wrap and refrigerate.

LEMON MOUSSE

Beat 2 egg whites (large batch: 9.2 oz) to stiff peaks; fold into warm or room temperature lemon curd. Let curd cool slightly. Beat ¹/₂ cup heavy cream (large batch: 17 oz) to soft peaks and fold into lemon mixture. Refrigerate until cold.

CHOCOLATE MOUSSE

MAKES ABOUT 6 CUPS Chocolate mousse is a beloved dessert on its own, but it can also be used to fill cakes and tarts. Pasteurized eggs should be used, or the yolks will need to be cooked with the chocolate. Powdered egg whites can be used, or even Italian meringue, but Italian meringue will sweeten the mousse. Though the egg whites are deflated more by being incorporated first, the whipped cream must be folded in last or it will cause the warm chocolate to seize. Use 4 egg whites for a soft mousse, 2 for a firmer one.

8 ounces bittersweet chocolate, chopped	2 lb	
4 large egg yolks	8.8 oz	**LARGE BATCH**
2 Tbs rum, port, or bourbon	$^1/_2$ cup	
2 to 4 large egg whites	9.2 oz to 1 lb 2.4 oz	
1 cup heavy cream	1 qt	

In a small bowl, melt the chocolate over simmering water. Whisk in the yolks and liquor or desired flavoring. Transfer to a larger bowl. Whip the egg whites to stiff peaks; very gently fold into the chocolate in two additions. Whip the heavy cream to firm peaks; fold into the chocolate mixture. Mound into parfait or serving bowls before chilling, but refrigerate before piping mousse.

WHITE CHOCOLATE MOUSSE

Follow the recipe above, substituting white chocolate for the bittersweet chocolate. Avoid strongly flavored liqueurs for this mousse. Since white chocolate is sweet, the mousse should be paired with tart or nutty flavors, such as strawberry, passion fruit, lemon, hazelnut, or toasted coconut.

RASPBERRY MOUSSE

MAKES 4 CUPS This is the basic formula for any fruit mousse; 1¹/₂ cups (large batch: 6 cups) of raspberry coulis may be substituted for the berries and sugar. Be sure to adjust the sugar when using different fruits. Also remember that the yield of fruit purée based on total amount of fresh fruit will vary with the fruit. Fresh pineapple, mango, papaya, and kiwifruit will not set up with gelatin, but canned fruit is fine. This mousse is the perfect texture for eating plain. Increase the gelatin to 2¹/₄ teaspoons (.25 oz envelope; 1 oz) if using the mousse as a filling for a cake or charlotte.

	LARGE BATCH
1 lb frozen raspberries, or 4 cups fresh	4 lb
¹/₂ cup plus 2 Tbs granulated sugar	1 lb 1.5 oz
2 Tbs Chambord, framboise, or Cointreau	¹/₂ cup
2 Tbs water	¹/₂ cup
1¹/₂ tsp powdered gelatin	2 Tbs
1¹/₄ cups heavy cream	5 cups

Thaw the raspberries, if frozen. Purée the fruit; strain it to remove the seeds. Stir in the sugar until it begins to dissolve. Sprinkle the gelatin over the liqueur and water; let soften 5 minutes. Melt the gelatin gently over low heat until completely dissolved, or in the microwave for 10 to 15 seconds. Whisk into fruit. (Make sure the fruit is not too cold when stirring in the gelatin, or the gelatin will harden immediately). Stir the mixture over an ice water bath, or refrigerate until it begins to set. When the fruit mixture has the consistency of raw egg whites, whip the heavy cream and fold it into the fruit. Chill for 4 to 6 hours, until cold and set.

FROZEN SOUFFLÉS

Frozen soufflés are actually frozen mousses. Typically they are molded in ceramic soufflé dishes that have been fitted with a parchment collar. The collar is removed after the mixture sets, giving the mousse the illusion of being a risen soufflé.

WARM CHOCOLATE SOUFFLÉ

MAKES ONE 8-CUP SOUFFLÉ For restaurant service, the best soufflés contain flour, which makes the egg structure more stable. Most soufflés are simply a starch-thickened, egg-yolk custard base (similar to pastry cream or white sauce, for savory soufflés) with egg whites folded in at the last minute. The base must be strongly flavored since it will be diluted by the large volume of egg whites. Typically, a soufflé will have an equal number of yolks and whites. Chocolate soufflés are more stable than other dessert soufflés. This delicate soufflé has no starch, making it especially light. Though it will lose some volume upon cooling, it is delicious cold.

	LARGE BATCH
$^1/_2$ cup unsalted butter	1 lb
7 oz semisweet chocolate, chopped	1 lb 12 oz
3 Tbs Dutch-processed unsweetened cocoa powder	2.8 oz
2 large egg yolks	4.4 oz
1 tsp vanilla extract	4 tsp
5 large egg whites	1 lb 7 oz
$^1/_4$ tsp salt	1 tsp
$^1/_2$ cup granulated sugar	14 oz

Butter and sugar an 8-cup straight-sided soufflé dish. Melt the butter and chocolate together over low heat. Whisk in the cocoa, egg yolks, and vanilla; transfer to a large bowl. Beat the egg whites until foamy; add the salt and beat the egg whites to soft peaks. With mixer running at medium speed, add the sugar a tablespoon at a time. Beat until shiny. Fold the egg whites into the chocolate mixture in two additions. Spread the mixture into the prepared dish. (The dish should be no more than three-fourths full unless a parchment collar has been attached.) Bake at 400°F for 5 minutes; reduce temperature to 350°F and bake until puffed and set in center. For best rise, bake near the bottom of the oven. Serve warm with Crème Anglaise (page 141) or Chocolate Sauce (page 247).

TIRAMISÙ

MAKES ONE 9-INCH SQUARE PAN This light but rich Italian dessert appeared on almost every restaurant menu in the past fifteen years. Though many unusual variations popped up, nothing compares to the original. If you have access to fresh-brewed espresso, by all means use it. Upscale versions of tiramisù use sabayon, or more properly zabaglione, made with marsala and folded into a mixture of mascarpone lightened with whipped cream. This keeps four to five days.

	LARGE BATCH
¹/₄ cup hot water	1 cup
¹/₃ cup brandy or marsala	1¹/₃ cups
2 Tbs espresso powder	2 oz
2¹/₄ tsp (.25 oz envelope) powdered gelatin	1 oz
One 8-oz container mascarpone cheese	2 lb
One 8-oz package cream cheese	2 lb
²/₃ cup granulated sugar	1 lb 2.67 oz
1 pint heavy cream	1 qt
¹/₂ recipe **LADYFINGERS** (page 101)	2 times recipe
Unsweetened cocoa powder, for dusting	

Combine the water, brandy, and espresso powder in a bowl. Reserve ¹/₄ cup of this mixture for brushing the ladyfingers. Sprinkle the gelatin over the remaining espresso mixture; let soften 1 to 2 minutes. Microwave the gelatin on high at 15-second intervals, stirring, until completely dissolved. Beat the mascarpone, cream cheese, and sugar until smooth and light; beat in the gelatin. In another bowl, beat the heavy cream to stiff peaks. Fold half the whipped cream into the cheese mixture to lighten it, then fold in the remaining cream. Brush the ladyfingers with the reserved espresso mixture. Line the bottom of a 9-inch square pan with the ladyfingers; top with half the cheese mixture. Repeat. Cover surface directly with plastic wrap. Refrigerate 4 hours, until cold. Dust the top with cocoa before serving.

ZABAGLIONE

MAKES 4 SERVINGS The French call this a light Italian dessert sabayon. It can be served warm as a dessert sauce or cold as a parfait. The most traditional version is made with marsala, a fortified wine. If using other wines, the amount should be increased. This keeps 24 hours.

		LARGE BATCH
$^3/_4$ cup Champagne, white wine, red wine, or $^1/_2$ cup marsala	3 cups, 2 cups	
4 large egg yolks	8.8 oz	
$^1/_4$ cup granulated sugar	7 oz	
Pinch of salt	$^1/_2$ tsp	
$^1/_2$ cup heavy cream (optional)	2 cups	

Whisk the Champagne, wine, or marsala with the egg yolks, sugar, and salt in a bowl set over a pan of simmering water. Cook, whipping constantly with the whisk, until the mixture is thick and light and it registers 160°F on a candy thermometer. Remove from heat. Serve immediately, if serving warm.

For the chilled version, whisk the sabayon over a bowl of ice water until cold. Whip the cream to soft peaks; fold into the egg mixture. Chill until ready to serve.

BAKED CUSTARDS

These custards generally contain little starch, if any, and must be cooked carefully and slowly to prevent curdling. They are usually baked in a slow to moderate oven (300° to 350°F) in a protective water bath. A water bath, or *bain-marie,* is made by placing the custard dish in a larger pan that is filled with enough hot water to come halfway up the side of the custard dish. A towel may be placed under the custard dishes to insulate them from the hot bottom of the pan. For ease of transport and to prevent sloshing the custard with water, the large pan containing the custard dish is placed directly on the extended oven rack *before* the water is poured in.

Custards are done cooking once their top surface no longer wiggles, except in the very center, when the pan is gently shaken. Each type of recipe, however, may have its own test for doneness. Custards will set upon cooling, and if they are overcooked they may crack or curdle. Prompt removal from the water bath is essential, since its residual heat will continue the cooking process. Except for bread pudding, they are chilled before serving.

CRÈME BRÛLÉE

MAKES EIGHT 4-OUNCE SERVINGS Crème brûlée translates as "burnt cream," referring to the crisp crust of burnt sugar that tops the custard. The custards are baked ahead, chilled, and then caramelized just before serving. Any sugar can be used for caramelizing, even powdered, but the dry, pourable version of brown sugar (known as *brownulated*) tastes the best. Though it sounds dangerous, a blowtorch is the safer bet for even caramelizing, rather than the broiler. Beginners should pack the custard-filled shallow ramekins in ice to keep the dessert cool as the top caramelizes. Espresso powder, brown sugar, liqueurs such as amaretto, rum, or bourbon are great additions to this recipe, but vanilla is the all-time favorite.

		LARGE BATCH
3 cups heavy cream	3 qt	
1 cup whole milk	1 qt	
1/3 cup granulated sugar	9.33 oz	
1/2 vanilla bean, split and scraped	2	
2 large eggs	13.6 oz	
8 large egg yolks	1 lb 1.6 oz	

Heat the cream, milk, sugar, and vanilla bean together over medium-low heat, stirring, until the sugar is dissolved. In a large bowl, combine the eggs and yolks. Slowly whisk the hot cream into the eggs. Strain the mixture. Place shallow crème brûlée dishes or ramekins onto the bottom of a hotel pan (roasting pan) or sheet pan lined with a wet towel. Pour the custard into each ramekin.

Place the hotel pan on the center rack of a 325°F oven. Make sure each ramekin is completely full of custard, as the custard will settle when baked. Fill the pan with enough hot water to come at least halfway up the sides of the dishes. Bake for 30 minutes, or until the custard is just set in the center but still wobbles slightly. Remove the custards from the pan; refrigerate until cold before caramelizing the tops.

QUICHE

MAKES ONE 9-INCH QUICHE Quiches are savory custards. Sautéed vegetables, such as onions, mushrooms, and artichokes, and meats, such as bacon, ham, shellfish, and salmon, are common ingredients. Though French versions remain popular, such as the bacon and gruyère-filled quiche lorraine, these savory pies invite creativity. Hearty southwestern-style quiches with cheddar, roasted corn, and smoked peppers have become commonplace in recent years.

1 1/2 to 2 cups filling, seasoned as desired	6 to 8 cups	**LARGE BATCH**
One 9-inch blind baked pie shell with a fluted crust	4 shells	
Pinch of salt and pepper	1/2 tsp each	
6 large eggs plus enough half-and-half to equal 3 cups total	2 lb 8.8 oz eggs plus half-and-half to equal 3 qt	
Shredded or crumbled cheese (optional)		

It is important for any vegetables in the filling to be thoroughly sautéed, or they will leak water into the custard, causing it to appear curdled. Place the filling in the shell. Add a pinch of salt and pepper to the egg mixture, then pour it into the shell. Sprinkle the cheese on top. Bake at 350°F for 30 to 40 minutes, or until custard is set or a knife inserted in the center comes out clean. Cool to just warm before serving.

POTS DE CRÈME

MAKES 4 SERVINGS Similar to crème brûlée in richness, pots de crème are silky puddings that are baked rather than stirred. This version is flavored with Nutella, a hazelnut spread that provides the flavor of gianduja—chocolate and hazelnut.

1½ cups half-and-half	6 cups	
⅔ cup Nutella spread	1 lb 5 oz	
4 large egg yolks	8.8 oz	LARGE BATCH
6 ounces milk chocolate, chopped	1 lb 8 oz	

Heat the half-and-half and Nutella together over medium-low heat, stirring until smooth. Increase the heat to medium; bring the mixture just to a boil. In a large bowl, stir the yolks. Slowly whisk the hot cream into the yolks. Stir in the chopped chocolate. Let stand 1 minute; stir until smooth. Strain the mixture. Place four 6-ounce ramekins or tea cups onto the bottom of a hotel pan (roasting pan) lined with a wet towel. Pour custard into each ramekin. Place the hotel pan on the center rack of a 325°F oven. Fill the pan with enough hot water to come at least halfway up the sides of the ramekins. Bake for 20 to 25 minutes, or until the custard just barely wobbles in the center. Remove the custards from the pan; refrigerate 30 minutes uncovered. After the custards are no longer warm, cover loosely with plastic wrap. Chill until cold.

CHEESECAKES

Cheesecakes are custards baked in a crumb or cookie crust. Home cooks constantly fight soggy crusts resulting from ineffective springform pans, but professional bakers simply use round cake pans with 2- to 3-inch sides. If the pan has been greased, running a knife around the inside edge and a quick pass or two over a warm burner will easily release the cooled cheesecake. The cheesecake can be inverted onto a plastic-wrapped cardboard cake circle, and then flipped right side up. Creamy cheesecakes contain sour cream or heavy cream and very little starch. They are baked in a water bath to ensure gentle, even cooking, which preserves their silky texture and prevents cracking. Dense New York–style cheesecakes are different. Their formula includes more flour and less liquid. They cook in a moderate oven, without a water bath, and rest in the turned-off oven for an hour after baking. When cool, New York–style cheesecakes fall a little, leaving a characteristic rim around the edge.

PLAIN CHEESECAKE

MAKES ONE 8-INCH CHEESECAKE

		LARGE BATCH
Four 8-oz packages (2 lb) cream cheese	8 lb	
1¼ cups granulated sugar	2 lb 3 oz	
3 Tbs all-purpose flour	3.2 oz	
4 large eggs	1 lb 11.2 oz	
2 large egg yolks	4.4 oz	
½ cup sour cream	2 cups	
½ cup heavy cream	2 cups	
2 tsp vanilla extract	2 Tbs plus 2 tsp	
One 8-inch crumb crust, prebaked in an 8 by 3-inch cake pan		

Beat the cream cheese, sugar, and flour together at medium speed until light and fluffy, 5 to 8 minutes. One at a time, beat in the eggs and yolks. On low speed, beat in the sour cream, heavy cream, and vanilla. Pour into the prepared crust. Bake at 350°F in a water bath for 65 to 75 minutes, or until the center barely wobbles. Remove from water bath and let cheesecake cool. Refrigerate until cold before removing from pan.

ESPRESSO CHEESECAKE

Dissolve 2½ tablespoons instant espresso powder (2.5 oz) in some of the cream and add to the batter. Stir in 1 cup mini semisweet chips (1 lb 8 oz), if desired.

CHOCOLATE CHEESECAKE

MAKES ONE 9 BY 3-INCH CHEESECAKE OR THREE 6 BY 2-INCH CHEESECAKES

10 oz semisweet chocolate, chopped	2 lb 8 oz	
2 oz unsweetened chocolate, chopped	8 oz	
Four 8-oz packages (2 lb) cream cheese	8 lb	**LARGE BATCH**
1¹⁄₂ cups granulated sugar	2 lb 10 oz	
4 large eggs	1 lb 11.2 oz	
2 large egg yolks	4.4 oz	
1¹⁄₂ cups heavy cream	6 cups	
2 tsp. vanilla extract	2 Tbs plus 2 tsp	
One 9-inch crumb crust, prebaked in a 9 by 3-inch cake pan		

Melt the semisweet and unsweetened chocolates together. Beat the cream cheese and sugar together at medium speed until light and fluffy, 5 to 8 minutes. One at a time, beat in the eggs and yolks. On low speed, beat in the heavy cream and vanilla. Stir in the melted chocolates. Pour into the prepared crust. Bake at 350°F in a water bath for 65 to 75 minutes, or until the center barely wobbles. Remove from the water bath and let the cheesecake cool. Refrigerate until cold before removing from pan.

WHITE CHOCOLATE RASPBERRY CHEESECAKE

MAKES ONE 9 BY 3-INCH ROUND CHEESECAKE

		LARGE BATCH
8 ounces white chocolate, chopped	2 lb	
Four 8-oz packages (2 lb) cream cheese	8 lb	
1 cup granulated sugar	1 lb 12 oz	
4 large eggs	1 lb 11.2 oz	
2 large egg yolks	4.4 oz	
1 cup heavy cream	1 qt	
1 tsp vanilla extract	4 tsp	
1 cup fresh raspberries	4 cups	
One 9-inch crumb crust, prebaked in a 9 by 3-inch cake pan		

Melt the white chocolate. Beat the cream cheese and sugar together at medium speed until light and fluffy, 5 to 8 minutes. One at a time, beat in the eggs and yolks. On low speed, beat in the heavy cream and vanilla. Stir in the melted chocolate and raspberries. Pour into the prepared crust. Bake at 350°F in a water bath for 65 to 75 minutes, or until the center barely wobbles. Remove from the water bath and let the cheesecake cool. Refrigerate until cold before removing from pan.

ORANGE COINTREAU CHEESECAKE

Eliminate the raspberries and add 3 tablespoons Cointreau ($^3/_4$ cup) and 1 teaspoon orange extract or grated zest (4 tsp). Use a gingersnap crumb crust instead of a chocolate or graham crust.

PUMPKIN CHEESECAKE

MAKES ONE 9-INCH CHEESECAKE

		LARGE BATCH
Four 8-oz packages (2 lb) cream cheese	8 lb	
1 cup packed light brown sugar	2 lb	
$^1/_2$ cup granulated sugar	14 oz	
2 Tbs all-purpose flour	2.125 oz	
1 tsp ground cinnamon	4 tsp	
1$^1/_2$ tsp ground ginger	2 Tbs	
$^1/_4$ tsp ground nutmeg	1 tsp	
5 large eggs	2 lb 2 oz	
1$^3/_4$ cups (15-oz can) pumpkin purée	3 lb 12 oz	
$^1/_3$ cup heavy cream	1$^1/_3$ cups	
3 Tbs dark rum	$^3/_4$ cup	
1$^1/_2$ tsp vanilla extract	2 Tbs	
One 9-inch gingersnap graham crust, prebaked in a 9 by 3-inch cake pan		

Beat the cream cheese, sugars, flour, and spices together at medium speed until light and fluffy, 5 to 8 minutes. One at a time, beat in the eggs. On low speed, beat in the pumpkin purée, heavy cream, rum, and vanilla. Pour into the prepared crust. Bake at 350°F in a water bath for 65 to 75 minutes, or until the center barely wobbles. Remove from the water bath, and let cheesecake cool. Refrigerate until cold before removing from pan.

NEW YORK CHEESECAKE

MAKES ONE 9-INCH CHEESECAKE New York–style cheesecake is taller, denser, and more solid than the previous cheesecake recipes. It gets its deep golden top from a unique baking method that begins with an extremely hot oven. A water bath is not used.

		LARGE BATCH
Five 8-oz packages (2$\frac{1}{2}$ lb) cream cheese	10 lb	
1$\frac{2}{3}$ cups granulated sugar	2 lb 14.67 oz	
3 Tbs all-purpose flour	3.2 oz	
5 large eggs	2 lb 2 oz	
1 cup sour cream	1 qt	
2 tsp vanilla extract	2 Tbs plus 2 tsp	
1 tsp grated lemon zest	4 tsp	
One 9-inch graham crust, prebaked in a 9 by 3-inch cake pan		

Beat the cream cheese, sugar, and flour together on medium speed until light and fluffy, 5 to 8 minutes. One at a time, beat in the eggs. On low speed, beat in the sour cream, vanilla, and lemon zest. Pour into the prepared crust. Place in the center of a 450°F oven for 8 minutes; reduce the oven temperature to 200°F. Bake for 1 hour; turn off the oven. Leave the cheesecake in the oven for 1 more hour. Let the cheesecake cool. Refrigerate until cold before removing from pan.

BREAD PUDDING

This comfort food is a great way to use day-old bread or croissants. Basically, the dessert is a dry bread baked with a rich custard—a very rich custard, along the lines of crème brûlée. The two recipes below show how much variety is possible with this dessert.

CINNAMON BREAD PUDDING WITH APPLES

MAKES SIX 8-OUNCE PUDDINGS

2 tart apples (1 lb), peeled, cored, and chopped	4 lb	
$^1/_4$ cup packed light brown sugar	8 oz	
1 tsp ground cinnamon	4 tsp	**LARGE BATCH**
2 Tbs unsalted butter	4 oz	
1 loaf day-old cinnamon raisin bread, cubed (about 8 cups)	32 cups	
4 large eggs	1 lb 11.2 oz	
4 large egg yolks	8.8 oz	
$^1/_2$ cup granulated sugar	14 oz	
4 cups half-and-half	4 qt	
1 tsp vanilla extract	4 tsp	

Sauté the apples, brown sugar, and cinnamon in the butter until the sugar has dissolved and the mixture is bubbly and thick. Toss the apples in a bowl with the cubed bread; divide among six 8-ounce buttered ceramic ramekins. Whisk the eggs, yolks, and sugar together in a large bowl. Bring the half-and-half to a boil and slowly whisk it into the eggs. Stir in the vanilla. Pour the hot custard over the bread cubes, pressing the cubes to immerse them in the liquid. Let the ramekins stand 15 minutes. Place the ramekins in a roasting pan or hotel pan; fill the pan with enough hot water to come halfway up the sides of the ramekins. Bake at 350°F for 45 minutes, or until the bread puddings are set in the middle. Serve warm.

CHOCOLATE
BREAD PUDDING

MAKES TWO 8-CUP PUDDINGS

		LARGE BATCH
1 loaf day-old brioche bread, cubed (about 10 cups)	40 cups	
1 cup granulated sugar	1 lb 12 oz	
12 large egg yolks	1 lb 10.6 oz	
4 cups half-and-half	4 qt	
3 Tbs unsweetened cocoa powder	2.8 oz	
8 oz bittersweet chocolate, finely chopped	2 lb	
1 tsp vanilla extract	4 tsp	
1/4 tsp salt	1 tsp	

Place the bread cubes on a sheet pan and dry them in a low (200° to 300°F) oven. Place the cubes in a buttered 9 by 13-inch baking pan or two buttered 8-cup ceramic ramekins. Whisk the sugar and egg yolks together in a large bowl. Bring the half-and-half to a boil with the cocoa powder. Gradually whisk the hot cream into the eggs. Stir in the chopped chocolate, vanilla, and salt until the chocolate is melted and the mixture is smooth. Pour the custard over the bread cubes. Place plastic wrap over the pan and weight the top down to immerse the bread cubes. Let stand 30 minutes to 1 hour. Remove the weights; cover the custard with foil and cut vent holes through the foil and plastic. Bake at 325°F in a hot water bath for 75 to 90 minutes, or until the custard is set and the liquid is absorbed by the bread. Cool slightly on a wire rack. Serve warm or cold.

MERINGUES

As soon as an egg white foam is combined with sugar, it becomes a meringue. Sugar makes the beaten egg whites smooth, stable, flexible, and resistant to overbeating. There are several different methods, such as for **French, Swiss,** and **Italian** meringues. But fundamentally, there are two types of meringue, soft and hard. The amount of sugar is the variable: more sugar makes a smoother, more stable hard meringue. Thus, meringues are not so much recipes as formulas.

Soft meringue is used to top pies and desserts such as baked Alaska. Generally it is an equal weight of egg whites and sugar, but it can be made sweeter if desired. Hard meringue, used to make crisp shells to hold soft desserts and the crisp round layers in dacquoise, contains twice the sugar as egg whites by weight. It is baked on parchment in a very low oven, between 200° and 225°F. Hard meringue should completely dry out and harden without browning.

MERINGUE-MAKING TIPS

Eggs are easiest to separate when cold, but warm whites whip faster and provide better finished volume.

Egg whites should be beaten with grease-free utensils.

A copper bowl is useful for creating a more stable meringue that resists overwhipping.

For a very stable meringue, substitute confectioners' sugar for up to half of the granulated sugar (by volume).

For foam with lots of small bubbles, beat the egg white at medium-high rather than high speed.

Cream of tartar, an acid that prevents overbeating, is added near the beginning of mixing.

Superfine sugar dissolves faster than granulated sugar.

Do not add the sugar until the egg whites are near the soft peak stage.

In small mixers, the sugar should be added to the running mixer a tablespoon at a time. In large mixers, the amount is increased to around $^1/_4$ cup.

The meringue should be shiny, fluffy, with no grittiness from undissolved sugar.

Bake hard meringue at the end of the day, turn off the oven, and leave the meringue overnight. This ensures the meringue is completely dry, since meringue absorbs moisture from the air.

FRENCH MERINGUE

French meringue is the basic meringue. Quite simply, it is room-temperature egg whites beaten to soft peaks, with added sugar. The sugar amount is variable, 1 to 2 ounces sugar per egg white, depending on the end use of the meringue. Salt, cream of tartar, and vanilla are optional.

DACQUOISE DISKS

MAKES 2 MERINGUE DISKS Dacquoise is a dessert formed by rounds of crisp meringue flavored with toasted nuts, even coconut. The meringue disks are sandwiched together with ganache, buttercream, or sometimes even whipped cream. Usually the outside is coated with buttercream and garnished with chopped nuts or chocolate shavings, so that the dessert resembles an elegant cake or torte. Often the nut-flavored meringue disks themselves are called dacquoise. The recipe for them is simply a variation of French meringue, made with a sugar to egg white ratio greater than 2 to 1.

		LARGE BATCH
1/2 cup whole hazelnuts, skinned and toasted	10 oz	
1 Tbs plus 1 1/2 tsp potato starch	6 Tbs	
6 large egg whites	1 lb 11.6 oz	
1/4 tsp salt	1 tsp	
1 3/4 cups superfine sugar	3 lb 3.3 oz	

Grind the nuts with the potato starch in a food processor. In a mixer bowl, beat the egg whites with the salt to soft peaks. With the mixer running at medium speed, add the sugar, a tablespoon at a time. Increase speed to high and beat meringue another minute, until stiff and shiny. Fold in the nut mixture. Place the meringue in large pastry bag fitted with a 1/2- to 3/4-inch plain tip. Line a sheet pan with parchment. Using a 9-inch round cake pan as a guide, trace two circles onto the parchment. Flip the parchment over; you should still be able to see lines. Pipe, starting just inside the template lines and continuing concentrically, toward the center. Bake at 250°F until hard and dry, about 1 hour.

SWISS MERINGUE

Swiss meringue is rarely used except in making buttercream. The classic formula for Swiss meringue is 2 ounces of sugar for every egg white, but in buttercream this can be reduced to avoid an overly sweet frosting. It is heavier than either basic meringue or Italian meringue. To make Swiss meringue, combine the egg whites and sugar in the mixing bowl. Place the bowl over a low burner or over simmering water. If making a large batch, place the whites in a small bowl and transfer to the mixer later. Stir the eggs until they are warm and the sugar is dissolved. If no grains of sugar can be detected, beat the whites at medium-high speed until stiff peaks form.

ITALIAN MERINGUE

MAKES ABOUT 4 QUARTS Italian meringue is sweet, with twice the sugar as egg by weight. It is also lighter than the other meringues with the advantage of being fully cooked. Instead of granulated sugar, the whipped egg white foam is cooked with a hot sugar syrup. This meringue is safer than unpasteurized meringues used to top pies and baked Alaska, and it is more stable.

		LARGE BATCH
2 cups granulated sugar	3 lb 8 oz	
1 cup water	1 qt	
1 cup egg whites (about 7 large)	2 lb 2 oz	

In a saucepan, dissolve the sugar in the water over medium heat, stirring. Increase the heat to high; boil until syrup reaches 238°F on a candy thermometer. Once the syrup is boiling, begin whipping the egg whites in the mixer bowl. The egg whites should be at the stiff-peak stage when the syrup goes in. With the mixer running, carefully pour the hot syrup down the side of the bowl. Continue beating the meringue until it has cooled to just warm. Flavor with vanilla or salt if desired. (To ensure that the egg whites reach a high enough temperature to be cooked, 160°F instantly or over 3 minutes at 143°F, use a warm mixing bowl and room-temperature whites.)

MERINGUE FOR PIES

Pies are traditionally topped with French meringue and baked until golden. This is tricky business, however, since the interior and exterior cook at vastly different rates. An overcooked meringue will form beads of moisture on its surface as the egg proteins tighten and squeeze out moisture. A meringue that did not cook through in the center slowly dissolves and releases its liquid, which is called weeping. Two factors lead to success: First, the filling needs to be hot when the meringue is applied in order to ensure that it cooks through. Second, a hot oven temperature (425°F) for a shorter period of time prevents overcooking.

To avoid the problems of weeping and shrinkage, many chefs add a thickened cornstarch-water solution to meringue. Starch provides long-term stability and makes the meringue easy to slice. It takes only a teaspoon or two of cornstarch to stabilize meringue for a pie. The cornstarch must be brought to a boil in just enough water so that it can be beaten into the meringue without clumping. This is more efficient for large-scale use than for one pie: About 2 teaspoons of cornstarch should be cooked with $1/3$ cup water. A couple of teaspoons of this warm mixture will stabilize the meringue for one pie.

For pies that have cold fillings, Italian meringue is the best option. It is stable since it is precooked, and quick browning under a broiler or with a blow torch will finish it nicely. One last option is to whisk the whites and sugar over simmering water until their temperature

MERINGUE-BASED DESSERTS

Baked Alaska is an ice cream dessert. The ice cream is placed in a layer of sponge cake, or in a sponge cake–lined mold, and frozen. Just before serving, a layer of soft meringue is swirled over the unmolded ice cream and browned quickly in a hot oven. French meringue was once the standard, but today chefs prefer the stability and safety of Italian meringue, which can be browned with a blowtorch or in the oven.

Dacquoise is a dessert of two nut meringue disks filled with buttercream.

Marjolaine is a rectangular dacquoise, flavored with toasted nuts and filled with chocolate buttercream. Today a marjolaine may be flavored any number of ways.

Pavlova is an Australian dessert named for a famous Russian ballerina. It consists of a meringue shell or base filled with whipped cream and fruit.

reaches 160°F, and then beat them. This makes a fully cooked but heavy meringue.

Pasteurized egg whites or powdered pasteurized egg whites should be used for any meringue that may not reach temperatures high enough to be fully cooked. Pasteurized egg whites in cartons and powdered egg whites whip fast. But eggs pasteurized in the shell may not whip easily.

PÂTE À CHOUX

Pâte à choux, the dough used to make cream puffs, eclairs, profiteroles, and croquembuches, does not fit into any category well. Made from beating eggs into a paste of boiled water, butter, and flour, it does not resemble any other type of pastry. But since the high proportion of eggs makes it rise and gives the product its distinctive character, pâte à choux is placed here with egg cookery.

PÂTE À CHOUX

MAKES 16 LARGE PUFFS OR ECLAIRS

		LARGE BATCH
1/2 cup milk	2 cups	
1/2 cup water	2 cups	
1/2 cup unsalted butter	1 lb	
1 Tbs granulated sugar	1.75 oz	
1/2 tsp salt	2 tsp	
1 1/4 cups all-purpose flour	1 lb 5.25 oz	
4 to 5 large eggs	1 lb 11.2 oz to 2 lb 2 oz	

Bring the milk, water, butter, sugar, and salt to a boil in a medium saucepan. Remove from heat. Stir in the flour. The mixture will resemble thick paste. Stir the paste constantly over low heat until the flour has lost its raw flavor and the mixture pulls away from the sides of the pan. Do not overcook, or the flour will not be able to absorb the maximum amount of eggs. Transfer the flour mixture to the mixer; beat with the paddle attachment until it has cooled to just warm. One at a time, add the eggs to the running mixer. Before adding the last eggs, begin checking the consistency of the mixture. If it falls from a wooden spoon in blobs, it needs another egg; if it runs in a steady stream, it is too thin. The perfect consistency is a dough that can be piped without oozing. As soon as the mixture is shiny and falls into a drooped peak when pulled, it has absorbed enough egg and is ready to be piped.

HINTS FOR USING PÂTE À CHOUX

The pastry dough may be glazed with an egg wash to add shine.

A very small amount of sugar may be added to the dough, but too much causes overbrowning.

Milk makes the puffs richly flavored but tender; all water makes them crisp, and half of each is a compromise.

Choux paste is usually made with whole eggs, but for crisper puffs a few egg whites may be substituted.

All-purpose flour or bread flour may be used. Bread flour, which is higher in protein, can absorb more moisture (egg in this case) and makes a lighter puff.

Line sheet pans with parchment, using dabs of the pastry to glue the corners of the paper down. Use a $1/2$-inch plain tip for piping cream puffs and a star tip for eclairs. Pipe a $2^{1}/_{4}$-inch mound for large puffs and 1-inch mounds for small. For eclairs, pipe 5-inch-long tubes. With a wet finger, flatten any tips of dough that stick up from the piped tubes or rounds.

If you have a convection oven, you may need to turn off the fan when baking the puffs. Like soufflés, pâte à choux gets the best lift if baked near the heat source at the bottom of the oven. Place the pans in a 450°F oven, reducing the temperature immediately to 375°F. Eclairs will take 35 to 40 minutes to bake, the puffs less time. Remove the puffs from the oven and turn off the oven. When the oven has cooled to just warm, return the pans to the oven, leaving the door propped open so the puffs dry out. (Another method of preventing the puffs from getting soggy is to pierce them or slice them open to let steam escape.)

Before they are filled, the eggy interiors may be hollowed out with a knife. The cooked pastries freeze and reheat well.

FRITTERS OR BEIGNETS

Add $^1/_3$ cup granulated sugar and $^2/_3$ cup all-purpose flour to the recipe above. For apple fritters, stir in one apple, peeled, cored, and shredded. For banana-chip beignets, stir in one mashed banana and 2 to 3 tablespoons mini semisweet chocolate chips. Fry in 365°F oil for 3 to 5 minutes until golden. Drain and toss in cinnamon sugar or confectioners' sugar. Plain French doughnuts, called **crullers,** are made by piping this dough in circles and frying them.

CHOUX PASTRIES

Eclairs are oblong pastries filled with pastry cream and topped with chocolate glaze or flavored fondant.

Cream Puffs are simple rounds of pastry filled with sweetened whipped cream. When they are filled with ice cream or other savory and sweet fillings, they are called **profiteroles.**

Croquembouche is a tall, impressive dessert made from pastry cream-filled profiteroles stacked to form a cone or pyramid. Golden caramel, sometimes called golden syrup, is used to glue the puffs together and glaze them. The dessert is often garnished with spun sugar—more golden syrup that has been flicked with a fork or open whisk.

CHAPTER 6

PIES, TARTS, AND OTHER
FRUIT DESSERTS

Pies and tarts are simply crusts or shells with delicious fillings. The fillings can be virtually anything—mousse, fruit, pastry cream, custards, or chocolate ganache. Pies and tarts appear to be different versions of the same idea. The biggest difference is size: tarts are wide and shallow, pies are deeper and taller. At the local bakery, you are just as likely to see chocolate tart as chocolate pie, key lime tart as key lime pie, and caramel pecan tart as caramel pecan pie.

BASIC DOUGHS AND CRUSTS

AMERICAN PIE DOUGH

MAKES EIGHT 8-INCH PIES OR SEVEN 9-INCH PIES A combination of butter and shortening gives American pie crust its characteristic flakiness. All-shortening recipes are flakier, but most consumers prefer at least some butter for flavor. Hard shortenings, available through wholesale distributors, also produce good results. Though lard is not commonly used today, it does create the most velvety and flaky crust of any natural fat. The dough will keep for three days in the refrigerator or for several months frozen.

8 cups all-purpose flour	8 lb 8 oz	
1 Tbs salt	2 oz	**LARGE BATCH**
1³/₄ cups plus 2 Tbs (15 oz) unsalted butter, cold	3 lb 12 oz	
³/₄ cup shortening, cold	1 lb 1.25 oz	
1 to 1¹/₂ cups ice cold water	1 qt to 6 cups	

Place the flour and salt in a mixer bowl fitted with the paddle attachment; briefly combine. With the mixer running at medium-low speed, toss the cold butter into the bowl a tablespoon at a time. Add the shortening the same way. Once the fat has been reduced to ¹/₄ to ¹/₂-inch pieces (pea-size clumps), drizzle enough ice water into the bowl for the dough to start to come together. The dough will still be shaggy, not wet. Press the dough together, then divide into eight 8-ounce pieces for 8-inch diameter pies, or seven pieces just over 9 ounces each for 9-inch pies. For easier rolling, flatten each piece into a round disc. Wrap in plastic; let the dough rest for 2 hours or overnight before using. This is a very important step.

PÂTE BRISÉE

MAKES FIVE 9-INCH OR 10-INCH TART SHELLS This is the classic French dough for tarts and quiches. Less flaky than basic pie dough, it is crisp and very buttery.

		LARGE BATCH
4 cups all-purpose flour	4 lb 4 oz	
2 cups cake flour	2 lb	
2 tsp salt	2 Tbs plus 2 tsp	
2 cups (1 lb) unsalted butter, cold	4 lb	
2 large eggs	13.6 oz, cold	
$1/4$ cup ice cold water	1 cup	

Place flours and salt in mixer bowl fitted with the paddle attachment; briefly combine. With mixer running at medium-low speed, toss the cold butter into the bowl a tablespoon at a time. Whisk the eggs with the ice water. Once the butter has been reduced to $1/4$ to $1/2$-inch sized pieces (pea-size clumps), drizzle enough of the egg mixture into the bowl for the dough to start to come together. The dough will still be shaggy, not wet. Press the dough together. For 9 to 10-inch tart shells, divide the dough into five pieces about $9^{1}/4$ ounces each.

PÂTE SUCRÉE

MAKES SIX 9-INCH OR FIVE 10-INCH TART SHELLS Sweet tart dough is a variation of pâte brisée; using milk instead of water and adding a little sugar make this crust sweeter and more golden. Pâte sucrée can be mixed like regular pie dough; or, for a sturdier dough, the butter and sugar may be creamed together as if you were making cookies.

4 cups all-purpose flour	4 lb 4 oz	
2 cups cake flour	2 lb	**LARGE BATCH**
$^1/_2$ cup granulated sugar	14 oz	
2 tsp salt	2 Tbs plus 2 tsp	
2 cups (1 lb) unsalted butter, cold	4 lb	
2 large eggs	13.6 oz	
$^1/_4$ cup cold milk	1 cup	

Place flours, sugar, and salt in mixer bowl fitted with the paddle attachment; briefly combine. With mixer running at medium-low speed, toss the cold butter into the bowl a tablespoon at a time. Whisk the eggs with the milk. Once the butter has been reduced to $^1/_4$ to $^1/_2$-inch sized pieces (pea-size clumps), drizzle enough of the egg mixture into the bowl for the dough to start to come together. The dough will still be shaggy, not wet. Press the dough together. For 9-inch tart shells, divide the dough into six pieces about $8^2/_3$ ounces each, and for 10-inch shells, divide the dough into five pieces about $10^1/_2$ ounces each.

HAZELNUT SHORT CRUST

MAKES THREE 9 BY 13-INCH CRUSTS This dough tastes like a cross between pâte sucrée and shortbread, with the added flavor of toasted nuts. The type of nut used may be varied. It is the ideal crust for lemon bars.

		LARGE BATCH
2 cups toasted, skinned hazelnuts	2 lb 6 oz	
1¹/₂ cups granulated sugar	2 lb 10 oz	
6 cups all-purpose flour	6 lb 6 oz	
³/₄ cup cornstarch	1 lb	
1¹/₂ tsp salt	2 Tbs	
2¹/₄ cups (1 lb 2 oz) unsalted butter, cold	4 lb 8 oz	

Line three 9 by 13-inch baking pans with foil or parchment; grease foil. In a food processor, pulse the nuts with the sugar until they are finely chopped, but not pulverized. Transfer the nuts to a mixer bowl; add the flour, cornstarch, and salt. With the mixer running at medium-low speed, toss the butter into the bowl a tablespoon at a time. When the mixture resembles coarse crumbs, turn off the mixer. Press the crumbs into the bottom and ³/₄-inch up the side of the prepared pans. Prebake crust at 350°F for 25 minutes before adding filling, then bake until filling is set.

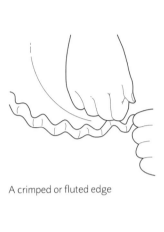

A crimped or fluted edge

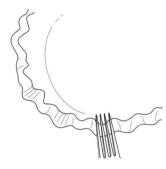

A textured edge made by using a fork or knife

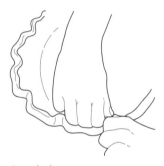

A petal edge

A lattice top

A top crust formed with decorative cut-outs

FIGURE 6.1 **Different styles of decorative crusts.**

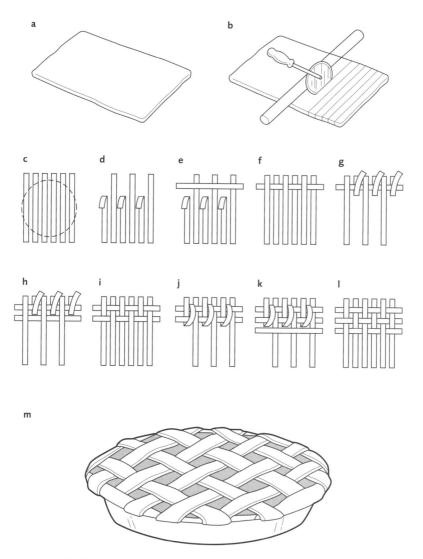

FIGURE 6.2 **Making a lattice top.**

ROLLING AND BAKING PIE AND TART DOUGH

The dough for pies and tarts is rolled to a ⅛-inch thickness. A dough sheeter makes fast, consistent work of rolling. When placing the dough into the pie or tart pan, do not to push or stretch the dough— it will spring back in the oven. Trim the overhanging dough to ½-inch, fold it toward the inside of the pan, and crimp it decoratively for a single-crust pie. For a double-crust pie, place the filling in the pan, arrange a second layer of dough on top, then trim and crimp the dough. After rolling and shaping, the dough for blind-baked (prebaked) shells should rest in the refrigerator for a half hour to relax the gluten. It is especially important to chill butter-rich doughs; the chilling prevents the butter from melting too rapidly in the oven and collapsing the decorative edge. The unbaked pie shells may be frozen if not needed right away.

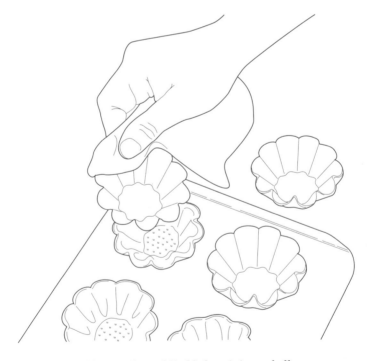

FIGURE 6.3 Double-panning to blind bake mini-tart shells.

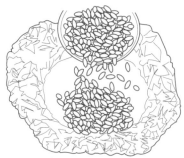

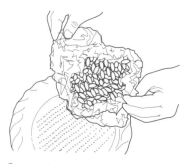

Line a chilled pie or tart shell with parchment or foil and fill with beans. Bake for 15 to 20 minutes, until the crust begins to set.

Remove the beans by lifting the parchment or foil off the dough.

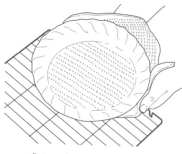

Return the pan to the oven and bake until golden.

FIGURE 6.4 Using dry beans or dry rice to prebake pie and tart shells.

Prebaking pie and tart shells is necessary if they will be filled with precooked custards or fruit. Prebaking is also helpful for pies with wet fillings, such as pecan, pumpkin, and quiche, that may make the dough soggy. In this case, the shells are baked only until just set and pale blond, since complete prebaking would cause the crusts to get too brown when they bake with the filling. Chefs go to many lengths to keep pie and tart shells crisp. Some pour leftover cake crumbs onto the bottom before adding the filling. Others brush the baked bottom crust with egg or fruit preserves, and then briefly bake it again until it is dry and sealed. Tart and cream pie shells may be brushed with melted chocolate. Obviously, this takes additional time. If the pies are promptly sold or served, the crust will be in good condition.

Blind-baking the shells is done at a high temperature, 400° to 425°F, to immediately set the crust and promote flakiness. The rolled and crimped dough should be well rested (to prevent shrinkage), and cold (to prevent sliding and collapsing). The pastry dough is docked if the shell will not be baked again with a liquid filling. Docking prevents large air bubbles from causing the pastry to rise unevenly, but some of the holes may remain after baking. Pouring a thin liquid filling into such a shell may cause leakage and sticking.

The easiest way to weigh down the dough is to place empty pie pans on top of the dough. This is called **double panning,** and it is done to prevent the dough from puffing as it bakes. The empty pans on top can be filled with dry rice or beans, or inverted onto sheet pans and weighted with a sheet pan. If extra pans are not available, line the chilled pie shells with parchment and pour dried beans or rice into the shell. After fifteen minutes, when the dough is set, remove the parchment and pie weights to let the crust brown.

The best pans for baking pies are inexpensive thin metal pie plates, either dark or light. Though dark pans absorb heat better than shiny metal pans, which reflect heat, dark pie plates are usually heavy and take longer to initially heat up in the oven. Bakeries, as opposed to restaurants, use disposable aluminum pie pans made for carry-out service. Once filled, these pans should be transported on sheet pans for support.

Baking crusts near the bottom of the oven creates a crisp bottom. For similar results, place sheet pans on oven racks and preheat them before placing the pies in the oven. The hot sheet pans will help the bottom crust cook faster, and will capture any pie liquid that dribbles over. Pies baked on sheet pans should be turned midway through cooking time, and if several racks are used, rotate the pans top to bottom.

The top of a double-crust pie is usually brushed with an egg wash before baking (egg whisked with a little water and salt to make it smooth) for color and shine. Butter, milk, or cream are used for mere browning. Cinnamon sugar or coarse-grained sugar can be sprinkled on the wash for textural appeal.

BASIC CRUMB CRUST

MAKES CRUMBS FOR ONE 9-INCH CHEESECAKE OR ONE 9-INCH DEEP-DISH PAN Crumb crusts form the base of cheesecakes, mousse-filled pies, and many cold pies such as Key lime and peanut butter pie. Basically, they are all formed from cookies that have been finely ground and mixed with enough melted butter to be pressed into a pan. Though many bakers purchase the cookies (or crumbs) for these shells, it is most economical to use leftover cookies from the kitchen. Biscotti and amaretti, for example, make wonderful crumb crusts. Be sure to adjust the sugar when using different cookies. Ground toasted nuts can be substituted for a portion of the crumbs in the recipe below.

1$^1/_2$ cups crumbs (see "Crumb Equivalents")	1 lb 8 oz	
2 Tbs to $^1/_4$ cup granulated sugar	3.5 oz to 7 oz	**LARGE BATCH**
4 to 6 Tbs unsalted butter, melted	1 lb to 1 lb 8 oz	

In bowl, combine all ingredients. Press firmly into the bottom and up the sides of your pan. Bake the crumb crust at 350°F for 10 to 15 minutes, until toasted and fragrant.

CRUMB EQUIVALENTS

- 30 2$^1/_2$-INCH SQUARE GRAHAM CRACKERS = 1$^1/_2$ CUPS CRUMBS
- 30 2$^1/_2$-INCH ROUND GINGERSNAPS = 1$^1/_2$ CUPS CRUMBS
- 24 CHOCOLATE WAFER COOKIES = 1$^1/_2$ CUPS CRUMBS

Tarts

APPLE TARTE TATIN

MAKES ONE 9-INCH TART Tarte tatin is traditionally prepared with puff pastry. The large amount of liquid from the apples, however, tends to make puff pastry soggy and compresses its layers. American pie dough or pâte brisée are better choices if you want a crisp pastry.

		LARGE BATCH
6 firm baking apples such as Golden Delicious or Granny Smith (3 lb), peeled, cored, and cut into $3/4$-inch wedges	12 lb	
1 Tbs lemon juice	$1/4$ cup	
$1/2$ to $2/3$ cup sugar, depending on sweetness of apples	14 oz to 1 lb 2.67 oz	
$1/3$ cup unsalted butter	10.66 oz	
1 portion (9 oz) **AMERICAN PIE DOUGH** (page 170)	4 portions	

Combine the apples, lemon juice, and sugar in a bowl; let stand until juicy, about 45 minutes. Drain, reserving the liquid. In a heavy 9-inch oven-safe skillet (cast iron is perfect), combine the reserved juices and the butter. Cook over medium-high heat, stirring frequently, until the sugar just begins to caramelize. Carefully arrange the apple wedges, overlapping slightly, in concentric circles in the skillet. Cover; cook 10 minutes. Uncover and continue cooking, pressing down on the apple wedges and spooning the juice over the fruit, until the apples are just tender, about 10 more minutes. Remove from heat. Roll out the pie dough to a $10^{1}/_{2}$-inch circle. Lay the pastry over the apples, tucking the edges around the apples, next to the edge of the skillet. Use an offset spatula to accomplish this task without burning yourself! Cut small vents in the center of the pastry. Bake 30 minutes in preheated 425°F oven or until deeply golden. Cool 10 minutes. To unmold, invert onto a serving dish with a lip and well to catch the caramel. Tarte tatin can be prepared ahead of time, left in the skillet, and reheated briefly on the stove top to melt the caramel.

PEAR TARTE TATIN

The pear version of tarte tatin is prepared with an equal weight of pears, preferably firm, but somewhat ripe Barlett or Anjou pears. Reduce the amount of sugar slightly; prepare and bake as above.

FRENCH APPLE TART

MAKES ONE 9-INCH TART The following method of arranging the apple slices creates the tallest tart, jam-packed with fruit, and it can be a bit tricky to master. Nestling simple rings of apple slices, one within another, is an attractive alternative that has a bit more applesauce to fresh apple, proportionally. This tart keeps for two to three days.

1^1/$_2$ cups **APPLESAUCE** (page 266)	6 cups	
One 9-inch partially baked tart shell using **AMERICAN PIE DOUGH** (page 170) or **PÂTE BRISÉE** (page 171)	4 shells	**LARGE BATCH**
3 tart apples such as Granny Smith, peeled, cored, halved, and thinly (^{1}/$_8$-inch-thick) sliced across (apple slices will look like the letter C)	6 lb	
Granulated sugar, for sprinkling		
Clear or strained apricot preserves, melted and thinned with water or Cointreau, for glazing		

Spread the applesauce evenly in the shell with a metal offset spatula. Arrange the apple slices in a continuous spiral ring. Begin by placing an apple slice with the bottom of the curve against the edge of the shell. Overlap the remaining slices, always keeping the end of the slice at right angles to the tart shell edge. Place small or irregular apple slices under the spiral for support as you work toward the center. Sprinkle with sugar. Bake on preheated sheet pan at 375°F for 45 to 50 minutes, or until the apples are well browned on the edges, the filling is bubbling, and the pastry is golden on the bottom. Some chefs use a knife to push the apples away from the edge to check; others push the tart bottom up (past the outer ring) to view the side. Brush the hot tart with the glaze to keep the apples from drying out.

FRESH BERRY TART

MAKES ONE 9-INCH TART This tart can be made using any seasonal fruit. To improve its keeping quality, place a thin disk of sponge cake or genoise under the pastry cream to prevent the tart shell from becoming soggy. The tart will keep for two days.

		LARGE BATCH
1¹/₂ cups **PASTRY CREAM** (page 142)	6 cups	
One 9-inch prebaked tart shell using **PÂTE SUCRÉE** (page 172)	4 shells	
About 3 cups fresh raspberries, blueberries, blackberries, and sliced strawberries	12 cups	
Red currant jelly, melted and thinned with water or Chambord, for glazing		

Spread the pastry cream in the shell; arrange the berries over the filling in concentric circles. Glaze with currant jelly and refrigerate.

LEMON TART

MAKES ONE 9-INCH TART Also known as *tart au citron*, this lemon tart is easily assembled from components. Keeps for three to four days.

		LARGE BATCH
2²/₃ cups **LEMON CURD** (page 146)	10²/₃ cups	
One 9-inch partially baked tart shell using **PÂTE SUCRÉE** (page 172)	4 shells	
Clear or strained apricot preserves, melted and thinned with water or Cointreau, for glazing		

Spread the lemon curd evenly in the shell with a metal offset spatula. Bake at 350°F for 20 to 25 minutes, or until lemon curd is set. Brush with glaze while warm to prevent skin from forming. Refrigerate until ready to serve.

LINZERTORTE

MAKES THREE 9-INCH ROUND TARTS Linzertorte has a buttery dough fragrant with ground nuts, spices, and lemon peel. Typically, raspberry jam is the second layer, but other preserves such as apricot or blackberry may be used. The dough is a versatile component—with the addition of another cup of flour, this soft, sticky dough becomes firm enough to roll (when chilled) and cut into decorative shapes for cookies. The cookies, fashioned after the tart, have a layer of jam sandwiched between them.

		LARGE BATCH
1 cup toasted blanched almonds	1 lb 4 oz	
1 cup toasted skinned hazelnuts	1 lb 4 oz	
1/2 cup graham cracker crumbs	8 oz	
2 1/2 cups all-purpose flour	2 lb 10.5 oz	
1 1/2 tsp ground cinnamon	2 Tbs	
3/4 tsp salt	1 Tbs	
1/2 tsp ground allspice (optional)	2 tsp	
1/4 tsp ground cloves	1 tsp	
2 cups (1 lb) unsalted butter	4 lb	
1 cup granulated sugar	1 lb 12 oz	
3 large eggs	1 lb 4.4 oz	
2 large egg yolks	4.4 oz	
1 to 2 tsp grated lemon zest	4 to 8 tsp	
2 1/4 cups raspberry jam	6 lb 12 oz	
Confectioners' sugar, for dusting		

Grind the nuts with the graham crumbs and 1/2 cup of the flour in a food processor. Sift the remaining flour with the cinnamon, salt, allspice, and cloves. In a mixer bowl, cream the butter with the sugar. One at a time, beat in the eggs and yolks. Beat in the lemon zest. Gradually beat in the flour and nuts at low speed. Divide the dough into three pieces, about 1 pound each (1 pound of dough will make a 9-inch tart). Press 10 ounces of dough, almost two-thirds of a 1-pound piece, into the bottom and up the side of a tart pan. Spread the dough with

$^3/_4$ cup raspberry jam. Place the remaining 6 ounces dough into a pastry bag fitted with a $^3/_8$-inch plain tube. Pipe a lattice over the jam. Form two remaining tarts with remaining ingredients. Bake at 350°F for 35 minutes, or until golden and cooked through. Dust with confectioners' sugar before serving.

POACHED PEAR FRANGIPANE TART

MAKES ONE 9-INCH TART Frangipane, a buttery almond filling, pairs naturally with fruit, whether in this classic poached pear version or tarter versions featuring cherries or plums. For a fresh fruit tart with extended keeping qualities, simply fill a prebaked shell with frangipane, but skip topping with fruit. Bake for 30 to 35 minutes or until the filling is set and golden. Brush with apricot preserves while warm and top with an attractive arrangement of cut fresh fruit. Brush fruit with apricot glaze. For berry tarts, brush the baked frangipane shell with a complementary jam; top with whole or sliced berries and glaze with red currant jelly. This pear tart keeps for two to three days.

	LARGE BATCH
2 cups **FRANGIPANE** (page 265)	8 cups
One 9-inch partially baked tart shell using **AMERICAN PIE DOUGH** (page 170)	4 shells
2 to 3 poached pears halved lengthwise	8 to 12
Melted butter, for brushing	
Granulated sugar, for sprinkling	
Clear or strained apricot preserves, melted and thinned with water or Cointreau, for glazing	

Spread the frangipane evenly in the shell with a metal offset spatula. Slice the pears into fans, leaving the top 1 inch intact. Lay the pears over the frangipane, fanning the base with the tips pointing toward the center. Brush the pears with butter; sprinkle liberally with sugar. Bake on preheated sheet pan at 375°F for 45 to 50 minutes, or until the edges of the pears are browned and the frangipane is puffed, golden, and set. Brush hot tart with glaze.

SOUR CHERRY FRANGIPANE TART

Substitute 1$^1/_2$ cups pitted fresh sour cherries or thawed, well-drained frozen sour cherries for the pears. Arrange in an even layer over the frangipane. Brush with butter and sprinkle with cinnamon sugar. Bake as directed above. Glaze with thinned red currant jelly.

PLUM TART

Substitute 6 to 8 red or black plums for the pears. Pit and halve the plums. Cut into fans, leaving $^1/_2$ inch intact on one end. Lay the plums over the frangipane, fanning the base with the tips pointing toward the center; fill the center with more fans. Brush with butter; sprinkle with cinnamon-sugar. Bake as directed above. Glaze with thinned red currant jelly.

FRUIT PIES

Fruit pies of excellent quality can made be made from IQF (individual quick frozen) fruit as well as fresh fruit. Frozen fruit makes available year-round seasonal fruits of consistent quality, though fresh, ripe fruit is almost always preferable. Fresh fruit is less reliable than it used to be, since long-distance shipping has necessitated picking and packing the fruit before it is perfectly tender, ripe, and sweet. Since some fruits never get sweeter after picking and others do, creating a pie of consistent quality is challenging. Frozen fruit can be picked later, when the fruit may be too tender to ship, since it is usually processed nearby. Obviously, the variability of fruit requires adjustments in the amount of sugar and thickener. Fresh, ripe fruit at its peak almost always gives off the most juice.

There are three methods for making fruit pies. The recipes in this book are made with the homemade method, but you can experiment to find a technique that best suits your business.

HOMEMADE METHOD

Fruit pies with superior texture are made by placing the uncooked fruit mixture into the pastry dough. The filling is sometimes dotted with butter before it is topped with pastry dough. The dough is trimmed, crimped to seal, and vented. Most starch-thickened pies, such as those that contain flour or cornstarch, must be baked until the filling at the center of the pie is bubbling in order to properly set up.

The telltale sign of a homemade pie is the empty air space between the fruit and the top crust, created when the mounded fruit cooks down after the pie dough sets. Unbaked pies can be frozen and baked as needed, with no noticeable reduction in quality. Fresh or frozen fruit can be used, but pies made with frozen fruit should be baked or frozen immediately, before the fruit begins to thaw and make the crust soggy.

COOKED FRUIT METHOD

The fruit filling can be precooked on the stove top. After it has cooled, it is placed in the dough and then baked. There are two advantages to this method. One is that the chef can control and adjust the thickening of the fruit, assuring a consistent product. The second advantage is that precooked fruit will not collapse, so more fruit can be added to the pie. The disadvantage is that twice-cooked fruit can have the texture of baby food.

COOKED JUICE METHOD

A compromise between the homemade and cooked fruit methods, this method prethickens only the juice, sugar, and spices. The cooked juice is combined with the uncooked fruit, and then baked in a pie shell. The juice will have to be substantially thickened, since the fruit will release liquid as it cooks. Also, juice must be added to the recipe, since uncooked fruit has not released its juices.

CHOOSING A STARCH

Grain starches, such as flour and cornstarch, behave differently from root starches, such as tapioca, potato starch, and arrowroot. Below are tips for choosing between the two types. Special instant starches (usually made from modified waxy cornstarch) are becoming more and more available. These starches will thicken even with cool water, and leave pie fillings translucent.

CHARACTERISTICS OF STARCHES

- Root starches thicken at a lower temperature than grain starches. Grain starches must be brought to a boil to prevent a raw cereal aftertaste.

- Pies that will be frozen will not weep moisture from the gelled filling (syneresis) if root starches or waxy cornstarch is used.

- Pies that will be reheated and served warm stay thicker if grain starches, such as cornstarch or flour, are used.

- For shiny, transparent juices that don't dull the bright color of fruit, like berries, use a root starch to thicken.

- Instant tapioca granules should not be used for pies with a lattice top or open-topped pies with decorative cut-outs. The pellets must be submerged in liquid to dissolve or they will remain hard. Double-crust pies hold in moisture and steam, but open pies expose fruit and tapioca granules to the hot, dry oven air.

- It takes 2 tablespoons of flour to thicken 1 cup of liquid to the consistency of gravy, but only 1 tablespoon or so of the other starches.

Though the recipes for fruit pies have general suggestions, each can be made as a single or double-crust pie, with streusel or not. The fluting and crimping style is left up to you, as is glazing of the top crust. Adjust the sugar level to suit the sweetness of the fruit.

BLUEBERRY PIE

MAKES ONE 9-INCH PIE

		LARGE BATCH
6 cups blueberries, fresh or frozen	6 qt	
2 Tbs lemon juice	$^1/_2$ cup	
$^2/_3$ cup granulated sugar	1 lb 2.67 oz	
3 Tbs instant tapioca	6 oz	
$^3/_4$ tsp ground cinnamon	1 Tbs	
$1^1/_2$ tsp grated lemon zest	2 Tbs	
$^1/_8$ tsp ground allspice	$^1/_2$ tsp	
Pinch of salt	$^1/_2$ tsp	
One 9-inch pie shell and pastry for top crust	4 shells	
4 tsp unsalted butter	3.33 oz	

In a bowl, toss the blueberries with the lemon juice. Stir in the remaining filling ingredients except the butter. Place in unbaked 9-inch pie shell; dot with butter. Cover with top crust; crimp, flute, and vent. Bake at 375°F on a preheated sheet pan for 50 to 60 minutes, or until center of pie is bubbling.

CHERRY PIE

MAKES ONE 9-INCH LATTICE-TOP PIE Sour cherries are essential for a good cherry pie. Though they are not always available in grocery stores, they are easy to obtain wholesale, in both canned and frozen forms. Almond extract is a popular flavor addition to cherry pie. Since cherry pie is almost always topped with a lattice crust, cornstarch is used in the filling instead of flour or tapioca.

		LARGE BATCH
6 cups fresh, frozen, or canned sour cherries, drained	6 qt	
$^2/_3$ cup granulated sugar	1 lb 2.67 oz	
2 Tbs cornstarch	2.67 oz	
$^1/_8$ tsp salt	$^1/_2$ tsp	
$^1/_8$ tsp ground cardamom	$^1/_2$ tsp	
$^1/_8$ tsp ground allspice	$^1/_2$ tsp	
One 9-inch pie shell and pastry for lattice top	4 shells	
1 Tbs unsalted butter	2 oz	

In a mixing bowl, combine all the filling ingredients except the butter. Place in a 9-inch unbaked pie shell; dot with butter. Top with lattice crust. Bake at 375°F on a preheated sheet pan for 50 to 60 minutes, or until center of pie is bubbling.

PLUM PIE

MAKES ONE 9-INCH PIE WITH STREUSEL TOPPING While other fruits, such as peaches, vary widely in juiciness, plums can be mouth-puckering tart or pleasantly sweet. Thus, a range of sugar has been given. Plum pie is less common these days, but for people who prefer fruit with a bit of tartness, it is delicious.

	LARGE BATCH
2¹/₂ lb prune plums, pitted and sliced	10 lb
3 Tbs lemon juice	³/₄ cup
¹/₄ tsp almond extract	1 tsp
³/₄ to 1¹/₄ cups granulated sugar	1 lb 5 oz to 2 lb 3 oz
3 to 4 Tbs all-purpose flour	3.2 oz to 4.25 oz
1 Tbs grated fresh ginger	¹/₄ cup
1 Tbs minced crystallized ginger	¹/₄ cup
¹/₈ tsp salt	¹/₂ tsp
One 9-inch pie shell	4 shells
¹/₂ recipe **WHITE ALMOND STREUSEL** (page 274)	2 recipes

In a mixing bowl, toss the plum slices with the juice. Stir in the remaining filling ingredients. Place in an unbaked 9-inch pie shell; top with white almond streusel. Bake at 375°F on a preheated sheet pan for 65 to 75 minutes, or until edges of pie are bubbling and streusel is browned.

PEACH OR NECTARINE PIE

MAKES ONE 9-INCH PIE

		LARGE BATCH
3 lb peaches or nectarines, peeled, pitted, and sliced	12 lb	
1 Tbs lemon juice	$1/4$ cup	
$2/3$ cup granulated sugar	1 lb 2.67 oz	
$1/4$ cup instant tapioca	8 oz	
$1/4$ tsp ground cinnamon	1 tsp	
$1/4$ tsp ground nutmeg	1 tsp	
$1/8$ tsp salt	$1/2$ tsp	
One 9-inch pie shell and pastry for top crust	4 shells	
1 Tbs unsalted butter	2 oz	

In a mixing bowl, toss the peach slices with the lemon juice. Stir in the remaining filling ingredients except the butter. Place in an unbaked 9-inch pie shell; dot with butter. Cover with top crust; crimp, flute, and vent. Bake at 425°F on a preheated sheet pan for 60 to 70 minutes, or until center of pie is bubbling.

APPLE PIE

MAKES ONE 9-INCH PIE This recipe for apple pie is very simple because many feel that this American emblem should not be tampered with. However, for the more adventurous, a cheddar cheese streusel topping or apple butter in the filling are tasty variations.

	LARGE BATCH
6 to 8 tart apples (3 lb), such as Granny Smith, peeled, cored, and sliced	12 lb
2 Tbs lemon juice	$^1/_2$ cup
$^1/_2$ cup granulated sugar	14 oz
$^1/_4$ cup all-purpose flour	4.25 oz
1 tsp grated lemon zest	4 tsp
1 tsp ground cinnamon	4 tsp
$^1/_8$ tsp ground cloves	$^1/_2$ tsp
$^1/_8$ tsp salt	$^1/_2$ tsp
One 9-inch pie shell with pastry or streusel for top layer	4 shells

In a mixing bowl, toss the apples with the lemon juice. Stir in the remaining filling ingredients. Place in an unbaked 9-inch pie shell. Cover with top crust or streusel. Bake at 375°F on a preheated sheet pan for 55 to 65 minutes, or until center of pie is bubbling.

STRAWBERRY-RHUBARB PIE

MAKES ONE 9-INCH PIE WITH STREUSEL TOPPING

		LARGE BATCH
4 cups diced rhubarb (about 1$^1/_4$ lb)	5 lb	
4 cups halved strawberries	4 qt	
1$^1/_4$ cups granulated sugar	2 lb 3 oz	
$^1/_4$ cup cornstarch	5.33 oz	
$^1/_4$ tsp ground cardamom or ginger	1 tsp	
$^1/_8$ tsp salt	$^1/_2$ tsp	
One 9-inch pie shell with pastry for lattice crust	4 shells	
2 Tbs unsalted butter	4 oz	

In a mixing bowl, combine all ingredients for the filling except the butter. Place in a 9-inch unbaked pie shell; dot with the butter. Top with lattice crust. Bake at 400°F on a preheated sheet pan for 20 minutes; reduce heat to 350°F. Bake another 40 minutes, or until center of pie is bubbling.

OTHER PIES

KEY LIME PIE

MAKES ONE 9-INCH PIE Key lime pie was not originally a baked custard. The recipe came from the Florida Keys, with ingredients convenient to locals: key limes and canned sweetened condensed milk; before refrigeration and without land for grazing dairy herds, canned milk was the norm in that hot area. Home cooks whisked egg yolks, the sweetened milk, lime juice, and zest together and poured it into a prepared pie shell. The mixture was not even baked, since the acid in the limes caused the proteins in the milk and egg to set without any heat.

The egg whites were used to make a meringue topping. Modern pies are baked unless pasteurized yolks are available. Graham cracker crust and a whipped cream topping are modern changes to this old recipe (see Anderson, 337). Tart Persian limes are more available than sweet key limes, and taste perfectly fine. Key lime pie is pale yellow, but a few drops of green food coloring may be added. This pie keeps three or four days.

		LARGE BATCH
1 Tbs powdered gelatin	$^1/_4$ cup	
3 Tbs water	$^3/_4$ cup	
1$^1/_3$ cups key lime juice	5$^1/_3$ cups	
One 14-oz can sweetened condensed milk	3 lb 8 oz	
4 large egg yolks	8.8 oz	
1 Tbs grated lime zest	$^1/_4$ cup	
Few drops green food coloring (optional)		
1$^1/_2$ cups heavy cream, whipped (3 cups volume)	6 cups	
One 9-inch graham or gingersnap crumb crust	4 crusts	
Sweetened whipped cream, for topping		

Sprinkle the gelatin over the water; let stand 5 minutes to soften. In a medium saucepan, combine the lime juice and condensed milk; bring to a boil. In a bowl, whisk the yolks. Slowly whisk in part of the hot milk; return to pan. Cook the custard over medium-low heat until thick enough to coat the back of a wooden spoon. Stir in the zest and softened gelatin mixture. If desired, add food coloring. Refrigerate until cool. Place the cool custard in a mixer bowl and beat with paddle attachment until smooth. Fold in the whipped cream; spread into the prepared crust, briefly freezing part of the filling, if necessary, until it is firm enough to mound. Top with sweetened whipped cream, piped decoratively over pie. Refrigerate.

LEMON MERINGUE PIE

MAKES ONE 9-INCH PIE Traditional recipes for lemon meringue pie economically use whole eggs: the yolks go into the lemon custard and the whites are used for meringue. This is not true for today's pies, which use differing amounts of yolks and whites. For one thing, plain meringue bakes unevenly, which leads to shrinkage and beading if it is overcooked and weeping if it is undercooked. Even cooking is difficult for pies topped with more than three egg whites. Unless you have pasteurized eggs, or dried pasteurized egg whites, Italian meringue is safest for pies. It is also more stable. (There is another option for pies, and that is to cook the egg whites briefly before making the meringue; see page 165 for details.) There is a lot of science behind the cooking of this humble pie: the lemon juice is added after the cornstarch has thickened the mixture, because acids inhibit the starch's thickening ability. The custard can be brought to a boil because the starch and sugar protect the yolks from scrambling.

6 large egg yolks	13.2 oz	**LARGE BATCH**
1$^1/_3$ cups granulated sugar	2 lb 5.33 oz	
$^1/_2$ cup cornstarch	10.67 oz	
$^1/_8$ tsp salt	$^1/_2$ tsp	
1$^2/_3$ cups water	6$^2/_3$ cups	
$^2/_3$ cup lemon juice	2$^2/_3$ cups	
3 Tbs unsalted butter	6 oz	
4 tsp grated lemon zest	$^1/_3$ cup	
One prebaked 9-inch pie shell	4 shells	
6 cups **ITALIAN MERINGUE** (page 164)	6 qt	

In a bowl, whisk the yolks to combine. Combine the sugar, cornstarch, and salt in large saucepan; whisk in the water, stirring until no lumps remain. Cook over medium-high heat, whisking constantly, until the mixture thickens. Slowly whisk some of this liquid into the yolks to warm them; return to the pan. Put the mixture over medium heat, and bring the mixture to a boil, stirring. Cook for 1 minute. Remove from heat; stir in lemon juice, butter, and lemon zest. Pour into prepared pie shell; top with meringue, making sure to attach the meringue to the crust to prevent shrinkage. Bake at 425° to 450°F just until the meringue begins to turn golden at the edges.

RASPBERRY CHIFFON PIE

MAKES ONE 8- OR 9-INCH PIE Since chiffon pie is made from components, any other fruit coulis or sweetened fruit purée can be used instead of the raspberry. Remember that as a gelatin-stabilized pie, only canned (pasteurized) pineapple, papaya, kiwifruit, or mango can be used. Chunks of fruit may be added to the filling for texture, and the finished pie may be garnished with a piped whipped cream border. This pie keeps for three days.

		LARGE BATCH
$^3/_4$ cup raspberry coulis (see page 270)	3 cups	
3 Tbs Cointreau or Chambord	$^3/_4$ cups	
$1^1/_2$ tsp powdered gelatin	2 Tbs	
3 large pasteurized egg whites	13.8 oz	
$^1/_8$ tsp cream of tartar	$^1/_2$ tsp	
Pinch of salt	$^1/_2$ tsp	
$^3/_4$ cup heavy cream	3 cups	
One 8- or 9-inch prebaked graham crumb crust	4 crusts	

Warm the coulis in a saucepan. In a microwave-safe bowl, sprinkle the gelatin over the Cointreau; let stand 5 minutes. Heat the gelatin gently in the microwave until dissolved, stirring. Whisk the gelatin into the fruit coulis. Refrigerate the fruit mixture or stir over an ice water bath until it has thickened to the consistency of raw egg whites. Beat the egg whites with the cream of tartar and salt to stiff peaks; fold into the fruit mixture. Whip the cream to soft peaks; fold into the fruit. Mound filling in the pie shell. If the filling is too soft to mound, chill it first.

PUMPKIN PIE

MAKES ONE 9-INCH PIE Soft fillings such as pumpkin and sweet potato can make pie crusts soggy. If you have a good convection oven, then placing the filling in an uncooked shell in the lower third of the oven may do the trick. If not, partially bake the crust before filling it. The crust will get soggy over time, but there is no reason a pie should start out that way.

	LARGE BATCH
²/₃ cup packed light brown sugar	1 lb 5.33 oz
4 large eggs	1 lb 11.2 oz
One 15-oz can pumpkin purée	3 lb 2 oz
2 Tbs dark molasses	¹/₄ cup
1 tsp ground cinnamon	4 tsp
1 tsp ground ginger	4 tsp
³/₄ tsp ground cardamom (optional)	1 Tbs
¹/₂ tsp ground mace	2 tsp
¹/₄ tsp salt	1 tsp
1¹/₄ cups half-and-half	5 cups
¹/₄ cup dark rum	1 cup
One 9-inch partially baked pie shell	4 shells

In a bowl, whisk the brown sugar and eggs together until the sugar begins to dissolve. Whisk in the pumpkin, molasses, spices, and salt. Whisk in the half-and-half and the rum. Pour into prepared shell; bake at 375°F for 45 to 50 minutes, or until just set in middle.

SWEET POTATO PIE

For best flavor, use 2 large baked fresh sweet potatoes, scooped out to yield 2 cups potato purée (8 cups). Follow the recipe above, substituting the sweet potato for the pumpkin. Purée the sweet potato with the molasses or some of the half-and-half until smooth. Strain if the potatoes are stringy. Omit the cardamom, and use half the cinnamon and mace. This keeps for three days.

PECAN PIE

MAKES ONE 9-INCH PIE Browned butter gives a butterscotch, caramel flavor to this traditional pie.

6 Tbs unsalted butter	12 oz	
3 large eggs	1 lb 4.4 oz	
1¹/₂ cups dark corn syrup	6 cups	
³/₄ cup packed light brown sugar	1 lb 8 oz	
2 Tbs bourbon	¹/₂ cup	LARGE BATCH
1 tsp vanilla extract	4 tsp	
¹/₈ tsp salt	¹/₂ tsp	
¹/₂ cup finely chopped toasted pecans	8 oz	
2 cups toasted pecan halves	2 lb	
One 9-inch partially baked pie shell	4 shells	

Cook the butter over medium heat until golden and fragrant; cool until just warm. In a bowl, whisk together the eggs, corn syrup, and brown sugar until smooth. Whisk in the butter, bourbon, vanilla, and salt. Stir in the chopped pecans. Place the pecan halves in the pie shell; pour the filling over the nuts. Bake at 425°F for 15 minutes; reduce temperature to 350°F and cook another 30 minutes, until set. Cool completely before serving.

MINCEMEAT FILLING

MAKES ENOUGH FILLING FOR FIVE 9-INCH PIES, ABOUT 3¹/₂ QUARTS Mincemeat went out of favor long ago, but this historical recipe is actually delicious. More fruit can be used instead of the meat, and, honestly, the pie tastes the same either way. Mincemeat filling needs to mellow and mature in the refrigerator at least two weeks before being used to make pies. Though most recipes in this chapter are for one pie, the time and trouble it takes to make mincemeat is such that a larger batch size makes sense. Also, this recipe is merely doubled, not quadrupled like the others, to keep it a reasonable size for a stockpot. The filling will last a couple of months in the refrigerator, and for at least 6 months frozen.

	LARGE BATCH
2 lb London broil or top round of beef	4 lb
$^1/_2$ lb beef suet or butter	1 lb
6 cups granulated sugar	5 lb 4 oz
4 lb apples or pears (about 8 to 10), peeled, cored, and diced	8 lb
2 lb raisins or currants	4 lb
1 lb dried cherries or cranberries	2 lb
$^1/_2$ lb candied citron	1 lb
$1^1/_2$ Tbs grated orange zest	3 Tbs
$1^1/_2$ Tbs grated lemon zest	3 Tbs
1 Tbs ground cinnamon	2 Tbs
$1^1/_2$ tsp ground mace	1 Tbs
1 tsp ground cloves	2 tsp
$^3/_4$ tsp black pepper	$1^1/_2$ tsp
$1^1/_2$ tsp salt	1 Tbs
3 cups apple cider	6 cups
$^1/_2$ cup dark rum	1 cup
$^1/_2$ cup bourbon	1 cup

Grind the beef and suet in a food processor, or have it ground by a butcher. In a stockpot, simmer everything together, covered, for $3^1/_2$ to 4 hours. As the filling cooks, skim any foam or scum from the surface. Let the filling mellow in the refrigerator for at least two weeks.

CREAM PIES

Associated with roadside diners, cream pies are stirred custards poured into prebaked pie shells, cooled, and topped with whipped cream. Regular or stabilized whipped cream may be used; see page 275 for options. The custard is basically a richer version of pastry cream. These pies are also known as pudding pies, since the filling is simply a firmer version of a creamy pudding. Any prebaked crust may be used, whether crumb or pastry. These pies generally keep three days.

COCONUT CREAM PIE

ONE 9-INCH PIE

One recipe **COCONUT CREAM PIE FILLING** (page 143)	4 recipes	
One 9-inch prebaked pie shell	4 shells	
4 cups lightly sweetened whipped cream, either stabilized or regular	4 qt	
$^1/_3$ cup toasted unsweetened flaked coconut or sweetened	1 lb	

LARGE BATCH

Pour the custard into the prepared pie shell. Cover the surface with plastic; refrigerate until cold. Top with whipped cream. Sprinkle toasted coconut over pie.

BANANA CREAM PIE

ONE 9-INCH PIE

One recipe **CREAM PIE FILLING** (page 142)	4 recipes
One 9-inch prebaked pie shell	4 shells
2 medium bananas, cut lengthwise into $^1/_4$-inch-thick pieces	8 bananas
2 Tbs lemon or pineapple juice	$^1/_2$ cup
4 cups lightly sweetened whipped cream, either stabilized or regular	4 qt

(LARGE BATCH)

Pour half the custard into the prepared pie shell. Toss the bananas with the lemon juice. Arrange the bananas over the custard; spread the remaining custard over them. Cover the surface with plastic; refrigerate until cold. Top with whipped cream.

BANANA SPLIT PIE

A graham crumb crust, a layer of chocolate ganache, and a sprinkling of chopped roasted peanuts turn the banana cream pie into a banana split pie.

CHOCOLATE CREAM PIE

ONE 9-INCH PIE

One recipe **CHOCOLATE CREAM PIE FILLING** (page 143)	4 recipes
One 9-inch prebaked pie shell	4 shells
4 cups lightly sweetened whipped cream, either stabilized or regular	4 qt
$^1/_3$ cup semisweet chocolate curls or shavings, or 2 Tbs chocolate sprinkles	$1^1/_3$ cups

(LARGE BATCH)

Pour the custard into the prepared pie shell. Cover the surface with plastic; refrigerate until cold. Top with whipped cream. Garnish with chocolate curls.

PEANUT BUTTER CREAM PIE

ONE 9-INCH PIE This all-American pie is traditionally topped with whipped cream, but a layer of chocolate ganache makes a nice variation.

		LARGE BATCH
1 cup smooth peanut butter (not natural style)	2 lb	
1/2 cup packed dark brown sugar	1 lb	
One 8-oz package cream cheese	2 lb	
1 tsp vanilla extract	4 tsp	
1 cup heavy cream	1 qt	
One 9-inch graham or chocolate crumb crust	4 crusts	
4 cups lightly sweetened whipped cream, either stabilized or regular	4 qt	
2 Tbs chopped roasted peanuts	1/2 cup	

OTHER FRUIT DESSERTS

Fruit cobbler is basically a pie filling cooked without a bottom crust and topped with thinly rolled biscuit or shortcake dough. It is a homey dish not usually served in restaurants.

Like the humble fruit cobbler, **fruit crisp** begins with a starch-thickened, sweetened-fruit filling (pie filling) baked without a bottom crust. A streusel topping is what gives fruit crisp its crunch. Though it is a comfort food, fruit crisps can be made in individual ramekins and thus find their way onto restaurant menus. Both desserts are served warm with ice cream on the side.

Cream the peanut butter with the brown sugar until the sugar granules dissolve and the mixture is smooth. Beat in the cream cheese until smooth, light, and fluffy. Beat in the vanilla. Transfer mixture to a bowl. In a mixer with the whip attachment, beat the heavy cream to soft peaks; fold into the peanut butter mixture. Spread filling in crust. Refrigerate until firm, 3 to 4 hours. Top with whipped cream and chopped peanuts before serving.

CHARLOTTES

There are several types of charlottes. The most common is a fruit bavarian set inside a cake-lined mold. Charlotte russe and charlotte royal fall into this category (for more information, see "Bavarians," in Chapter 5).

FALL FRUIT CHARLOTTE

Apple and pear charlottes consist of a sautéed fruit filling poured into a buttered and brioche-lined mold that is baked and served warm. The following recipe can be adapted for individual service by preparing in 4-inch ramekins. Persimmons and quince are also interesting candidates for this treatment. The marmalade or preserves helps stabilize the unmolded charlotte. Approximately 4 cups Applesauce (page 266), can be substituted for the cooked fruit. Simply heat with the amount of preserves and liqueur called for below and proceed with the recipe as directed.

	LARGE BATCH
4 lb pears or apples (about 8 to 10), peeled, cored, and roughly chopped	16 lb
$^3/_4$ cup sugar	1 lb 5 oz
Grated zest and juice of 1 lemon and 1 orange	4 each
1 vanilla bean, split and scraped	4 beans
1$^1/_2$ tsp ground cinnamon	2 Tbs
$^1/_2$ tsp ground ginger	2 tsp
$^3/_4$ cup orange marmalade, ginger preserves, or apple jelly	3 cups
3 Tbs apple brandy or Poire William	$^3/_4$ cup
About 24 slices of brioche, about $^1/_4$-inch thick	96 slices
1 cup butter	2 lb
1$^1/_2$ cups **CRÈME ANGLAISE** (page 141)	6 cups

Combine the fruit, sugar, zests and juices, vanilla seeds and pod, cinnamon, and ginger in a pot over low heat; cook until very soft, about 1 hour. Remove from heat. Remove vanilla bean pod. Stir in $^1/_2$ cup marmalade (large batch: 2 cups) or ginger preserves and 2 tablespoons liqueur (large batch: $^1/_2$ cup). Purée in a food processor, in batches, until smooth. Return to the pot; continue cooking over medium heat until thickened, about 30 minutes. Cool completely. Arrange four bread slices with sides touching to form a large square. Place a soufflé dish over the square; trim bread to fit dish. Cut this circle of bread into twelve fan-shaped slices. Cut a 2-inch circle from another bread slice. Melt 2 tablespoons butter (large batch: $^1/_2$ cup) in a large skillet. Cook the fan-shaped slices and cir-cle until lightly browned, 1 to 2 minutes per side. Butter the soufflé dish and place the circle in the bottom. Arrange fan-shaped slices, points facing inward, to cover bottom of dish. Set aside six slices brioche. Cut the remaining slices vertically into thirds. Melt the remaining $1/4$ cup butter (large batch: 1 cup); brush over bread strips. Arrange some of strips vertically around edge of dish, overlapping slightly. Spoon in one-third of the filling. Top with half of the remaining bread strips, another one-third of the filling, the remaining bread strips, and the remaining filling. Filling will be $1/2$ inch above the top of the dish. Cover the filling with the remaining six bread slices, trimming to fit dish. Bake at 425°F 40 minutes or until golden and beginning to pull away from side of dish. Invert onto a serving plate, leaving the soufflé dish in place over the charlotte as it cools. After 40 minutes, reinvert. Run a spatula around the edges of the dish to loosen. Invert again with the serving plate; this time remove the soufflé dish. Heat the remaining $1/4$ cup marmalade or preserves (large batch: 1 cup) and remaining 1 Tbs liqueur (large batch: $1/4$ cup) until melted. Brush over the top and sides of the charlotte. Serve warm or at room temperature with crème anglaise.

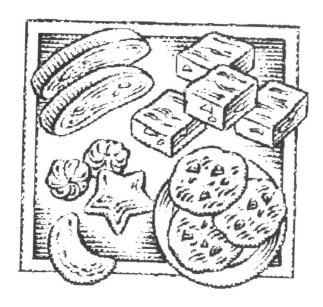

COOKIES

The key to great cookies is flavor from the finest ingredients. We have all been lured by gorgeous cookies that tasted flat, dull, and even dry. Often the bottom line dictates ingredients, so that even beautiful specimens disappoint at the first bite. The finest and freshest butter is key, but it is also expensive. Shortening is most often the primary or sole fat in lesser bakery items, producing a tall, shelf-stable, more impressive-looking cookie, but a rather tasteless one. In some of the recipes for American classics, like chocolate chip cookies, you'll find I've used a small amount of shortening to achieve a better union of texture and flavor. Most recipes call for butter only.

In butter cookies, creaming has such an immediate impact on the appearance, spread, and texture of cookies that it deserves some special attention. Though many cake and muffin batters are aerated by beating the sugar into butter until "light and fluffy," chemical leavening agents such as baking powder and soda ensure consistent results in rise and texture. Butter is the best-tasting fat in baked goods, but the small amount of water it contains causes cookies to spread when baked. If your butter isn't beaten to the right texture when you are making langues du chat, for example, you will have a mess on your hands. To ensure consistent results, try the following technique taught to me by Lisa Bell by way of chef Alex Miles.

Start with slightly softened butter, but not room-temperature butter which will be too warm. The butter should feel cold to the touch and your finger should leave an impression when you press it. At this point the butter is about 60°F. Place the butter in the mixer and beat it until it is shiny and holds a peak when the beater is pulled away.

Sometimes you will not have the luxury of time and must start with very cold butter straight from the refrigerator. In this case, melt one-fourth of the total butter and place it in the mixer with the cold butter, preferably cut into chunks. Start beating the butter on low speed, increasing the speed as the two butters are combined. You should be able to achieve the same texture as above. Some chefs find it easiest to put all the butter in the mixer and hold a blowtorch to the bowl while the butter begins mixing.

Each style of cookie has a different shelf life. You'll notice that biscotti keep for a month while peanut butter cookies should be baked daily. With a few exceptions, large batches of cookie dough can be made and refrigerated or frozen, making it easy to provide a freshly baked product.

ROLLED, DROP, AND SHAPED COOKIES

BASIC BUTTER COOKIES

MAKES 5 DOZEN COOKIES These crisp butter-rich cookies are perfect un-adorned, but they make beautiful decorated sugar cookies for holidays and special occasions. They are not too sweet and, therefore, are a good foil for royal icing or piped chocolate decoration. The cookies themselves will keep for two to three days, but the dough can be frozen for up to six months or refrigerated for up to a week.

	LARGE BATCH
$1\frac{1}{2}$ cups unsalted butter	3 lb
1 cup granulated sugar	1 lb 12 oz
3 large egg yolks	6.6 oz
$1\frac{1}{2}$ tsp vanilla extract	2 Tbs
$3\frac{3}{4}$ cups all-purpose flour	4 lb
$\frac{3}{4}$ tsp salt	1 Tbs

Beat the butter on medium speed until smooth, shiny, and holds a peak when the paddle is pulled away from the bowl. Add the sugar; beat until mixture is light and fluffy. One at a time, add the yolks until incorporated. Beat in the vanilla. Add the flour and salt; beat on low speed just until the dough forms. Refrigerate the dough until firm enough to handle. On a lightly floured surface or between sheets of parchment paper, roll the dough to a $\frac{3}{8}$-inch thickness. Freeze the dough sheets until firm. Cut dough into rounds or decorative shapes, keeping cut-outs cool until ready to bake. Bake cookies at 350°F until edges are golden, 12 to 15 minutes for $2\frac{1}{2}$-inch cookies.

CHOCOLATE CHIP COOKIES

MAKES 3 DOZEN COOKIES The most famous recipe for chocolate chip cookies is printed right on the package of Nestle's semisweet chocolate morsels. Their buttery flavor is incomparable, but I have always been disappointed in the thin, flat shape of the Toll House cookies. To give the cookies more height, shortening here replaces a small amount of the butter. To reduce the cakey texture, less egg is used. The result is crisp-edged cookies with chewy centers. Chocolate chip cookies keep only for a day, but the dough can be frozen for up to six months or refrigerated for up to a week.

	LARGE BATCH
³/₄ cup unsalted butter	1 lb 8 oz
¹/₄ cup shortening	5.75 oz
1 cup packed dark brown sugar	2 lb
¹/₂ cup granulated sugar	14 oz
1 large egg	6.8 oz
1 large egg yolk	2.2 oz
1 tsp vanilla extract	4 tsp
2¹/₃ cups all-purpose flour	2 lb 8 oz
1 tsp baking soda	4 tsp
¹/₂ tsp salt	2 tsp
1 cup semisweet chocolate chips	1 lb 8 oz
1 cup chopped toasted nuts (optional)	1 lb

Beat the butter and shortening on medium speed until smooth. Add the sugars; beat until the mixture is light and fluffy. Add the egg, yolk, and vanilla and beat until smooth. Add the flour, baking soda, and salt. Beat on low speed just until dough forms, adding the semisweet pieces and nuts before the flour is fully incorporated. Using a scoop with a capacity of 2 tablespoons, drop the dough onto ungreased half-sheet pans. Bake the cookies at 350°F until the edges are golden and centers are puffed and almost set, 12 to 14 minutes. Let cookies cool 5 minutes on pans to set before transferring them to wire racks. Increase the baking time for crisper cookies.

PEANUT BUTTER COOKIES

MAKES 3 1/2 DOZEN COOKIES I use regular peanut butter for this recipe, not the natural style with the oil at the top of the jar. For best flavor, choose a brand that is not overly sweet. Peanut butter cookies keep only for a day, but the dough can be frozen for up to six months or refrigerated for up to a week.

	LARGE BATCH
1 cup creamy peanut butter	2 lb
3/4 cup unsalted butter	1 lb 8 oz
1/2 cup packed dark brown sugar	2 lb
1/2 cup granulated sugar	14 oz
2 large eggs	13.6 oz
1 tsp vanilla extract	4 tsp
2 1/2 cups all-purpose flour	2 lb 10.5 oz
1 tsp baking soda	4 tsp
1/2 tsp salt	2 tsp

Beat the peanut butter and butter on medium speed until smooth. Add the sugars; beat until mixture is light and fluffy. One at a time, add the eggs and beat until smooth. Beat in the vanilla. Add the flour, baking soda, and salt. Beat on low speed just until the flour is incorporated. Form the dough into 1 1/2-inch balls; place on half-sheet pans. Using the tines of a fork, press into dough to make criss-cross patterns, dipping tines in sugar to prevent sticking. Bake cookies at 375°F until edges are golden and centers are puffed and almost set, 12 to 14 minutes. Let cookies cool 5 minutes on pans to set before transferring them to wire racks. Increase baking time for crisper cookies.

OATMEAL RAISIN COOKIES

MAKES ABOUT 4 DOZEN COOKIES This is your basic all-American oatmeal cookie, complete with raisins and a hint of cinnamon. Only imagination limits the flavor combinations possible with this dough: chocolate chips with dried cherries or espresso powder with toasted coconut and pecans make great variations. Oatmeal cookies are best the day they are made, but the dough can be frozen for up to six months or refrigerated for up to a week.

		LARGE BATCH
³/₄ cup unsalted butter	1 lb 8 oz	
¹/₄ cup shortening	5.75 oz	
³/₄ cup packed dark brown sugar	1 lb 8 oz	
³/₄ cup granulated sugar	1 lb 5 oz	
2 large eggs	13.6 oz	
1 tsp vanilla extract	4 tsp	
1¹/₂ cups all-purpose flour	1 lb 9.5 oz	
1 tsp salt	4 tsp	
³/₄ tsp baking soda	1 Tbs	
³/₄ tsp ground cinnamon	1 Tbs	
3 cups old-fashioned rolled oats	2 lb 10 oz	
1¹/₂ cups raisins	2 lb 4 oz	

Beat the butter and shortening on medium speed until smooth. Add the sugars; beat until mixture is light and fluffy. One at a time, add the eggs and beat until smooth. Beat in the vanilla. Add the flour, salt, baking soda, and cinnamon. Beat on low speed just until the flour is incorporated. Gently beat in the oats and raisins just until combined. Using a scoop with a capacity of 2 tablespoons, drop dough onto ungreased half-sheet pans. Bake cookies at 350°F until edges are golden and centers are puffed and almost set, 12 to 14 minutes. Let cookies cool 5 minutes on pans to set before transferring them to wire racks. Increase baking time for crisper cookies.

GINGER SNAPS

MAKES 3 DOZEN COOKIES Check your ground ginger for freshness before making these cookies, or you won't get the same flavorful zing. Minced candied ginger can be added, or even orange zest, but the basic recipe is plenty spicy without these additions. Unlike other cookies, ginger snaps are actually better the second day because the flavors come together. The cookies will stay at their peak for up to four days if kept in an airtight container. Ginger dough can be frozen for up to six months or refrigerated for up to a week, improving in flavor as it rests.

		LARGE BATCH
¹/₂ cup butter	1 lb	
¹/₄ cup shortening	5.75 oz	
1 cup granulated sugar	1 lb 12 oz	
1 large egg	6.8 oz	
2 Tbs dark molasses	¹/₂ cup	
2 cups all-purpose flour	2 lb 2 oz	
1 Tbs ground ginger	¹/₄ cup	
1 tsp baking soda	4 tsp	
¹/₂ tsp ground cinnamon	2 tsp	
¹/₄ tsp salt	1 tsp	
¹/₈ tsp ground cloves	¹/₂ tsp	

Beat the butter and shortening on medium speed until smooth. Add the sugar; beat until mixture is light and fluffy. Add the egg and molasses, and beat until smooth. Add the dry ingredients. Beat on low speed just until dough forms. Form dough into 1¹/₂-inch balls; roll in granulated sugar. Place balls on ungreased half-sheet pans; flatten by one-half with the bottom of a glass, dipping the glass in sugar to prevent sticking. Bake cookies at 350°F until edges are golden and centers are puffed and almost set, 10 to 12 minutes. Let cookies cool 5 minutes on pans to set before transferring them to wire racks. Increase baking time for cookies that snap when you break them.

CHOCOLATE FUDGE COOKIES

MAKES 2 DOZEN COOKIES White chocolate chunks are delicious in these dark, not-too-sweet chocolate cookies, but milk or semisweet chocolate can be substituted for chocolate lovers. For the best fudgy texture, these cookies should be eaten the day they are made. The dough, however, keeps a week in the refrigerator and up to six months in the freezer.

		LARGE BATCH
2 Tbs heavy cream	$^1/_2$ cup	
2 oz semisweet chocolate, finely chopped	8 oz	
$^1/_2$ cup unsalted butter	1 lb	
$^1/_2$ cup packed dark brown sugar	1 lb	
$^1/_2$ cup granulated sugar	14 oz	
1 large egg	6.8 oz	
1 tsp vanilla extract	4 tsp	
1 cup plus 2 Tbs all-purpose flour	1 lb 3.125 oz	
$^1/_3$ cup unsweetened Dutch-processed cocoa powder	5 oz	
$^1/_2$ tsp baking soda	2 tsp	
$^1/_8$ tsp salt	$^1/_2$ tsp	
$3^1/_2$ oz chopped white chocolate (about $^2/_3$ cup)	14 oz	

Place the cream in a small saucepan set over medium-low heat. When cream is warm, stir in chocolate. Turn off the heat; stir until the chocolate is melted and the ganache is smooth. Meanwhile, beat the butter on medium speed until it is smooth, shiny, and holds a peak. Beat in the sugars until light and fluffy. Beat in the egg and vanilla until smooth. Sift the flour, cocoa powder, baking soda, and salt together. On low speed, beat in the sifted dry ingredients just until combined. Gently incorporate the ganache and, last, the chopped white chocolate. Refrigerate the dough until firm enough to handle. Using a 2-tablespoon capacity scoop, drop mounds of dough onto half-sheet pans. Bake at 350°F for 12 minutes, or until centers are almost set. Cool cookies on pans for 5 minutes before transferring to wire racks.

GINGERBREAD CUT-OUTS

MAKES ABOUT 4 DOZEN COOKIES Gingerbread cookies are not as moist as gingersnaps, since the dough must hold the decorative shape of the cutters without spreading. For a more robust and complex flavor, replace $^1/_4$ cup of the flour with cocoa powder. Espresso powder also adds depth to these cookies. If possible, refrigerate the dough for 24 hours before baking to let the flavors develop. Once baked, the flavor of these cookies helps them age well, which makes them great for holiday decorating. Their texture, however, becomes purely crisp after the first day. The dough will keep a week in the refrigerator and up to six months in the freezer.

	LARGE BATCH
1 cup unsalted butter	2 lb
$^3/_4$ cup granulated sugar	1 lb 5 oz
$^3/_4$ cup packed light brown sugar	1 lb 8 oz
1 large egg	6.8 oz
2 Tbs dark molasses	$^1/_2$ cup
$3^1/_4$ cups all-purpose flour	3 lb 7.25 oz
1 Tbs ground ginger	$^1/_4$ cup
2 tsp instant espresso powder	2 Tbs plus 2 tsp
1 tsp ground cinnamon	4 tsp
1 tsp baking soda	4 tsp
$^1/_2$ tsp salt	2 tsp
$^1/_4$ tsp ground cloves	1 tsp
Royal icing, optional	

Beat the butter at medium speed until it is smooth, shiny, and holds a peak. Beat in the sugars until light and fluffy. Beat in the egg and molasses until smooth. Sift the dry ingredients together. On low speed, beat in the dry ingredients just until combined. Refrigerate the dough about 45 minutes until firm enough to handle.

On a lightly floured surface or between sheets of parchment paper, roll the dough to a $^3/_8$-inch thickness. Cut the dough into rounds or decorative shapes, keeping the cut-outs cool until ready to bake. Bake the cookies at 350°F on parchment-lined baking sheets until the edges are golden and crisp, 12 to 15 minutes for $2^1/_2$-inch cookies. Cool cookies on pans for 5 minutes before transferring to wire racks. Decorate with royal icing, if desired.

LINZER COOKIES

MAKES 16 SANDWICH COOKIES These cookies are simply a variation of Linzertorte (page 183). Usually, the bottom cookie is spread with jam and the top cookie, whose center is cut out to reveal the jam, is dusted with confectioners' sugar. Because this dough has more flour and is rolled thin, the cookies are more crisp than the tart. Filled cookies will keep two days before getting soggy, but unassembled the cookies are fresh for almost a week. The dough is good for up to a week in the refrigerator or six months in the freezer.

		LARGE BATCH
$^1/_3$ cup all-purpose flour	5.6 oz	
1 pound **LINZERTORTE** dough (page 183)	2 lb	
Confectioners' sugar, for dusting		
Raspberry jam		

Knead or stir the flour into the dough. Refrigerate the dough until firm enough to handle. On a lightly floured surface or between sheets of parchment paper, roll dough to $^3/_8$-inch thickness. Cut the dough into rounds or decorative shapes. For cookie tops, remove the centers from half the cookies by using a slightly smaller cutter of the same shape. Keep cut-outs chilled until ready to bake. Bake cookies at 350°F on parchment-lined baking sheets until the edges are golden and crisp, 12 to 15 minutes for $2^1/_2$-inch cookies. Bake the cookie tops separately as their baking time will be a few minutes shorter. Cool cookies on pans for 5 minutes before transferring to wire racks. Dust the cookie tops with confectioners' sugar. Spread the cookie bottoms with a thin layer of jam; assemble cookies.

SHORTBREAD

MAKES ABOUT 5¹/₂ DOZEN 2-INCH COOKIES Shortbread is butter, sugar, flour, and salt—the simplest of all butter cookies and also the richest. The dough can be pressed into a large cookie mold or round, or chilled, rolled, and cut into shapes. Many chefs use shortbread instead of pâte sucre for the base of bar cookies like lemon bars. Because it is sandy, crumbly, and crisp, shortbread is traditionally scored before baking and is cut while still warm.

There is no one way to make shortbread. Most recipes are a variation of the following ratio: 1 pound butter, 1 cup sugar, and 4 cups flour. Since shortbread is prized for its delicate sandy crumb, some recipes use confectioners' sugar, cornstarch, cake flour, or rice flour to tenderize the dough. Traditional Scottish shortbread often calls for some whole wheat flour or oats.

		LARGE BATCH
2 cups unsalted butter	2 lb	
1 cup granulated sugar	1 lb 12 oz	
1 tsp vanilla extract (optional)	4 tsp	
4 cups all-purpose flour	4 lb 4 oz	
³/₄ tsp salt	1 Tbs	

Cream the butter and sugar until light and fluffy. Beat in the vanilla, if using. Beat in the flour and salt on low speed. Press the dough into a pan so that it is an even ¹/₂ inch thick. Chill until firm; dock with a fork. Bake at 325°F until golden, 30 to 40 minutes.

To roll cookies, chill dough until firm enough to roll between sheets of parchment paper. Refrigerate until firm before cutting with decorative cookie cutters. Bake at 350°F on parchment-lined sheet pans for 10 to 15 minutes.

Shortbread is rich with butter, which makes the dough difficult to roll and the cookies prone to spreading. Using part confectioners' sugar with the granulated, and using a little cake flour for part of the all-purpose, will help prevent spreading. An extra ¹/₂ cup flour will make the dough easier to handle and prevent spread. Adding an egg or two yolks to the recipe will make sturdier cookies. Browned butter, toasted nuts, brown sugar, espresso, and mini-chocolate chip are just some of the flavor variations possible. For delicate, crumbly cookies, put all the dry ingredients in the mixer first and cut in cold chunks of butter.

ALMOND BISCOTTI

MAKES ABOUT 6 DOZEN COOKIES The word *biscotti* translates as "baked again," indicating how these butterless Italian cookies get their ultra-crisp texture. Biscotti of all flavors have sprung up on this side of the Atlantic, but I include only two traditional flavors here. Once you are accustomed to the feel of the dough, however, it isn't much of a stretch to develop new ones like lemon-pistachio and dried cranberry with ginger. For chocolate biscotti, reduce the flour by $^1/_2$ cup and add $^2/_3$ cup cocoa. Mini chocolate chips can be added for more chocolate flavor. Biscotti actually get better in time, and under the right conditions (protected from humidity in an airtight container) will keep for a month. The dough can be shaped into logs and frozen for several months.

This is a classic Tuscan cookie. For best results, make sure the almonds are finely ground without turning into a paste. Because the friction of the food processor brings the nuts' natural oils to the surface, the nuts should be ground with sugar or flour to keep them dry. The grinder attachment for a Kitchen-Aid or Hobart mixer is a great way to grind the nuts, and if you are making a small batch, a rotary cheese grater will do the trick nicely.

	LARGE BATCH
$2^1/_4$ cups blanched whole almonds, toasted	2 lb 13 oz
$^2/_3$ cup granulated sugar	1 lb 2.67 oz
2 cups all-purpose flour	2 lb 2 oz
$^2/_3$ cup light brown sugar	1 lb 5.33 oz
2 tsp baking powder	2 Tbs plus 2 tsp
$^1/_4$ tsp salt	1 tsp
3 large eggs	1 lb 4.4 oz
2 Tbs vegetable oil	$^1/_2$ cup
2 tsp almond extract	2 Tbs plus 2 tsp
2 tsp vanilla extract	2 Tbs plus 2 tsp

Coarsely chop $1^1/_2$ cups of the almonds; reserve. Grind the remaining $^3/_4$ cup almonds with the granulated sugar in a food processor. Sift the nut mixture with the flour, brown sugar, baking powder, and salt into a bowl. Stir in the chopped almonds. In a liquid measuring cup, beat the eggs, oil, and extracts together.

Stir just enough of the egg mixture into the dry ingredients to form a rather dry, shaggy dough. Reserve the remaining egg mixture. Knead the dough briefly to smooth it out and incorporate all remaining dry particles. The dough will become slightly sticky.

Divide the dough into four pieces. With your hands, roll each piece into a log 12 inches long. Flatten the top of the logs slightly, until the width of each log is 1 1/2 inches. If the dough is overly sticky and impossible to shape, too much liquid has been added. In this case, knead with a small amount of flour. Place two logs on parchment-lined half-sheet pans, spacing them at least 4 inches apart. Brush the tops of the logs with the remaining egg mixture. Bake the cookies at 325°F for 25 to 30 minutes, or until the edges are crisp and centers puffed but still slightly soft. When the logs are cool enough to handle, gently cut them crosswise with a serrated knife into 1/2-inch-thick slices. Return the sliced biscotti to the baking sheets, bottom side down, and bake at 300°F for another 20 to 30 minutes, until dry.

HAZELNUT-ANISE BISCOTTI

Follow the recipe for the almond biscotti, above, substituting 1 1/2 cups toasted skinned hazelnuts (large batch: 1 lb 6.5 oz) for the almonds. Chop 1 cup of the hazelnuts (large batch: 15 oz). Grind the remaining 1/2 cup nuts with the granulated sugar, adding 2 tsp toasted anise seed (large batch: 2 Tbs plus 2 tsp), 1 teaspoon orange zest (large batch: 4 tsp), 1 teaspoon lemon zest (large batch: 4 tsp), and 1/4 teaspoon ground cinnamon (large batch: 1 tsp) to the food processor. Omit the almond extract, and increase the vanilla extract to 1 tablespoon (large batch: 1/4 cup). Shape and bake as directed above.

SPRITZ (PIPED BUTTER) COOKIES

MAKES 4 DOZEN COOKIES Piped with a $^1/_2$-inch star tip, these cookies are shaped into round, shells, S-shapes, and long fingers. The rounds may be filled with jam, and the tips of long (Viennese) fingers are dipped in chocolate after baking. Piping the cookies is hard work, since the dough must be stiff enough to retain the piped edge during baking. Confectioners' sugar prevents spread more than other sugars, but granulated sugar may be substituted for those who prefer its texture. For these cookies, it is essential that the butter be cool enough to beat without melting—cold rather than warm.

	LARGE BATCH
1 cup unsalted butter	2 lb
$^3/_4$ cup confectioners' sugar	1 lb 8 oz
1 large egg	6.8 oz
1$^1/_2$ tsp vanilla extract (2 Tbs) or $^1/_2$ tsp almond extract	2 tsp
2$^1/_3$ cups all-purpose flour	2 lb 8 oz
$^1/_2$ tsp salt	2 tsp
1 large egg white, if needed	4.6 oz

Beat the butter until smooth and shiny, but still cold. Gradually beat in the sugar, then the egg and vanilla. Add the flour and salt at low speed. If the dough feels too stiff to pipe, add the remaining egg white a tablespoon at a time, until the dough is workable. The dough will be stiff, and it may be necessary to twist off the filled pastry bag in the center, creating two smaller sections for easier piping (this is called putting a break in the bag). Pipe the dough onto parchment-lined sheet pans; bake at 350°F for 10 to 15 minutes.

FLORENTINES

MAKES 5 DOZEN COOKIES Florentine batter is versatile, good for much more than the crisp, flat cookie coated with chocolate for which it is named. As the cookies cool, they are briefly malleable and can be rolled into cigarette cookies or shaped into bowls or cones to hold fillings. This batter can also be poured over a partially baked sweet dough crust and baked again to create chewy, caramel bar cookies. The batter will keep a week in the refrigerator but must be melted over low heat before it can be reused. If it separates, whisk in a small amount of cream. If your cookies are full of holes rather than solid, add more sugar to the batter. Florentine cookies keep a week if the air is not humid.

		LARGE BATCH
1/2 cup toasted sliced almonds	6 oz	
6 Tbs all-purpose flour	6.375 oz	
1/3 cup old-fashioned rolled oats	4.67 oz	
1/4 cup toasted skinned hazelnuts	5 oz	
1/8 tsp salt	1/2 tsp	
6 Tbs unsalted butter	12 oz	
3/4 cup granulated sugar	1 lb 5 oz	
1/3 cup corn syrup	1 1/3 cups	
1/4 cup heavy cream	1 cup	

Grind the nuts with the flour, oats, nuts, and salt in a food processor until finely chopped but not pulverized. Bring the butter, sugar, corn syrup, and cream to a boil, stirring until the sugar dissolves. As the mixture reaches a boil, stir in the dry ingredients. Cook over low heat for another 30 seconds to a minute, stirring. Drop batter by teaspoonfuls onto lightly buttered sheet pans, spacing the mounds 4 to 5 inches apart. Bake at 350°F for 8 to 10 minutes, or until dark golden and bubbly. Let the cookies sit for a minute or two before gently lifting off the sheet with a metal offset spatula. Quickly shape, if desired, and place on racks to cool. If you do not have help, bake only one sheet pan at a time.

TULIPE PASTE

MAKES 2 DOZEN COOKIES Tulipe paste is a unique batter used for shaped cookies. The cookies are flexible for the first minute after baking, and can be shaped into bowls and cones that will hold mousse or ice cream. Often, stencils are used to create decorative shapes for garnishing desserts, but the paste may be spread freehand with an offset spatula for rounds. For a two-tone effect, 1 tablespoon of Dutch-processed cocoa powder may be added to a quarter of the batter. After the plain batter has been spread on sheet pans, the chocolate mixture can be piped decoratively on top. Unless you have help to quickly shape the warm cookies, bake one sheet pan at a time.

		LARGE BATCH
³/₄ cup plus 2 Tbs all-purpose flour	14.87 oz	
1 cup confectioners' sugar	1 lb	
¹/₈ tsp salt	¹/₂ tsp	
¹/₂ cup unsalted butter, melted	1 lb	
4 large egg whites	1 lb 2.4 oz	
1 tsp vanilla extract	4 tsp	

Combine the flour, sugar, and salt in a bowl. Whisk in the butter, egg whites, and vanilla until smooth. Refrigerate 1 hour before using to let the batter hydrate evenly. Lightly grease sheet pans. Using a small metal offset spatula, spread 1 tablespoon of batter into a very thin round (less than ¹/₈ inch thick) on the prepared pan. Repeat, leaving at least 2 to 3 inches between the cookies. Bake at 400°F for 4 to 5 minutes, or until the edges are browned. Carefully loosen the cookie with a spatula and quickly shape as desired.

COCONUT MACAROONS

MAKES 20 COOKIES These macaroons are more crisp than chewy. Dip the right side of the cookies in tempered chocolate for a garnish. The unsweetened coconut used in this recipe is the small flake variety, not the large. Cream of coconut is thick and sweetened; do not confuse this product with coconut milk. These cookies last for a week at room temperature in dry conditions.

	LARGE BATCH
2^3/$_4$ cups unsweetened shredded coconut	1 lb 6 oz
^{2}/$_3$ cup canned cream of coconut	1 lb 10.67 oz
2 large egg whites	9.2 oz
1 tsp vanilla extract	4 tsp
^{1}/$_8$ tsp salt	^{1}/$_2$ tsp

Gently toast the coconut until barely blond, but not golden. Combine all the ingredients in a small bowl; chill until firm. Line a sheet pan with parchment paper; butter the paper. With wet fingers, shape 1 tablespoon and 1 teaspoon dough into a three-sided pyramid. Place on prepared pan; repeat. Bake at 325°F for 18 to 20 minutes, or until edges are dry and golden.

BROWNED BUTTER MADELEINES

MAKES 2 DOZEN MADELEINES Madeleines are ephemeral. Usually a rather plain French tea cake, their delicate flavor and texture lasts only a day. This recipe is more moist and light than the typical version. Brushing warm madeleines with a flavored sugar syrup, like lemon or rum, preserves some moisture, but a dusting of confectioners' sugar is the customary garnish.

	LARGE BATCH
1 cup cake flour	1 lb
2 Tbs toasted skinned hazelnuts or almonds	2.5 oz
$^1/_2$ tsp baking powder	2 tsp
$^1/_8$ tsp salt	$^1/_2$ tsp
3 large eggs	1 lb 4.4 oz
2 large egg yolks	4.4 oz
$^2/_3$ cup granulated sugar	1 lb 2.67 oz
1 tsp vanilla extract	4 tsp
10 Tbs unsalted butter, browned until golden and cooled slightly	1 lb 4 oz
Topping of choice	

Grind the flour and nuts together in a food processor. Sift the flour mixture, baking powder, and salt together; repeat. Meanwhile, using the whip attachment, beat the eggs and yolks together at high speed until doubled in volume. With the mixer running, slowly pour the sugar down the side of the bowl a tablespoon at a time. Continue beating the eggs until pale yellow, thick, and quadrupled in volume. Beat in the vanilla. Gently fold in the flour mixture, adding the butter before the flour is completely incorporated. Refrigerate the batter for 20 minutes. Dollop the batter into greased and floured 3-inch madeleine molds. Bake at 375°F for 12 to 15 minutes, or until the centers are puffed and spring back when touched. Cool 2 minutes; invert into cooling racks. Brush with syrup or dust with cocoa powder or confectioners' sugar, if desired.

RUGELACH

MAKES ABOUT 4 DOZEN RUGELACH Rugelach's distinctive cream cheese pastry has made it an everyday favorite. Though technically a pastry, these bite-size sweets are consumed just like cookies. Though the richness of the dough extends rugelach's shelf life beyond other pastries, the dough can be rolled in advance, sliced, and frozen to be baked later. The dough can be made by the creaming method, but it will not be as flaky. Rugelach keep three days.

		LARGE BATCH
2 cups all-purpose flour	2 lb 2 oz	
1/2 tsp salt	2 tsp	
1 cup unsalted butter, cold	2 lb	
One 8-oz package cream cheese	2 lb	
Filling of your choice (see Note)		
Granulated sugar, or confectioners' sugar, for dusting		

Combine the flour and salt in a bowl. Cut in the butter and cream cheese until the mixture is crumbly. (This can be done in a mixer.) Gather the dough into a disk, wrap in plastic, and refrigerate at least 2 hours before rolling.

Divide the dough into two pieces. On a well-floured surface, roll the dough into a rectangle that is 1/8-inch thick. Spread the filling over the dough, leaving a 3/4-inch border. Brush the border with water, then roll up the dough, beginning with the long side. Pinch seam to seal. Cut the dough into 1-inch pieces; refrigerate or freeze briefly.

Bake the chilled dough seam side down on parchment-lined sheet pans at 450°F for 10 to 15 minutes, or until golden. Dust with confectioners' sugar, or if desired, brush dough with water and sprinkle with granulated sugar before baking.

NOTE Consider apricot preserves, raspberry jam, or cinnamon sugar with chopped toasted nuts and chopped semisweet chocolate. Dried fruit and toasted coconut may also be used.

BAR COOKIES

FRUIT STREUSEL BARS

MAKES ONE 9 BY 13-INCH PAN This is one of the easiest and most adaptable bar cookies you'll ever find. Though the recipe calls for fig or prune filling, apricot preserves can be substituted. For an even richer cookie, try spreading a layer of bittersweet chocolate ganache under the fruit filling. These bars keep for almost a week; their components keep for months in the freezer.

¹/₂ recipe **ALMOND-OAT STREUSEL** (page 273)	2 recipes	LARGE BATCH
1 recipe **FIG OR PRUNE FILLING** (page 267)	4 recipes	

Press half the streusel into the bottom and 1 inch up the sides of a greased foil or parchment-lined 9 by 13-inch baking pan. Bake at 350°F for 15 to 20 minutes, or just until firm. Cool slightly. Spread the fruit filling over the crust. Crumble the remaining streusel over the filling. Bake for an additional 45 minutes, or until the streusel topping is golden and crisp. Cool completely before cutting into squares.

BLUEBERRY LEMON BARS

MAKES ONE 9 BY 13-INCH PAN A variation of the recipe above, this bar cookie has fresh blueberries set in a lemon cream.

3 times the recipe for **OAT STREUSEL** (page 273)	12 times	LARGE BATCH
One 14-oz can sweetened condensed milk	3 lb 8 oz	
¹/₂ cup lemon juice	2 cups	
1 large egg	6.8 oz	
1 large egg yolk	2.2 oz	
2 Tbs all-purpose flour	2.125 oz	
2 tsp lemon zest	2 Tbs plus 2 tsp	
3 cups blueberries	12 cups	

Press half the streusel into the bottom and 1 inch up the sides of a greased, foil or parchment-lined 9 by 13-inch baking pan. Bake at 350°F for 15 to 20 minutes, just until firm. Cool slightly. Meanwhile combine the condensed milk, lemon juice, egg, yolk, flour, and lemon zest until smooth; stir in the blueberries. Spread the fruit filling over the crust. Crumble the remaining streusel over the filling. Bake for an additional 40 minutes, until the streusel topping is golden and crisp. Cool until warm over a rack, then refrigerate until cold before cutting into squares.

BROWNIES

MAKES ONE 9-INCH SQUARE PAN These are rich, fudgy brownies. If you don't like fudgy, cook them until a toothpick inserted in the center comes out with moist crumbs. Otherwise, leave the very center a little gooey. The brownies will set up as they cool. Brownies will keep for three days at room temperature, or for several months if frozen after they are baked. Brownies are wonderful unadorned, but espresso powder, nuts, or chips are nice additions.

		LARGE BATCH
³/₄ cup unsalted butter	1 lb 8 oz	
10 oz bittersweet chocolate, chopped	2 lb 8 oz	
4 large eggs	1 lb 11.2 oz	
1 cup granulated sugar	1 lb 12 oz	
1 tsp vanilla extract	4 tsp	
¹/₂ cup all-purpose flour	8.5 oz	
¹/₄ tsp salt	1 tsp	
1 cup chopped toasted walnuts (optional)	1 lb	

Grease and flour a 9-inch square baking pan. In a saucepan, melt the butter over low heat; stir in the chopped chocolate. Cook, stirring frequently, until the chocolate is melted and smooth. Meanwhile, in a medium bowl, whisk the eggs, sugar, and vanilla together. Stir in the melted chocolate mixture. Stir in the flour and salt just until combined. Spread the batter into the prepared baking pan. Bake at 350°F for 35 to 40 minutes, or until a skewer inserted two inches or so from the center comes out with only moist crumbs clinging to it. Cool brownies before removing from pan.

BLONDIES

MAKES ONE 9-INCH SQUARE PAN Though the perennial favorite is blondies with chocolate chips, there are other ways to enjoy these chewy, butterscotch bars. Espresso powder and toasted pecans, coconut macadamia-nut, or even browned butter are popular variations. As with brownies, test for doneness near the center, but not at the center, for the best texture. They will keep two to three days at room temperature, or for several months if frozen after they are baked.

	LARGE BATCH
$^3/_4$ cup unsalted butter	1 lb 8 oz
1 cup dark brown sugar	2 lb
3 large eggs	1 lb 4.4 oz
$1^1/_2$ tsp vanilla extract	2 Tbs
$2^1/_4$ cups all-purpose flour	2 lb 6.25 oz
$^1/_2$ tsp salt	2 tsp
$^1/_4$ tsp baking soda	1 tsp
1 cup semisweet chocolate chips	1 lb 8 oz
1 cup chopped toasted pecans (optional)	1 lb

Grease and flour a 9-inch square baking pan. In a saucepan, melt the butter. Place the brown sugar in a medium bowl; whisk in the melted butter. One at a time, whisk in the eggs, then the vanilla. Stir in the flour, salt, and baking soda just until combined. Stir in the chocolate chips and nuts. Spread the batter into the prepared pan. Bake at 350°F for 35 to 40 minutes, or until a skewer inserted two inches or so from the center comes out with only moist crumbs clinging to it. Cool blondies before removing from pan.

LEMON BARS

MAKES ONE 9 BY 13-INCH BAKING PAN This recipe uses lemon curd and a short cookie crust. Pâte sucrée may be substituted. It doesn't matter if the curd is cold or warm when beginning this recipe. Once baked, the bars are good for up to four days, refrigerated. Lemon bars are commonly dusted with confectioners' sugar and garnished with candied lemon peel.

	LARGE BATCH
⅓ recipe **HAZELNUT SHORT CRUST** (page 173)	1⅓ recipes
6 cups **LEMON CURD** (about 1½ times the basic recipe; page 146)	6 recipes
Confectioners' sugar, for dusting	

Roll or press the dough into the bottom and 1 inch up the side of a greased foil- or parchment-lined 9 by 13-inch baking pan. Partially bake the dough at 350°F for 25 to 30 minutes, or until barely golden. Spread the lemon curd evenly over the dough; bake an additional 25 to 30 minutes, or until curd is just set in the middle. Cool completely before cutting into squares.

LINZER BARS

MAKES ONE 8-INCH SQUARE PAN These bar cookies are simply a sturdy variation of linzertorte. The cookies will keep two days before getting soggy, but the dough is good for up to a week in the refrigerator or six months in the freezer.

	LARGE BATCH
1 pound **LINZERTORTE** dough (about ⅓ basic recipe; page 183)	1⅓ recipes
⅓ cup all-purpose flour	5.67 oz
¾ cup raspberry jam	2 lb 4 oz
Confectioners' sugar, for dusting	

Knead the dough with the flour. Divide the dough into two pieces, roughly 11 oz and 6$^1/_2$ oz. Press or roll out the larger piece of dough to fit the bottom and 1 inch up the sides of a greased 8-inch square pan. Spread the jam onto the dough. With your fingers, roll the remaining dough into $^3/_8$-inch diameter ropes. Form lattice with ropes over jam. Bake at 350°F until the edges and top of the lattice is browned, about 35 minutes. Cool before cutting into squares. Dust with confectioners' sugar.

CHAPTER 8

WORKING
WITH SUGAR

Though it seems improbable, the same principle guides both the making of peanut brittle and the making of fondant. Controlled crystallization of varying concentrations of sugar syrups is the foundation for all candymaking, which for most pastry chefs centers on making syrup for Italian meringue or making golden caramel for croquembuche, rather than on making taffy or hard candy. Still, if you can make praline, you can make lollipops.

The finished texture of candy is defined by two things: the size of sugar crystals formed and the concentration of the sugar in the syrup. Each type of candy requires a specific concentration of sugar to form properly, and the easiest way to determine sugar concentration is to use a candy thermometer. The temperature range between 234° and 310°F is broken down into smaller intervals. These intervals are named for the shape a spoonful of syrup takes after it is dropped into ice cold water, removed, then pressed or pulled. See "Stages of Sugar Syrups," below.

SUGAR SYRUP

Each stage of candymaking falls within a temperature range. This temperature range reflects the sugar concentration, which affects the texture the final product will have. Thus, formulas for making sugar syrups and caramel are not even necessary: No matter how much sugar and how much water you start with, once you reach a given temperature the syrup has a specific sugar concentration. Naturally, beginning with a lot of water will prolong the cooking time, since more time is needed to boil off the excess moisture.

Sugar attracts moisture from the air, especially any invert sugar that has been formed from boiling the syrup in the presence of a crystal-inhibiting acid, such as lemon juice or cream of tartar. On rainy days, candy may turn out sticky or not set up properly. As a preventive measure, bring the sugar syrup to the top edge of the range to reduce the moisture present in the candy. For fondant, this would be 240°F rather than the more conservative temperature of 238°F.

STAGES OF SUGAR SYRUP

Thread	220°–233°F	simple syrup
Soft ball (a soft ball that flattens when pressed)	234°–240°F	fondant, fudge, syrup for Italian meringue
Firm ball (a ball that resists flattening when pressed)	242°–249°F	soft caramel candies, marshmallows
Hard ball	250°–265°F	nougat, divinity
Soft crack (flexible strands that can be shaped)	270°–290°F	taffy
Hard crack (brittle, easily broken strands)	300°–310°F	brittle, toffee, pulled sugar, blown sugar
Caramel	320°–370°F	praline

NOTE These temperature ranges are accurate at sea level. They decrease 1 degree for every 500-foot increase in altitude.

FOOLPROOF SUGAR SYRUPS

When 2 cups of sugar are combined with only 1 cup of water in a pan over low heat, the sugar will not completely dissolve at first, but as the solution approaches a boil, the sugar granules slowly disappear. When the pan is removed from the stove and the syrup begins to cool, the solution becomes **supersaturated**, meaning that the water is holding (temporarily) more sugar in solution than it normally can for that given temperature. Because the sugar molecules are packed beyond the

point at which they are able to remain dissolved, any agitation or ex-
posure to any foreign particle, such as a grain of sugar stuck to the side
of the pan, will cause the sugar molecules to cling to one another and
fall out of solution (recrystallize). This is called **precipitation.** Follow
the tips below to prevent sugar syrups from crystallizing prematurely.

1. Heat the sugar and water gradually, stirring frequently, to give the sugar time
   to dissolve. When the syrup reaches a boil, cover the pot for a minute or two to
   let steam and condensation dissolve any remaining granules clinging to the side
   of the pot. The lid must be removed for the water to evaporate and for the
   sugar concentration to increase. Continue to boil the syrup without stirring,
   which may instigate crystallization.

2. Prewarm your thermometer before inserting it into the hot syrup.

3. Have a pastry brush sitting in a cup of hot water. Use it to wash down crystals
   that form on the side of the pan.

4. Always use utensils that do not conduct heat for stirring, such as wooden
   spoons. Use a fresh spoon if the one you start cooking with becomes en-
   crusted with crystals, and never redip a spoon (that has not been washed) into
   the syrup.

5. Ingredients that inhibit crystal formation when making candy and syrups may
   be added during the early stages of cooking. They are glucose syrup, corn
   syrup, and acids, such as lemon juice, vinegar, and cream of tartar.

SIMPLE SYRUP

Simple syrup is any sugar-and-water solution that has been brought to
a boil to ensure complete dissolution of the sugar granules. The syrups
can vary in viscosity, depending on the amount of water present. The
most common syrup used in the kitchen consists of equal weights of
sugar and water. This is also called **heavy syrup.** It may be flavored
with rum, fruit juice, or coffee and used to brush genoise layers. It is
also used to candy fruit peel. Simple syrup is a great way to sweeten
fruit coulis with out adding the graininess of sugar. It will keep indefinitely in the refrigerator and may be thinned as needed.

SYRUP FOR ITALIAN MERINGUE

Sugar syrup is brought to the soft ball stage, preferably 238° to 240°F, for cooking whipped egg foams. If the syrup exceeds this temperature, the egg mixture will have a thicker, stickier texture. If the temperature is lower, the eggs may not get hot enough to be cooked and stabilized. Eggs must reach 160°F for a second or two, or be held at 143°F for almost four minutes to be safe. Beginning with a ratio of twice as much sugar as water by weight minimizes the cooking time while ensuring that the sugar granules dissolve.

FONDANT

Fondant is an ultra-smooth candy used as a coating for petits fours, napoleons, pastries, and smooth-surfaced wedding cakes. Fondant is created by the formation of millions of minuscule crystals that are so small the tongue cannot discern them. Like syrup for Italian meringue, fondant begins by cooking a sugar syrup to 238°F, often with the addition of cream of tartar or corn syrup to prevent crystallization. The syrup is poured onto a marble or Formica surface and left to cool, undisturbed, until it reaches 120°F. With a bench scraper (or two), the fondant is then kneaded until it turns milk white and opaque. The kneading process initiates crystallization and must be done quickly. It can be strenuous work by hand, since the fondant becomes stiffer as it is worked. Many chefs prefer using a mixer fitted with the paddle attachment.

Fondant is usually covered with simple syrup and left to sit for twenty-four hours in an airtight container to smooth out and ripen. It can be gently heated (to around 100°F) and thinned with sugar syrup to make a pourable glaze, or rolled and cut for draping over cakes. Fondant may be flavored as desired. If it is heated above 110°F, it will become grainy. Store fondant in an airtight container.

ALMOND TOFFEE

MAKES ONE HALF SHEET PAN Toffee is cooked to the hard crack stage, well below the temperature that pure caramel praline reaches. Though toffee is crunchy, it has a meltingly smooth texture because of the addition of butter, unlike praline, which is just plain hard. The milk solids in the butter caramelize (brown) at a lower temperature than sugar, so toffee is caramel in color despite the lower cooking temperature. Toffee may be topped with tempered milk or semisweet chocolate and more chopped almonds. It will keep indefinitely if the weather and storage environment is dry.

1¹/₂ cups unsalted butter	3 lb	
1 cup granulated sugar	1 lb 12 oz	
1 cup packed light brown sugar	2 lb	LARGE BATCH
¹/₄ cup corn syrup	1 cup	
¹/₄ plus ¹/₈ tsp salt	1¹/₂ tsp	
2 cups natural sliced almonds, toasted and chopped	1 lb 8 oz	

In a medium, heavy, nonreactive saucepan, melt the butter over medium-high heat. When the butter is almost melted, stir in the sugars, corn syrup, and salt. Continue to stir until the sugar dissolves and the mixture is smooth. Stop stirring once the mixture comes to a boil. Brush the sides of the pan with a pastry brush dipped in water to dissolve any sugar crystals. At about 300°F the mixture will begin to caramelize. The toffee is done cooking at 310°F; the mixture will be a deep golden to pale amber color. Remove the pan from the heat; stir in the chopped nuts. Pour the candy onto a lightly buttered half-sheet pan; spread with a greased metal offset spatula to an even thickness of about ¹/₄ inch. Cool until hard and then break into shards, or score with a knife while semisoft for uniform pieces.

SPUN SUGAR, CARAMEL, AND PRALINE

The point at which sugar begins to turn gold is called the caramel stage. First the syrup turns pale blond, then golden, amber, and dark amber.

Beyond this, the sugar is simply burned because all the sucrose will have been destroyed. Since the flavor of caramel is determined by the depth of its color, a thermometer is not necessary. When sugar cooked to the caramel stage is poured onto a sheet pan to cool, it forms a hard, glassy candy.

Interestingly, the hardest candy is formed by pale blond or colorless hard crack–stage syrup, not amber. Though praline is hard, technically it is less hard than spun sugar, since more sugar has been converted or "burned." The crystallization of sucrose is what gives candy its texture, so as sucrose is destroyed, the resulting candy will be softer.

DRY METHOD FOR MAKING CARAMEL

Since there is almost no moisture left at the caramel stage, the fastest way to make caramel is to simply melt sugar without water. This is called the dry method for making caramel. Eliminating the water saves time, but it is less foolproof for beginners. Dry sugar melts at 320°F and quickly darkens from there. The pan shape best suited for caramel is disputed by chefs. Some prefer a wide, shallow skillet to keep as much sugar in contact with the heated surface as possible. But a wide pan with its large surface area is harder to stir and control once the sugar melts and darkens.

WET METHOD FOR MAKING CARAMEL

The foolproof method for making caramel is called the wet method, which involves adding a small amount of water to the sugar, usually less than half the weight of the sugar. This helps the sugar melt slowly and evenly.

SPUN SUGAR

Pale, blondish straw-colored caramel is used for making **caramel cages**, for **golden syrup** for drizzling over croquembouche, and for making **spun sugar** decorations. The syrup usually reaches this color near 310° to 320°F, and to ensure that the syrup does not darken too quickly, the wet method for making the caramel is best. Keep the syrup fluid by placing the pan in a larger pan of hot water and return to heat if necessary. A fork may be used to flick the pale caramel into a greased bowl, for a sugar cage, or directly over a dessert, but the best tool is a thin wire whisk whose ends have been cut and straightened.

PRALINE AND PRALINE POWDER

MAKES ABOUT ³/₄ CUP GROUND PRALINE Praline is caramelized sugar with the addition of toasted almonds or hazelnuts. The mixture is poured onto a greased marble slab or sheet pan and left to cool and harden. Praline is crushed or ground in a food processor. It is added to fillings and buttercreams for caramel flavor. Large pieces can be used as a garnish.

		LARGE BATCH
1 cup granulated sugar	1 lb 12 oz	
¹/₂ cup water	2 cups	
1 cup toasted slivered almonds or chopped toasted hazelnuts	1 lb 2 oz	

Cook the sugar with the water over medium heat, stirring until the sugar is dissolved. Once the syrup reaches a boil, stop stirring. Cook until the caramel is light to medium amber for maximum flavor, then stir the nuts into the pan. The nuts may be added earlier, when the temperature is near the soft ball stage, if they have not been toasted to give them time to color. Pour the candy onto a lightly buttered half-sheet pan; spread with a greased metal offset spatula to an even thickness of about ¹/₄ inch. Cool completely. Grind in a food processor.

CARAMEL SAUCE

MAKES ABOUT 3 CUPS Caramel sauce is simply sugar cooked to the caramel stage with added cream. If no cream were added, the candy would harden into praline. Warm water and room temperature cream work best.

2 cups granulated sugar	3 lb 8 oz	
1 cup water	1 qt	**LARGE BATCH**
2¹/₄ cups heavy cream	2 qt plus 1 cup	
2 Tbs unsalted butter	4 oz	
¹/₈ tsp salt	¹/₂ tsp	

In a medium, heavy, nonreactive saucepan, stir the sugar and water together over medium-high heat. Continue to stir until the sugar dissolves and the mixture is smooth. Stop stirring once the mixture comes to a boil. Brush the sides of the pan with a pastry brush dipped in water to dissolve any sugar crystals. Let the mixture caramelize to a deep amber; gently swirl the pan for even coloring. Remove the pan from the heat; carefully pour in the cream, butter, and salt (the mixture will foam). Stir until smooth, gently reheating if necessary to melt any sugar crystals that form. For thicker or thinner sauce, simply adjust the amount of cream.

WORKING WITH
CHOCOLATE

Since quality, flavor, and texture directly correspond to cost, chocolate is often among the most expensive ingredients in a pastry kitchen. Pastry chefs usually have strong brand preferences. While taste comparisons are key, keeping the end product in mind is just as important. Two high-end chocolates can have an equally pleasing taste, but one may have better flow for making hard shells and decorations. The most wonderful tasting chocolate may not make the best cake; the nuances of its flavor may be lost because combining chocolate with other ingredients can change or mask its flavor.

While taste is a personal issue, quality is not. Poor quality chocolates may be difficult to work with in addition to lacking good flavor. The quality of the beans, along with fermentation, roasting, and conching processes, affect the quality of the chocolate. Some deficiencies are easily detected. Chocolate that has undergone minimal conching is noticeably less smooth. Waxy chocolate may indicate the presence of vegetable fats other than cocoa butter. Quality chocolates will not contain artificial ingredients, such as vanillin.

Types of Chocolate and Cocoa

- **Unsweetened chocolate**, also called bitter chocolate, is pure chocolate liquor. It must contain at least 50 percent cocoa butter.

- **Bittersweet** and **semisweet chocolate** both must contain at least 35 percent chocolate liquor. Sugar, added cocoa butter, lecithin (usually derived from soybeans), and vanilla are other typical ingredients. There is no official distinction between the two chocolates. Bittersweet is generally less sweet than semisweet, but one company's semisweet may be less sweet than another's bittersweet. Bittersweet chocolates with a chocolate liquor content of more than 60 percent are intensely flavored and less sweet than typical bittersweet chocolates.

- **Milk chocolate** contains at least 12 percent milk solids and 10 percent chocolate liquor. Milk chocolate also contains lecithin, vanilla, and sugar.

- **White chocolate**, made from cocoa butter, contains no cocoa solids, and hence lacks chocolate flavor. At the time of this writing, there is no regulation of the labels on white chocolate. Sugar, vanilla, milk solids, and lecithin are added to cocoa butter to create white chocolate. Read labels carefully. If another vegetable fat has been substituted for cocoa butter, it is *confectionery* (also called *summer* or *compound*) *coating*. It will not perform in recipes the same way as white chocolate.

- **Couverture** chocolates have a high cocoa butter content, usually 32 to 39 percent. They are used for making chocolate candies, decorations, and ultra-smooth glazes. The higher percentage of cocoa butter promotes good flow of melted, tempered chocolate, ensuring thin coatings that have a good snap.

- **Dutch-processed cocoa,** also known as **alkalized cocoa** or **European-style cocoa,** is processed with an alkali to neutralize the natural acidity of cocoa powder. Once alkalized, the cocoa's pH is increased from 5.5 to between 7 and 8, which mellows the flavor. Dutch-processed cocoa is darker in color than regular cocoa powder, and its flavor is smoother. **Regular cocoa powder,** called natural, is reddish brown, with a fruity, robust flavor. These two types of cocoa powder are not always interchangeable, as they are often paired with specific leaveners in a recipe that complement their acidity or alkalinity. Most of the cocoa butter has been separated from cocoa powders. Both these cocoas are unsweetened and should not be confused with hot cocoa mixes.

- **Chocolate chips** contain different vegetable fats and special stabilizers that help them retain their shape during baking. They are not interchangeable with regular chocolate, whose cocoa butter behaves (and tastes) differently from other fats. The additional stabilizers mean that sauces, puddings, and mousses will set firmer than ones made with regular chocolate.

STORING CHOCOLATE

Chocolate should be stored in a cool, dry environment, preferably around 55° to 65°F. It will readily absorbs kitchen odors, and should be protected accordingly. Warmer or fluctuating temperatures can cause the cocoa butter to melt, separate, and recrystallize with white filmy streaks called **fat bloom.** Humidity changes may cause water to condense on the chocolate. Sugar is dissolved in the water, and then recrystallizes on the surface when the water evaporates. This is called **sugar**

bloom. Neither is harmful for baking, but only fat-bloomed chocolate may be tempered and used for coating truffles or candymaking.

MELTING CHOCOLATE

Chocolate can be melted over a hot-water bath, in a double boiler, or even in the microwave. Gentle heat to prevent scorching is the prime consideration, as cocoa butter will separate from cocoa solids at temperatures beyond 120°F. Care should be taken to prevent water droplets from touching the chocolate. Chocolate will tolerate added water, but only a drop or two causes it to seize: $1^1/_2$ teaspoons water per ounce of chocolate is the minimum liquid to add to prevent seizing (Corriher, p. 461), but thinning the chocolate to smooth it out also means the chocolate can no longer be used for hard shells and decorations.

TEMPERING CHOCOLATE

Cocoa butter—the fat in chocolate—has unique properties of crystallization. As melted cocoa butter cools, it begins to recrystallize into *four different types* of crystal formations. Each form multiples rapidly, or predominates, at specific temperatures. Only one of the four types, called the beta, results in a shiny, solid piece of chocolate. **Tempering** is simply melting and cooling chocolate at specific temperatures to ensure proper solidification.

An accurate thermometer is essential for tempering. There are thermometers specifically for chocolate work, which have a range between 80° and 130°F. Those who become proficient at tempering eventually use their wrist or upper lip to determine temperature. The following is the procedure for tempering chocolate:

1. Melt the chocolate to a temperature of 115° to 120°F. The chocolate must reach this temperature to ensure that all the cocoa butter crystals have been thoroughly dissolved. The temperature should not exceed 120°F, or the cocoa butter may separate from the cocoa solids. Remove from the heat.

2. Let the chocolate sit at room temperature, stirring occasionally, until the temperature of the chocolate falls to just over 80°F.

3. Carefully bring the chocolate back up to between 86° and 91°F, using the lower end of the range for white and milk chocolates and the higher temperatures for dark chocolates. The chocolate is now ready to use.

The tempered melted chocolate may be kept at its ideal range (which ensures good control of flow for making thin coatings) by placing it near a warm spot on the stove near the pilot light, over a hot-water bath, on a heating pad, or an even blast of hot air from a hair dryer aimed at the bottom of the bowl. If the temperature reaches 92°F, or falls below 77°F, the chocolate is no longer in temper and the process must be repeated.

If you have a small amount of chocolate on hand that is still in temper, it can be used to "seed" melted untempered chocolate. Let the melted chocolate cool slightly, then stir in the chopped tempered chocolate. For this method, the ratio of melted chocolate to chopped tempered chocolate is about 4 to 1. Some chefs use larger chunks of tempered chocolate as seeds, and simply remove the lumps that have not melted when the ideal temperature is reached.

Blocks of chocolate that are still in temper do not require these steps. If they are carefully melted so that the temperature never exceeds 91°F, the chocolate will remain in temper.

Correct tempering is checked by spreading a small amount of chocolate on a sheet pan or piece of waxed paper and then waiting to see if the chocolate sets with an even surface color and shine. If improperly tempered chocolate does not set up, it can be forced to harden in the refrigerator, but this means that it will revert back to being soft and dull at room temperature.

GANACHE

Basic ganache is a mixture of heavy cream and chocolate. However, that is just the beginning. Butter, coffee, tea, and even fruit purées may flavor ganache. Easy to make, ganache is one of the most versatile

DECORATING WITH TEMPERED CHOCOLATE

CHOCOLATE CURLS are made by coating the underside of a sheet pan with a thin film of tempered chocolate. When the chocolate begins to set, push the chocolate with a bench scraper or flat palette knife. For ringlet-style curls, the chocolate should be almost set. For tight cigarette curls, the chocolate should be a little softer.

CHOCOLATE LEAVES are made by brushing the underside of cleaned, pesticide-free, nontoxic leaves with warm tempered chocolate. The chocolate should be thicker by the central vein and thinner toward the edges. Once the chocolate sets, peel the leaf away.

CHOCOLATE BOWLS are created by coating the inside of shaped molds or bowls with a thin film tempered chocolate, letting it set, then gently loosening it from the bowl. An easier method is to dip the ends of inflated balloons into warm, tempered chocolate, let it set, and then pop the balloon.

CHOCOLATE SHAVINGS are made with a vegetable peeler from a block of chocolate. The chocolate does not have to be tempered. Warm the block of chocolate in the microwave, 5 seconds at a time, if it is too cool to work with. Chocolate shavings can be sprinkled on top of cakes and pies or pressed into the sides of tortes.

components in the pastry kitchen. The ratio of chocolate to cream determines its function in the kitchen. Ganache made with mostly chocolate is used to fill truffles, while equal parts chocolate to cream by weight is perfect for glazing tortes, when warm, or filling cakes, when cooled. Ganache made with mostly cream can be whipped into a silky, stable whipped cream.

MAKING GANACHE

For recipes that call for equal or greater amounts of heavy cream to chocolate, place the chopped chocolate in a bowl. Once the cream has been brought to a boil, pour it over the chocolate. Let the mixture stand for a minute or two, then gently whisk until smooth. If the recipe calls for more chocolate than cream, there will not be enough residual heat to melt the chocolate using the above method. Instead, use a larger pot to bring the cream to a boil. Remove the pot from the heat and stir in the chocolate. The heat held in the pan should melt the chocolate easily.

BROKEN GANACHE

Despite its simple appearance, ganache is actually a fat-in-water emulsion, much like mayonnaise. Milk solids and cholesterol present in the heavy cream stabilize the mixture; indeed, cholesterol itself is an emulsifier. But occasionally the ganache will break, and the fat will separate, giving the ganache a curdled appearance. If ganache breaks while on the stove top, more cream or sugar can be added immediately. However, the following method is best for preserving the consistency of the original formula. After all, adding large amounts of cream is not helpful if a thick ganache is the goal.

To bring back ganache, the same principle is employed as bringing back other broken emulsions, like mayonnaise. Gradually beat the broken sauce into a tiny amount of heavy cream. According to professional chocolatiers, as little as $1/4$ cup of cream will bring back a bathtub of broken ganache. The broken ganache and heavy cream should be at the same temperature, preferably just barely warm. Alternatively, a small amount of warm cream can be poured directly onto the top of the broken ganache. Begin whisking just on the surface of the ganache, and gradually move outward to incorporate the entire mixture.

GLAZING GANACHE

Equal parts heavy cream and chocolate are used to make a ganache for glazing cakes and tortes, but a thinner or thicker glaze can be created by adjusting the amount of cream. Let the ganache cool slightly before pouring, so that it is warm enough to flow smoothly but not so hot that it melts the crumb coat. If there is no crumb coating of buttercream, two coats of glaze may be needed to smoothly cover the torte. Or, a room-temperature ganache that is thick enough to spread can be used to crumb-coat the torte, making it smooth and ready for the top coat of glaze. Refrigerate the torte after the first coat before continuing with the second.

WHIPPED GANACHE

Whipping a ganache made from equal parts chocolate and cream creates a spreadable frosting or mousselike filling for cakes and tortes. It can also cause the cocoa butter to crystallize and solidify: First the mixture is smooth and spreadable, then stiff and grainy seconds later. To prevent this from happening, the ganache should mature overnight and chill slowly. Let the ganache rest in a cool spot (55° to 65°F is ideal) or in the refrigerator. Waiting at least 8 hours makes the ganache easier to whip without seizing.

Ganache should be cool when whipped, but it doesn't have to be truly cold. Some chefs prefer the ease of whipping cold ganache, which, like plain heavy cream, incorporates air quickly when chilled. Other chefs feel 55° to 65°F is safer, since it lessens the probability of sudden hardening. Ganache should be whipped only to soft peaks.

CHOCOLATE WHIPPED CREAM

Made the same way as whipped ganache, chocolate whipped cream has a ratio of three parts cream to one part chocolate. It is lighter than whipped ganache, and makes a nice frosting and filling for rich cakes. White chocolate whipped cream is a delicious frosting, much more stable than regular whipped cream. Choose a white chocolate with a nice vanilla flavor.

CHOCOLATE SAUCE

MAKES 1 CUP This sauce is thick at room temperature and pourable when warm. It can be thinned with water.

		LARGE BATCH
¹/₂ cup sugar	14 oz	
¹/₄ cup water	1 cup	
¹/₄ cup light corn syrup	1 cup	
6 ounces bittersweet chocolate, chopped	1 lb 8 oz	
2 Tbs unsalted butter, softened	4 oz	

Bring sugar, water, and corn syrup to a boil in saucepan, stirring to dissolve the sugar. Remove the pan from the heat; stir in the chocolate and butter until smooth.

CHOCOLATE GLAZE

MAKES ABOUT 3¹/₂ CUPS This glaze is used for eclairs, doughnuts, and Boston cream pie.

		LARGE BATCH
6 ounces bittersweet chocolate, chopped	1 lb 8 oz	
4 Tbs unsalted butter	8 oz	
1 cup light corn syrup	1 qt	
¹/₂ cup boiling water	2 cups	
2 cups confectioners' sugar, sifted	2 lb	

Melt the chocolate with the butter. Stir in the corn syrup and boiling water. Stir in the sugar until smooth. Let cool until spreadable, or pour while hot.

BASIC TRUFFLES

MAKES 18 TO 24 TRUFFLES

		LARGE BATCH
$^1/_2$ cup heavy cream	2 cups	
8 ounces semisweet chocolate, finely chopped	2 lb	
2 Tbs unsalted butter, softened	4 oz	
1 Tbs rum or other liquor of choice	$^1/_4$ cup	
Cocoa powder or confectioners' sugar, for dusting (optional)		
Chopped nuts, sprinkles, or toasted coconut, for dusting (optional)		

Bring the cream to a boil in a saucepan. Turn off the heat; stir in the chocolate until melted and smooth. Stir in the butter and desired flavoring. Transfer to a bowl. Freeze until firm; scoop and roll into $^3/_4$ or 1-inch balls. Dust with cocoa or confectioner's sugar, or roll in chopped nuts, sprinkles, or toasted coconut.

NOTE

If coating the truffles with tempered chocolate, refrigerate the ganache instead of freezing it. With a plain pastry tip, pipe $^3/_4$ or 1-inch rounds onto sheet pans. Chill rounds before dipping.

MOLDING (MODELING) CHOCOLATE

MAKES 1 POUND Also called chocolate paste, molding chocolate can be sculpted, rolled, and cut to form decorations for cakes and tortes. Different types (white or dark) and brands of chocolate require slightly different amounts of corn syrup, so amounts here are approximate.

12 ounces semisweet or white chocolate	3 lb	
$^{1}/_{2}$ cup corn syrup	2 cups	LARGE BATCH
Cornstarch or confectioners' sugar, for kneading		

Melt the chocolate and let it cool slightly. Stir in the corn syrup. Remove from the pan; wrap the mixture and let it rest at room temperature overnight to ripen.

The next day, knead the chocolate paste with a small amount of cornstarch or confectioners' sugar until it is smooth and pliable. Chocolate paste will harden as it cools, but will soften under a warm lamp or in your hands for reshaping.

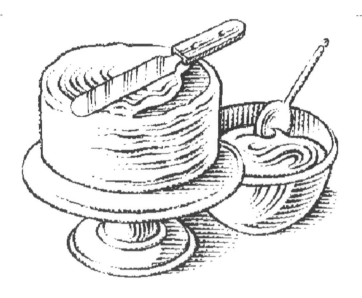

CHAPTER 10

FROSTINGS

This chapter includes recipes for icings and frostings. Fondant, chocolate glaze, and ganache are covered in Chapter 9.

BUTTERCREAMS

There are three major types of buttercream: Swiss, Italian, and French. Technically, buttercream describes anything that is made from beating butter into a base. Buttercream can be made by beating butter into a flavored pastry cream, which is both decadent and highly perishable. Crème anglaise with butter whipped into it makes a lovely but fragile buttercream that has the same silky richness as French buttercream.

Buttercream can be used as a base for creating other fillings and frostings. **Mousseline cream** is buttercream that has been mixed with pastry cream. A fluffy but silky frosting is made by combining French buttercream with Italian meringue. Once you think of buttercream as a component rather than just an end product, your dessert repertoire expands.

GENERAL GUIDELINES FOR BUTTERCREAM

Buttercream will appear curdled or broken when half the butter is added, but will smooth out by the time all the butter has been incorporated.

If the texture of the buttercream feels tight rather than fluffy, stir it over a bowl of hot water for a few seconds at a time until it loosens up.

For best results, the butter must be the same temperature as the beaten eggs. The exception to this is syrup-cooked buttercreams, which may be slightly warm when cool butter is added.

Lemon curd, espresso, orange zest—buttercream is a simple base that may be flavored with virtually anything, so long as the added flavor does not exceed half the total weight of the butter in the recipe.

Buttercream should be stored in the refrigerator if it will not be used right away. It must warm up to room temperature before it can be used. Simply stirring it or briefly beating it should smooth it out and make it spreadable. If it appears broken or greasy and refuses to smooth out even after it has been gently heated, more softened butter can be beaten into it.

SWISS BUTTERCREAM

MAKES 5 TO 6 CUPS At one time, this buttercream was preferred over other buttercreams. It is faster to prepare and less sweet than Italian buttercream, but is heavier in texture. Pasteurized egg whites should be used, since this butter-cream is uncooked. For the frosting to come together smoothly, it is essential that the whipped eggs and softened butter be at the same temperature.

1 cup pasteurized egg whites (about 7 large)	2 lb 2 oz	
1^1/$_2$ cups granulated sugar	2 lb 10 oz	**LARGE BATCH**
^{1}/$_4$ tsp salt	1 tsp	
2 cups unsalted butter, softened	2 lb	
2 tsp vanilla extract	2 Tbs plus 2 tsp	

Place the egg whites and sugar in a bowl. Stir constantly over a hot water bath or low burner until the sugar is completely dissolved. Place the mixture in a mixer bowl; whip to stiff peaks. Beat in the salt. With the mixer running at medium speed, toss the softened butter into the eggs a tablespoon at a time. Beat in the vanilla (and any additional flavorings).

ITALIAN BUTTERCREAM

MAKES 9 CUPS The lightest and most stable of the buttercreams is based on Italian meringue. It is also the most forgiving, easy to spread, and has a long shelf life. An equivalent amount of whole eggs may be used instead of whites for a richer buttercream. When making the sugar syrup, dissolve any sugar crystals that form on the side of the pan with a wet pastry brush. After the syrup reaches a boil, cover the pan for a minute or two to the let the condensing steam wash down the sides of the pan. Remember to remove the lid, or the syrup will not reach the proper temperature and sugar concentration.

	LARGE BATCH
2 cups granulated sugar	3 lb 8 oz
1 cup water	1 qt
1 cup egg whites (about 7 large)	2 lb 2 oz
$\frac{1}{2}$ tsp salt	2 tsp
3 cups ($1\frac{1}{2}$ lb) unsalted butter, softened but cool	6 lb
1 Tbs vanilla extract	4 tsp

In a saucepan, dissolve the sugar in the water over medium heat, stirring. Increase the heat to high; boil until the syrup reaches 238°F on a candy thermometer. Once the syrup is boiling, begin whipping the egg whites and salt together in the mixer bowl. Beat the egg whites to the stiff-peak stage. With the mixer running, carefully pour the hot syrup down the side of the bowl. Continue beating the meringue until it has cooled to just warm. Pinch off small pieces of butter and toss them into the mixer, one at a time. When the buttercream is smooth, beat in the vanilla (and any other desired flavorings).

CHOCOLATE BUTTERCREAM

Beat in 8 ounces bittersweet chocolate, melted, to the recipe above.

FRENCH BUTTERCREAM

MAKES ABOUT 7 CUPS French buttercream is made the same way as Italian buttercream, but with yolks instead of whites. Whipping hot sugar syrup into the egg yolks is also known as **pâte à bombe,** a component often used as the base for mousses and ice cream. Naturally, egg yolk–based buttercreams are richer in taste and denser in texture than egg white–meringue buttercreams.

		LARGE BATCH
1¹/₃ cups granulated sugar	2 lb 5.33 oz	
²/₃ cup water	2²/₃ cups	
12 large egg yolks (about ³/₄ cup)	1 lb 10.4 oz	
1 large egg	6.8 oz	
¹/₄ tsp salt	1 tsp	
3 cups (1¹/₂ lb) unsalted butter, at room temperature	6 lb	
1 Tbs vanilla extract	¹/₄ cup	

In a saucepan, dissolve the sugar in the water over medium heat, stirring. Increase the heat to high; boil until the syrup reaches 238°F on a candy thermometer. Once the syrup is boiling, begin whipping the egg yolks and whole egg together in the mixer bowl to the ribbon stage. With the mixer running, carefully pour the hot syrup down the side of the bowl. Beat in the salt, then beat the mixture until it has cooled to room temperature. Pinch off small pieces of butter and toss them into the mixer, one at a time. When the buttercream is smooth, beat in the vanilla.

HAZELNUT-PRALINE BUTTERCREAM

Stir 1 cup hazelnut praline paste into 1 cup of the butter used in the recipe above; add this mixture last.

CARAMEL BUTTERCREAM

MAKES 6 TO 7 CUPS This version of French buttercream is absolutely delicious. Ground praline (caramelized almonds) or instant espresso dissolved in rum are twists on this classic flavor.

1¼ cups packed dark brown sugar	2 lb 8 oz	
1¼ cups heavy cream	5 cups	
½ cup corn syrup	2 cups	
¼ tsp salt	1 tsp	**LARGE BATCH**
8 large egg yolks	1 lb 1.6 oz	
1 large egg	6.8 oz	
2 cups (1 lb) unsalted butter, at room temperature	4 lb	
2 tsp vanilla extract	2 Tbs plus 2 tsp	

In a saucepan, bring the brown sugar, cream, corn syrup, and salt to a boil, stirring over medium heat until the sugar has dissolved. Increase heat to high; boil until syrup reaches 238°F on a candy thermometer. Once the syrup is boiling, begin whipping the egg yolks and whole egg together in the mixer. The egg yolks should be at the ribbon stage when the syrup goes in. With the mixer running, carefully pour the hot syrup down the side of the bowl. Continue beating the meringue until it has cooled to just warm. Pinch off small pieces of butter and toss them into the mixer one at a time. When the buttercream is smooth, beat in the vanilla.

DECORATOR'S BUTTERCREAM

MAKES ABOUT 4 CUPS Also known as **mock buttercream,** this buttercream is a mixture of shortening, confectioners' sugar, and enough water to make it smooth and light. Some recipes call for beating shortening into meringue, but despite differences, these recipes share the same goal: a frosting that pipes easily, holds a piped edge well over a wide temperature range, and is shelf stable. Though it is a useful tool for practicing piping skills, this frosting is not the least bit palatable and should be avoided in a fine bakery. Shortening coats the mouth with a waxy film rather than melts on the tongue, creating an unpleasant sensation. If regular buttercream is too fragile for warm weather, for example, a better solution is to substitute shortening in place of a small amount of the butter ($^1/_4$ of the total), rather than use an all-shortening frosting.

		LARGE BATCH
1 cup shortening	1 lb 7 oz	
$^1/_4$ cup water	1 cup	
6 to 8 cups confectioners' sugar, sifted	1 lb 8 oz to 2 lb	
$1^1/_2$ tsp vanilla extract (optional)	2 Tbs	

Place the shortening in a mixer bowl. Beat with paddle, gradually adding the water. Gradually beat in the sugar until the desired consistency is reached. Beat in the vanilla. If frosting is for piping borders, soft peak is the proper consistency; for flowers, it should be stiffer.

OTHER FROSTINGS

CREAM CHEESE FROSTING

MAKES ENOUGH FROSTING FOR A THREE-LAYER 9-INCH CAKE This is the standard frosting for carrot, zucchini, and pumpkin cake. It can be flavored with lemon, orange, or ginger.

10 Tbs unsalted butter, softened but cool	1 lb 4 oz	
Two 8-oz packages cream cheese	4 lb	LARGE BATCH
2 cups confectioners' sugar	2 lb	
1 tsp vanilla extract	4 tsp	

With the paddle attachment, beat the butter until smooth. Beat in the cream cheese until smooth. Beat in the sugar and vanilla. Avoid overbeating the frosting, or it will become thin. The frosting may be thinned with milk, or chilled to make it firmer.

FUDGE FROSTING

MAKES 3¹/₂ CUPS This frosting is shiny, smooth, and thick. Since it has no confectioners' sugar or granulated sugar, it is never grainy or gritty. The egg yolks are not essential, but they do help keep the frosting emulsified.

		LARGE BATCH
1²/₃ cups sweetened condensed milk	4 lb 9.33 oz	
2 large egg yolks	13.6 oz	
8 ounces bittersweet chocolate, chopped	2 lb	
1 tsp vanilla extract (optional)	4 tsp	
1 cup unsalted butter, cold and cut into ¹/₂-inch dice	2 lb	

Warm the milk in a saucepan; whisk in the yolks. Cook 2 minutes, or until the temperature reaches 175°F. Remove pan from heat; stir in the chocolate until melted and smooth. Stir in the vanilla. Place the mixture in a mixer bowl. With the paddle attachment and mixer on low speed, toss in the cold butter a piece at a time. Once all the butter is blended, increase the speed briefly to ensure even consistency. Do not overbeat. The frosting should be just barely warm now. If it is not thick enough to spread, let it cool a few minutes. Use immediately.

COCONUT PECAN FROSTING

MAKES ENOUGH FROSTING FOR A TWO-LAYER 8- OR 9-INCH CAKE This is the traditional filling and topping for German chocolate cake, a chocolate layer cake made with German's brand (now Baker's) sweet chocolate. Any chocolate cake may be used, however. The original recipe does not call for the sides of the cake to be frosted.

1¹/₂ cups evaporated milk	6 cups	
1¹/₃ cups granulated sugar	2 lb 5.33 oz	**LARGE BATCH**
³/₄ cup unsalted butter	3 lb	
5 large egg yolks	11 oz	
2 cups sweetened flaked coconut	1 lb 8 oz	
1²/₃ cups chopped toasted pecans	1 lb 10.67 oz	

In a saucepan, whisk the milk, sugar, and butter together over medium-low heat until the butter is melted. Temper the eggs with the warm milk, then return to the pan. Bring to a simmer, stirring frequently, and cook until the mixture turns golden, 5 to 7 minutes. Transfer to a mixer bowl; beat with paddle attachment until cooled and spreadable. Stir in the coconut and pecans. Use immediately.

ROYAL ICING

MAKES ABOUT 6 CUPS Used for decorating cookies and piping designs on cakes, royal icing becomes hard and brittle when dry.

3 large pasteurized egg whites	13.8 oz	
1 lb box confectioners' sugar (about 4 cups)	4 lb	**LARGE BATCH**
Food coloring, if desired		

In a mixer bowl, whip all the ingredients together until stiff and glossy. Cover the surface with plastic wrap until ready to use or frosting will harden. For piping decorative patterns and borders, keep the frosting firm. Thin frosting with water for spreading over entire cookie or flooding within piped border. In warm, humid environments, the icing will dry with a dull, rather than shiny, finish.

CONFECTIONERS' SUGAR GLAZE

MAKES ABOUT ½ CUP Also known as **flat icing,** this glaze is drizzled over pastries, cinnamon rolls, hot cross buns, Bundt cakes, and cookies. It is a simple mixture of sifted confectioners' sugar and just enough liquid to make it thin enough to drizzle. Usually water, milk, or cream is used, but any flavorful liquid can be used, such as lemon, orange, or ginger juice or even rum or sherry. For cinnamon rolls, butter or cream cheese and heavy cream are used instead of water for added richness.

¼ cup confectioners' sugar
2 to 3 Tbs water or milk
½ tsp vanilla extract (optional)

In a bowl, gradually whisk the liquid into the confectioners' sugar until the glaze reaches the desired consistency. Adjust with additional liquid, if needed.

SEVEN-MINUTE FROSTING

MAKES 12 CUPS Also called **boiled icing,** this frosting has a texture somewhere between Italian meringue and marshmallow creme. It is an old-fashioned recipe used especially for layer cakes. It does not keep long but is prized as a light alternative to rich frostings. Seven-minute frosting got its name because it was beaten for seven minutes with a hand mixer over simmering water. Naturally, this is not practical for large production, and many bakeries use Italian meringue instead.

4 large egg whites	1 lb 2.4 oz	
2 cups granulated sugar	3 lb 8 oz	
$^2/_3$ cup water	$2^2/_3$ cups	**LARGE BATCH**
$^1/_4$ tsp salt	1 tsp	
$^1/_4$ tsp cream of tartar	1 tsp	
$1^1/_2$ tsp vanilla extract	2 Tbs	

Place all the ingredients except the vanilla in a bowl. Set the bowl over simmering water. Beat with an electric hand mixer for 5 to 7 minutes. Transfer the egg mixture to a mixer bowl. Whip until eggs have cooled to just warm. Beat in vanilla. The frosting should be fluffy, shiny, smooth, and spreadable. Use immediately.

CHAPTER 11

FILLINGS AND COMPONENTS

Component recipes are the building blocks common to almost every pastry kitchen. Occasionally, a component recipe may be an end product in itself, like a wine-poached pear; however, even the poached pear needs a little something extra—a sauce, be it fruit coulis, caramel, or chocolate—to work as a plated dessert. These recipes are generally versatile enough to be used in a variety of settings. For instance, frangipane can be used as the base for a fruit tart, or as a filling in Danish or a braided babka bread, or baked up as petit four cake. Having components on hand allows the pastry chef to be creative without having to make a different recipe for each new product. Keeping a par stock of components—never running out and never having to toss a batch—is one of the most difficult and most valuable skills a pastry chef can master.

EGG WASH

Brushing egg wash on top of bread and pastry dough gives the finished product color and shine. Pastry chefs usually keep egg wash on hand, but it will only keep for about three days in the refrigerator. Adding a small amount of water and salt keeps the egg smooth and easy to apply with a brush and prevents it from getting gummy in the refrigerator.

1 large egg
2 Tbs water
Pinch of salt (optional)

In a bowl, combine the egg, water, and salt, if using, and whisk together until fully combined.

NOTE For color but no shine, use only the yolk of the egg. For shine but no color, use only the white and 1 tablespoon of water instead of 2.

ALMOND FILLING FOR CROISSANTS

MAKES ABOUT 1¼ CUPS

		LARGE BATCH
1 scant cup (3 ounces) natural sliced almonds, toasted if desired	12 oz	
½ cup unsalted butter, melted	2 lb	
½ cup plus 1 Tbs granulated sugar	15.75 oz	
1 large egg yolk	2.2 oz	
½ tsp vanilla	2 tsp	

In a medium bowl, combine all the ingredients with your fingers until the almonds are crushed, or crush with the end of a rolling pin.

FRANGIPANE

MAKES 2½ CUPS This frangipane is semisoft under a crisp top when baked in a tart shell. For a firmer, more cakelike texture, add more flour and use whole eggs instead of yolks.

		LARGE BATCH
⅔ cup (6 ounces) almond paste	1 lb 8 oz	
6 Tbs unsalted butter	12 oz	
½ cup granulated sugar	14 oz	
2 large egg yolks	4.4 oz	
1 tsp vanilla extract	4 tsp	
⅓ cup all-purpose flour	5.67 oz	
¾ cup sliced natural almonds, toasted and crushed	9 oz	

Cream the almond paste with the butter and sugar until no lumps remain and the mixture is light and fluffy. Beat in the egg yolks and vanilla. Last, beat in the flour and almonds.

APPLESAUCE

MAKES 4 CUPS Making your own applesauce for French apple tart and turnovers is not only cost-effective, but tastes ten times better than anything you can buy. Use chopped fresh apples along with this flavorful sauce in turnovers and baked charlottes to make fillings that have a more solid, crunchy texture. The sauce keeps well in the refrigerator up to a week and can made in large batches and frozen for up to three months.

	LARGE BATCH
3 lb tart apples such as Granny Smith (8–10 apples), peeled, cored, and sliced	12 lb
1 cup sugar	1 lb 12 oz
$^1/_3$ cup water	$1^1/_3$ cups
$^1/_2$ vanilla bean, split and scraped	2 beans
$^1/_2$ cinnamon stick	2 sticks
$^1/_2$ lemon, seeded and quartered	2 lemons

Combine all the ingredients in a saucepan and bring to a boil. Reduce the heat to low and cook until the apples begin to disintegrate and the sauce thickens, about 40 minutes, stirring frequently. Remove the vanilla bean, cinnamon stick, and lemon pieces from the applesauce. Refrigerate for up to a week or freeze until ready to use.

FIG OR PRUNE FILLING

MAKES ABOUT 5 CUPS This filling can be used for prune Danish or fig bar cookies. The consistency can be controlled by adjusting the amount of liquid used in the recipe.

		LARGE BATCH
4 cups (about 1½ lb), packed dried figs or prunes	6 lb	
1 cup orange or cranberry juice	1 qt	
1 cup cognac, or bourbon, rum, or port	1 qt	
½ to 1 cup water	2 cups to 1 qt	
¾ cup granulated sugar	1 lb 5 oz	
Juice and zest of 1 lemon	4 lemons	
1 tsp orange zest	4 tsp	
1 cinnamon stick	4 sticks	
⅛ tsp ground cloves	½ tsp	

Simmer all ingredients in a covered saucepan until the liquid is absorbed, about 1 hour. Let the mixture cool slightly. Remove the cinnamon stick. Purée the mixture in batches, thinning with water if necessary. For Danish, the paste should be thick enough to hold its shape when baked as a filling, but thin enough to spread. It should be thicker for bar cookies.

CREAM CHEESE FILLING FOR DANISH

MAKES 1¹/₂ CUPS The filling will keep for two to three days in the refrigerator.

One 8-oz package cream cheese, softened	2 lb	
¹/₃ cup granulated sugar	9.33 oz	
2 Tbs all-purpose flour	2.125 oz	
1 large egg yolk	2.2 oz	**LARGE BATCH**
2 tsp brandy	2 Tbs plus 2 tsp	
1¹/₂ tsp lemon zest	2 Tbs	
¹/₂ tsp vanilla extract	2 tsp	
2 Tbs raisins or currants (optional)	3 oz	

With the paddle attachment, beat the cream cheese and sugar together until smooth and light; beat in the flour. Add the yolk, brandy, zest, and vanilla and beat until smooth.

KRINGLE FILLING

MAKES 1¹/₂ CUPS Kringles are long strips of Danish dough (often braided) filled with a brown sugar filling.

¹/₂ cup unsalted butter	1 lb	
1 cup packed brown sugar	2 lb	
1 tsp ground cinnamon	4 tsp	**LARGE BATCH**
¹/₂ tsp salt	2 tsp	
1 large egg white	4.6 oz	

Cream all ingredients until smooth.

APRICOT FILLING

MAKES 2³/₄ CUPS This component can be used to fill tarts and linzer cookies. The basic recipe is tart to complement sweet doughs; add water or corn syrup to thin to the consistency of apricot filling for use in mousse or bavarians. The filling may be frozen for several months.

3¹/₂ cups (1 lb) dried apricots, coarsely chopped	4 lb	
1 cup water	1 qt	**LARGE BATCH**
¹/₂ cup sugar	14 oz	
¹/₄ cup Cointreau	1 cup	
1 tsp vanilla extract (optional)	4 tsp	

Bring the apricots, water, and sugar to a boil. Reduce the heat and stir in the Cointreau. Simmer until the apricots are soft and begin to lose their shape. Turn off the heat; stir in the vanilla, if desired.

CANDIED CITRUS PEEL, ZEST, AND FRUIT SLICES

Most chefs make candied orange or lemon zest or slices for garnish, but candying the entire peel (pith and all) creates fabulous-tasting candied fruit for stollen, panettone, and fruitcake. Blanching the peel or zest removes the wax coating and any dirt.

To candy the zest, first the fruit must be carefully peeled with a vegetable peeler so that only the skin (and no pith) is removed. The zest is then sliced into the desired shape, blanched in boiling water for 1 minute, drained, and then boiled in sugar syrup until tender. For sugared peel, toss the drained zest in granulated sugar.

To candy thin slices of orange or lemon, follow the directions for candying zest, above. To candy citrus fruit for fruitcake, quarter the fruit and push it inside out to pull the skin away, pith and all. Boil the peel in water for 30 seconds. Drain and repeat two times. Last, boil the peel in sugar syrup until tender and translucent. Drain, cool, and chop as desired.

FRUIT COULIS

Fruit coulis can be used as a dessert sauce and as a flavor component for bavarians, chiffon pies, and soufflés. Fruit coulis can be made by cooking fruit with sugar to taste until the fruit softens and the liquid becomes syrupy. If the fruit does not release juice, add water. Coulis is then puréed and strained to ensure smoothness.

A simple, uncooked coulis can be made from puréed fresh fruit, individually quick-frozen fruit, and even sweetened frozen fruit, though it is best to control the sugar content yourself. Keep in mind that only canned pineapple and mango have been pasteurized, and therefore will not break down gelatin in bavarians and mousse. For uncooked coulis, use corn syrup to sweeten the fruit to avoid grainyness. Coulis may be frozen for six months.

SOUR CHERRY FILLING

MAKES 2²/₃ CUPS This filling is used for black forest cakes. Ideally, fresh or frozen sour cherries are best, but they are less available than canned sour cherries. If you have fresh or frozen, use water to replace the cherry-flavored juice in the can. Do not use regular cherries—they are too sweet. Canned sour cherries in water are dull red, and a drop or two of red food coloring may be necessary to make them more visually appealing. Black forest cake usually calls for kirschwasser, a brandy made from cherries, but cherry heering has an intense flavor that boosts the flavor of the cherries. The filling will keep for several days refrigerated.

		LARGE BATCH
One 24-oz can sour cherries in water	6 lb	
2 Tbs cornstarch	2.67 oz	
¹/₄ cup granulated sugar or corn syrup	7 oz or 1 cup	
2 to 3 Tbs cherry liqueur, such as cherry heering	¹/₂ to ³/₄ cup	

Drain the cherries, reserving the juice. You should have 2 cups cherries and 1¹/₂ cups juice. Whisk ¹/₄ cup of the juice with the cornstarch. Place the remaining juice in a saucepan with the cherries over medium-high heat. Stir in the cornstarch mixture and sugar. Bring the mixture to a boil, stirring constantly; cook until thickened. Stir in cherry heering.

RED WINE POACHED PEARS

MAKES 8 PEARS The liquid can be reduced to make a dessert sauce. Nectarines, peaches, or plums can also be poached, but pears are more popular. Pears will keep for up to two weeks. The poaching liquid may be used repeatedly.

		LARGE BATCH
1.5-liter bottle (about 6^1/$_2$ cups) dry red wine, such as cabernet or burgundy	4 bottles	
4 cups water	4 qt	
3 cups granulated sugar	5 lb 4 oz	
^{1}/$_2$ vanilla bean, split and scraped	2 beans	
1 lemon, quartered	4 lemons	
1 to 1^1/$_2$ cinnamon sticks	4 to 6 sticks	
1 star anise (optional)	4 star anise	
8 pears, peeled and cored	32 pears	

Bring all the ingredients except pears to a boil in a pot large enough to allow pears to stand upright in relatively close proximity while completely being submerged in liquid. Reduce heat to medium; simmer until pears just yield to gentle pressure. Remove pears with slotted spoon and cool on sheet pan to prevent overcooking; cover with plastic and refrigerate. Cool cooking liquid completely. Store poached pears in cooled cooking liquid in refrigerator until use.

WHITE WINE POACHED PEARS

MAKES 6 PEARS

8$^1\!/_2$ cups water	8$^1\!/_2$ qt	
1 cup dry white wine	1 qt	
$^1\!/_2$ cup tawny port	2 cups	
2 cups sugar	3 lb 8 oz	
$^1\!/_2$ vanilla bean, split and scraped	2 beans	
1 lemon, quartered	4 lemons	
1 cinnamon stick	4 sticks	
2 allspice berries or 2 whole cloves	8 berries or cloves	
6 pears, peeled and cored	24 pears	

LARGE BATCH

Follow the same directions as for the red wine poaching liquid.

Streusel Toppings

Streusels are used to top pies, crumb cakes, and muffins, and even serve as the foundation for filled bar cookies. Below are several streusel recipes. With the exception of the Cheddar cheese version, they may be frozen for six months.

ALMOND-OAT STREUSEL

MAKES ABOUT 8 CUPS, ENOUGH FOR ONE 9 BY 13-INCH PAN OF BAR COOKIES
This streusel is used as the foundation for fruit streusel bar cookies and also as
the topping for fruit crisps.

		LARGE BATCH
2 cups all-purpose flour	2 lb 2 oz	
2 cups old-fashioned rolled oats	1 lb 12 oz	
2 cups chopped toasted almonds	2 lb 8 oz	
2 cups packed light brown sugar	4 lb	
1 tsp salt	4 tsp	
1¼ cups unsalted butter, melted	2 lb 8 oz	

In a large bowl, whisk the flour, oats, almonds, brown sugar, and salt together
until well combined. Stir in the melted butter and mix well with your hands. The
streusel mix should be crumbly but form clumps when squeezed.

OAT STREUSEL

MAKES ABOUT 2 CUPS, ENOUGH FOR ONE 8- OR 9-INCH PIE This streusel is
used to top fruit pies or crisps.

		LARGE BATCH
1 cup all-purpose flour	1 lb 1 oz	
½ cup old-fashioned rolled oats	7 oz	
½ cup packed light brown sugar	1 lb	
⅛ tsp salt	½ tsp	
½ cup unsalted butter, melted	1 lb	

In a medium bowl whisk the flour, oats, brown sugar, and salt together until well
combined. Stir in the melted butter and mix well with your hands. The streusel
mix should be crumbly but form clumps when squeezed.

BROWN SUGAR STREUSEL

MAKES JUST OVER 1 CUP, ENOUGH FOR ONE 9 BY 13-INCH CRUMB CAKE This
streusel is used to top crumb and coffee cakes.

		LARGE BATCH
²/₃ cup all-purpose flour	11.33 oz	
¹/₂ cup packed light brown sugar	1 lb	
¹/₂ tsp ground cinnamon	2 tsp	
¹/₈ tsp salt	¹/₂ tsp	
¹/₄ cup unsalted butter, melted	8 oz	

In a small bowl, whisk the flour, brown sugar, cinnamon, and salt together until
well combined. Stir in the melted butter and mix well with your hands. The
streusel mix should be crumbly but form clumps when squeezed.

WHITE ALMOND STREUSEL

MAKES ABOUT 4¹/₂ CUPS, ENOUGH FOR TWO 9-INCH PIES White streusel is
preferred for crumb cake in some regions, but this white streusel is especially
for plum pie. For a plain white streusel, substitute granulated sugar for the
brown in the recipe above.

		LARGE BATCH
2 cups all-purpose flour	2 lb 2 oz	
1 cup chopped toasted almonds	1 lb 4 oz	
1¹/₂ cups granulated sugar	2 lb 10 oz	
Grated zest of 1 lemon (about 1 Tbs)	¹/₄ cup	
¹/₄ tsp ground allspice	1 tsp	
¹/₄ tsp ground cardamom	1 tsp	
¹/₄ tsp salt	1 tsp	
³/₄ cup unsalted butter, melted	1 lb 8 oz	

In a medium bowl, whisk the flour, almonds, sugar, lemon zest, spices, and salt together until well combined. Stir in the melted butter and mix well with your hands. The streusel mix should be crumbly but form clumps when squeezed.

CHEDDAR CHEESE STREUSEL

MAKES ABOUT 2¹/₂ CUPS, ENOUGH FOR ONE 9-INCH PIE Cheddar cheese streusel is used for tart apple pies and crisps.

		LARGE BATCH
1 cup all-purpose flour	1 lb 1 oz	
1 cup shredded sharp Cheddar cheese	1 lb	
¹/₂ cup granulated sugar	14 oz	
¹/₈ tsp salt	¹/₂ tsp	
¹/₄ cup unsalted butter, melted	8 oz	

In a medium bowl, whisk the flour, cheese, sugar, and salt together until well combined. Stir in the melted butter and mix well with your hands. The streusel mix should be crumbly but form clumps when squeezed.

STABILIZED WHIPPED CREAM

Whipped cream to be held at room temperature for any amount of time requires a small amount of added gelatin for support, about ¹/₂ teaspoon per cup of heavy cream. The gelatin is melted in a small amount of cream, then cooled to room temperature. After the remaining cold cream is whipped until slightly thickened, the gelatin mixture is added.

Whipped cream used as a topping on pies may gradually weep. To prevent the water from leaking out, cornstarch may be used to stabilize the cream. One-half to 1 teaspoon of cornstarch is cooked with any sugar and part of the cream until thickened. Once cooled to room temperature, the thickened cream can be beat into cold whipped cream.

MARZIPAN

MAKES ABOUT 4 CUPS Marzipan can be rolled thin to cover cakes or sculpted into various shapes and used to decorate cakes. Food coloring can be kneaded into marzipan for creating realistic-looking decorations.

One 8-oz can almond paste	2 lb
4 cups (1 lb) confectioners' sugar, plus 1 cup for kneading	4 lb
5 to 6 Tbs corn syrup	$1^1/_4$ to $1^1/_2$ cups

Using the paddle attachment of the mixer, beat the almond paste with 4 cups confectioners' sugar and the corn syrup until smooth (it is easier to add the confectioners' sugar gradually). On a clean surface, knead the marzipan with about 1 cup confectioners' sugar until it is smooth and malleable when rolled thin, and no longer sticky.

CHAPTER 12

ASSEMBLING AND
DECORATING CAKES

The caliber of a pastry chef is often based on the appearance of his or her products and techniques for assembling and decorating cakes could easily fill several volumes. This chapter will introduce you to the basics. Customers equate beautifully decorated cakes with quality, so it pays to develop your artistic side. Using a Styrofoam round, found in craft and floral shops, and a batch of mock buttercream (page 257) is the perfect way to practice decorative piping without wasting actual cake or frosting. A good decorator can disguise any number of superficial flaws in baked goods—a dented cake layer may taste great but need a little help in the appearance department—and good decorating skills give the cakes in your case flair and individuality.

USING CARDBOARD ROUNDS AND ROTATING CAKE STANDS

For ease of assembling, use a cardboard cake round that is slightly smaller in diameter than the cake itself. This makes holding the cake easy while frosting it. Once the cake has been filled, crumb-coated, and frosted, place it on a rotating cake stand to pipe designs more easily. When finished, ideally the cake is transferred to a larger, doiley-lined cardboard round that extends about $^3/_4$ inch beyond the cake. If you are in a hurry, however, you can always just place the smaller cake board directly onto the larger one.

TRIMMING AND SPLITTING LAYERS

Cake layers are typically leveled off with a long, serrated knife before the cake is assembled. Though homebaked layer cakes typically have a domed top, professional bakeries opt for a more polished, classic look.

Splitting a layer horizontally into two perfectly symmetrical halves is not easy; even seasoned chefs may not make perfect slices. Bruce Healy and Paul Bugat, authors of *The Art of the Cake*, have a clever solution. Before splitting the layer, they mark the outside edge, vertically or perpendicular to the top of the cake, with a knife in one spot. Once the layer is split and filled, it is easy to align the top layer of the cake by matching up the marks.

If you are using genoise or biscuit layers, they may be brushed with flavored syrup after being split.

FILLING THE LAYERS

American layer cakes are often filled and frosted with the same component, like cream cheese frosting for carrot cake. Assembling this type of cake is fast, unless the frosting becomes too warm from being in a hot kitchen. If the room is too hot, the frosting may become so soft that the filling oozes out from between the layers just as you are spreading the frosting over the top and sides of the cake. Refrigerating the cake a few times while frosting it will help keep the frosting firm.

When the filling in a cake differs from the frosting, assembling the cake is done in stages. Pastry-cream-filled Boston cream pie or cherry-filled black forest cake, for example, require more care to prevent the filling from leaking out the sides or bleeding into the frosting. The easiest way to solve both problems is to pipe a ring of buttercream around the outside edge of each cake layer and refrigerate it. Once the buttercream is chilled, it will be firm enough to hold the filling.

CRUMB COATING AND FROSTING A CAKE

Cakes and tortes are frosted in two stages. The first step, called the crumb coat, consists of a thin coating of buttercream or frosting, which seals in the crumbs and makes a smooth surface for the final application of frosting, glaze, or rolled marzipan or fondant. In this step, use the buttercream to correct the shape and lines of the cake, so that the side is perfectly parallel to the top and the top is level. Begin with the sides, coating the top last. Before continuing with the frosting, refrigerate the cake briefly.

If the crumb-coated cake is very cold, it should sit at room temperature until it is merely cool. This will prevent the frosting from setting up too quickly as the cake is frosted. The buttercream or other frosting should be applied as quickly as possible to prevent tearing the cake by overworking the frosting and to prevent the frosting from becoming warm enough to slide down the cake. European-style cakes are frosted to have smooth sides, which is a skill that must be aquired through practice with a long metal offset spatula or bench scraper. American-style layer cakes have swirled frosting. For making beautiful swirls, an ice tea spoon is the best tool.

GLAZING A TORTE

Many tortes and small cakes are glazed with ganache rather than frosted. Crumb-coat the torte or cake first, with either a complementary buttercream or a thick spreadable ganache. For successful glazing, the torte should be cool but not cold, and the glaze should be warm but not overly hot. If the glaze is too hot or the cake too warm, the crumb coat will melt when the glaze hits it. If the torte or glaze is too cold, the glaze will thicken and set up before the whole torte is covered. Pour the warm ganache from a measuring cup with a pouring spout directly over the center of the torte. Once the glaze reaches the sides, begin pouring around the edge of the cake to ensure the sides are coated. For glazing, set the torte on a wire rack set over a sheet pan to catch the ganache. The ganache can be scraped up, melted, and used again so long as it doesn't have crumbs in it.

Decorative patterns may be piped over the cake in a contrasting glaze, such as melted fondant or white chocolate ganache, using a parchment cone. This must be done while the initial glaze is still soft. (See Figure 12.1.)

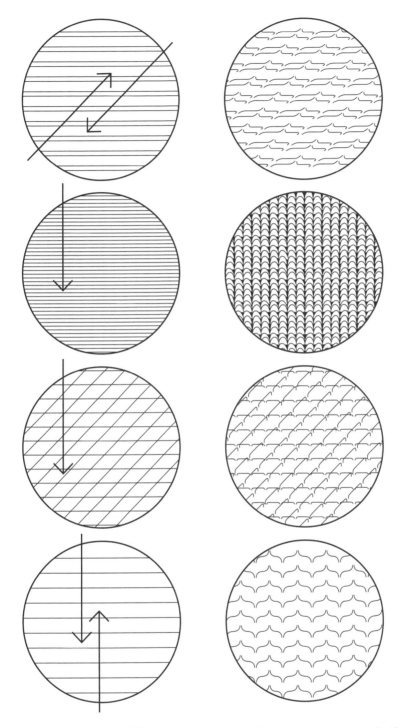

FIGURE 12.1 Creating different patterns (at right) by drawing a skewer or knife through the glaze in the directions indicated (at left).

Garnishing and Decorating a Cake

Attaching Chopped Nuts or Crumbs to a Cake

Chopped nuts, toasted coconut, chocolate shavings, coarsely ground praline, or even cake crumbs make a nice garnish when pressed around the side of a cake or sprinkled on top. For the best sticking power, this should be done before the frosting or glaze sets. Hold the cake over a sheet pan to catch the excess.

Making Parchment Cones

Parchment cones are essential for piping lines of contrasting glaze, frosting, or fondant over pastries, and they are used for writing on cakes. When decorating cookies with royal icing, parchment cones are the easiest tools for piping designs. They are easy to make, and unlike pastry bags, they do not leak out the bottom until the tip is snipped with the scissors. (See Figure 12.2, page 284.)

Cake Combs

Cake combs are square or triangular pieces of plastic or metal with toothed edges. Often each side has a different pattern. Cake combs are dragged around the side of the frosted cake to create decorative lines. These lines also hide any imperfections in the frosting.

Pastry Tips

There are several different pastry tips that are used frequently to decorate cakes. Each is available in different sizes.

- Star tip: This tip is used for simple rosettes, shell borders, reverse-shell borders, fleurs-de-lys, and rope borders. (See Figure 12.3, page 285.)

- Leaf tip: Leaves and ruffles may be piped with this tip. (See Figure 12.4, page 285.)

- Rose tip: In conjuction with a flower nail, roses are made by first piping a cone-shape core onto the nail. Then, with the narrow end of the tip facing up, petals are piped around the central core. Buttercream flowers can be made ahead and refrigerated. (See Figure 12.5, page 286.)

- Basketweave tip: This tip is used for ribbons and for creating a basketweave pattern around a cake. (See Figure 12.6, page 287.)

- Plain tip: Also called a writing tip, this tip is perfect for drawn designs and detail work, such as lace borders. (See Figure 12.7, page 288.)

WEDDING CAKE SUPPORT

Though plastic separaters can be purchased, wooden dowels (and a small saw for trimming them) are the only items necessary for stacking layers of cardboard-supported cake. The dowels are usually $3/8$-inch thick. The nicest but most challenging method for stacking the tiers is to insert the dowels (the number of dowels for adequate support depends on the size of the layer above it) into each layer and trim them so they stick out $1/8$-inch above the surface of the frosting. This means that each tier *appears* to be stacked on the next, but the frosting is not marred. Any imperfection in measuring or sawing compromises the structure, however. More often, bakers trim the dowels flush with the surface of the frosting. This is structurally sound but messes up the buttercream below each cake layer.

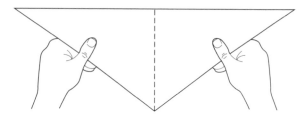

Cut a square of parchment diagonally to create 2 triangles.
Hold one triangle in front of you, long side up.

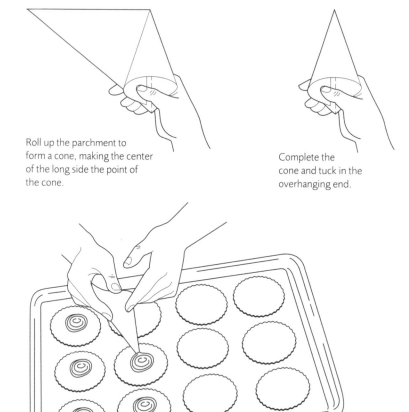

Roll up the parchment to
form a cone, making the center
of the long side the point of
the cone.

Complete the
cone and tuck in the
overhanging end.

Fill the cone with frosting, ganache, or melted chocolate; twist and fold
the end over to close the cone. Apply pressure with your thumb to
pipe, using the other hand to steady the cone.

FIGURE 12.2 **Making decorating cones from parchment paper.**

FIGURE 12.3 Rosettes and shell patterns made using small and large star tips.

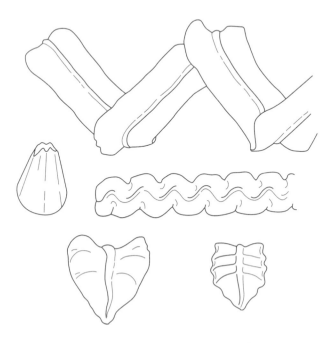

FIGURE 12.4 Leaves and ruffles made using a leaf tip.

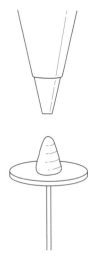

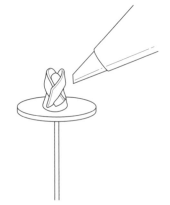

Pipe a cone-shaped mound of frosting onto the flower nail.

With the narrow end of the petal tube facing up, make a ribbon of icing that runs halfway around the cone. Repeat on the other side.

For the next layer, create three petals that wrap around the first layer.

For the final layer, make four to five petals. Be sure to overlap the petals and stagger them slightly.

Flowers made using a petal tip.

FIGURE 12.5 **Making buttercream roses with the petal tip.**

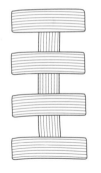

Pipe a vertical line down surface or side of a cake. Pipe horizontal lines across the vertical line, as if you are crossing *T*s, leaving a space (one piped line wide) between the lines.

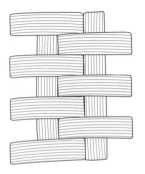

Pipe a vertical line to the right of the first line, joining the ends of the horizontal lines. There should be a small gap between the vertical lines. Pipe horizontal lines across this second vertical line, fitting them between the first set of horizontal lines.

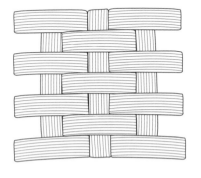

Continue in this fashion until the entire surface or side of the cake is covered.

FIGURE 12.6 **Making a basketweave pattern.**

FIGURE 12.7 Designs that can be made using a plain tip, the tip used to write and create intricate drawings and patterns on cakes and cookies.

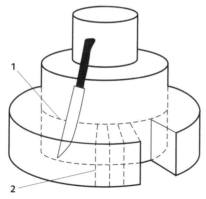

Cut vertically through the bottom layer at the edge of the second layer, as indicated by dotted line 1; then cut out wedge-shaped pieces as shown by dotted line 2.

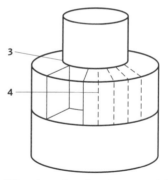

When these pieces have been served, follow the same procedure with the middle layer; cut vertically through the second layer at the edge of the top layer, as indicated by dotted line 3; then cut out wedge-shaped pieces as shown by dotted line 4.

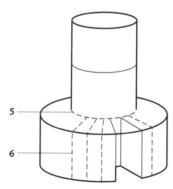

When pieces from the second layer have been served, return to the bottom layer and cut along dotted line 5; cut another row of wedge-shaped pieces, as shown by dotted line 6.

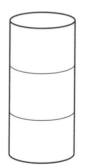

The remaining tiers may be cut into the desired size pieces.

FIGURE 12.8 **Slicing a cake with multiple tiers.**

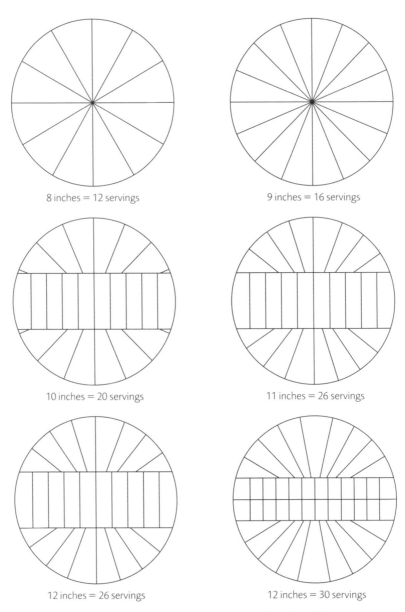

8 inches = 12 servings

9 inches = 16 servings

10 inches = 20 servings

11 inches = 26 servings

12 inches = 26 servings

12 inches = 30 servings

FIGURE 12.9 **Slicing round layer cakes.** Three-layer cakes should be cut as shown, but reduce the size of each serving by approximately one-third in order to increase the number of servings.

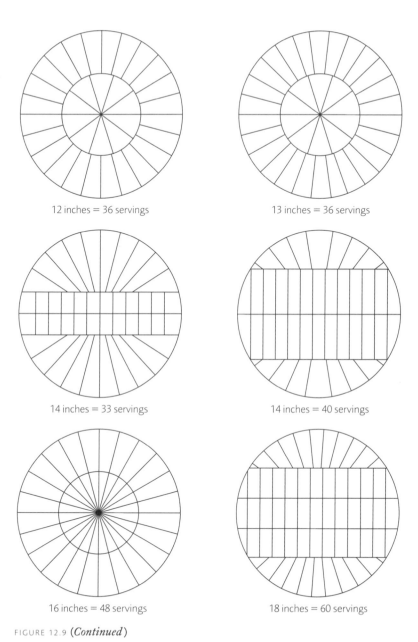

12 inches = 36 servings

13 inches = 36 servings

14 inches = 33 servings

14 inches = 40 servings

16 inches = 48 servings

18 inches = 60 servings

FIGURE 12.9 (***Continued***)

DESSERT GLOSSARY

1-2-3-4 CAKE: A classic American layer cake made with 1 cup butter, 2 cups sugar, 3 cups flour, and 4 large eggs. Its recipe also includes 1 cup milk, vanilla, baking powder, and salt.

AMBROSIA: A fruit salad associated with the American South, consisting of orange segments, shredded coconut, bananas, and marshmallows. Some recipes include whipped cream and maraschino cherries.

BABA AU RUM: Buttery, slightly sweet yeasted bread much like brioche, usually made with raisins or currants, baked in a small cylindrical mold and soaked with rum simple syrup.

BAKED ALASKA: Ice cream–topped sponge cake covered with piped or spread meringue and lightly browned.

BAKLAVA: Greek dessert composed of layers of phyllo dough brushed with butter and sprinkled with chopped nuts (walnuts or pistachios) and spices. After baking, the pastry is drizzled with honey-lemon syrup.

BANANA SPLIT: American ice cream dessert consisting of a banana split lengthwise and topped with scoops of ice cream; hot fudge, caramel, or butterscotch sauce; and whipped cream. Chopped nuts and maraschino cherries are typical garnishes. Without the banana, the concoction is merely an ice cream sundae.

BANANAS FOSTER: A dessert of bananas sautéed in butter and brown sugar, flambéed with rum, and topped with vanilla ice cream.

BAVAROIS: French for Bavarian cream.

BEAR CLAW: Filled Danish dough rectangles that are sliced almost halfway through down one long side before baking and then curved to imitate the shape of a bear claw. After baking, they are commonly drizzled with confectioners' sugar glaze.

BEIGNET: French for fritter. Beignets are usually deep-fried rounds of choux paste (flavored and sweetened), but they can be made from batters or yeast-doughs.

BELLE HÉLÈNE: A classic French dessert of chilled poached pear served with vanilla ice cream and warm chocolate sauce. Also called poire Hélène.

BETTY: An old-fashioned American dessert of fruit slices, such as apple, pear, or pineapple, sweetened and spiced, layered alternately with buttered bread crumbs, and baked. Bettys are served warm.

BIALY: Not as chewy or dense as bagels, bialys are yeasted rolls that have a depression, not a hole, in the center.

BLACK AND WHITE COOKIES: Associated with New York delis, these large, slightly soft sugar cookies are iced with plain fondant on one half and chocolate fondant on the other.

BLANCMANGE: A molded pudding made from sweetened milk and blanched, pulverized almonds, thickened with cornstarch and chilled. The dessert is unmolded just before serving.

BLINI: Buckwheat pancakes leavened with yeast.

BOMBE GLACÉ: Any frozen dessert that is made with pâte à bombe and poured into a mold to set. A bombe glacé usually has an outer layer of ice cream or sorbet, and the flavored bombe mixture is in the center. The unmolded bombe is decorated and served with a sauce. **Pâte à bombe** is made by pouring hot sugar syrup into beaten egg yolks, much like making Italian meringue. After the pâte à bombe is cooled, whipped cream is folded into it.

BUCKLE: A buckle is made by layering fresh fruit (blueberries are popular) between layers of plain muffin or cake batter. Streusel crumb toppings are common. After baking, the buckle is cooled and sliced into squares or wedges.

CANNOLI: An Italian dessert made from dough wrapped around metal tubes (cannoli molds or tubes) and deep-fried. The cooled cannoli shells are filled with ricotta, whipped cream, and grated chocolate or candied fruit.

CASSATA: An Italian dessert traditionally served at Easter consisting of layers of rum-brushed sponge cake and marzipan filled with a fluffy sweetened ricotta cheese mixture flavored with chocolate and orange. Cassata can also be translated as "case"; then the dessert consists of cake slices arranged on the bottom and sides of a mold that is then filled with custard, ice cream, or another of a wide variety of fillings. The mold is usually topped with a final slice of cake, chilled, and then unmolded.

CHERRIES JUBILEE: Pitted cherries flambéed with kirsch and sugar, then served over vanilla ice cream.

CHESS PIE: An open-faced pie with a baked filling made with eggs, butter, sugar, and flour; chess pies may be any flavor, such as chocolate and vanilla. They are popular in the American South.

CHIBOUST CREAM: Chiboust cream is made by combining warm pastry cream with beaten egg whites. Gelatin is usually added to bolster the light mixture, which can be piped. Chiboust cream is the traditional filling for gâteau Saint-Honoré.

CHOCOLATE MARQUISE: Firmer than a mousse, chocolate marquise is usually rich and silky with butter. It is commonly chilled in a mold and may be coated with a chocolate glaze.

CLAFOUTI: A simple French dessert consisting of an eggy batter poured over fruit (usually cherries) and baked. The texture may be firm or custard-like.

CLOTTED CREAM: Also known as Devon cream, since it is made in that region of England, clotted cream accompanies fresh fruit, desserts, and warm scones. It is made by allowing milk to stand for up to 24 hours, letting the cream rise to the top. The entire mixture is gently heated, then cooled, and the resulting cream is almost 60 percent fat. Today, the process is hastened in factories. Clotted cream has a slightly cooked taste, and it is thick enough to dollop onto food.

CLOVERLEAF ROLL: Dinner roll baked in a muffin tin (made with three or four balls of dough, one on the bottom, three on top) to resemble a three-leafed clover.

COMPOTE: A dessert of fresh or dried fruit cooked in a flavored poaching syrup, usually served with some of the syrup.

CRÈME CARAMEL: The French version of flan, crème caramel is a custard baked in a caramel-lined ramekin or dish. Like all baked custards, crème caramel is baked in a water bath. It is cooled after baking and unmolded before serving.

CRÈME CHANTILLY: Sweetened whipped cream.

CRUMBLE: The English version of a fruit crisp, fresh fruit topped with a crumbly oat-shortbread pastry and baked.

CRUMPET: A yeasted roll cooked on a griddle in a ring mold, similar to an English muffin except that it is not split and toasted before being eaten. Crumpets are cooked nearly through on one side, flipped, and just barely browned on the other side. The top side, to be spread with jam, is pale and full of tiny holes.

DERBY PIE: Derby Pie is a trademarked name. The pie is similar to pecan pie, but it is made with walnuts and chocolate chips. Variations include Kentucky bourbon pie (which is not trademarked), basically pecan pie with added bourbon and, sometimes, chocolate chips.

DEVON CREAM: See Clotted cream.

DIPLOMAT PUDDING: A cold dessert made of layers of liquor-soaked ladyfingers alternating with custard or Bavarian cream and dried fruit. The dessert is unmolded just before serving, and accompanied with a fruit sauce or crème anglaise. Some versions use brioche instead of ladyfingers and are made like bread pudding.

EGGNOG: This rich, cold Christmas beverage is like a nutmeg-scented crème anglaise. Eggnog traditionally contains hefty amounts of whisky, rum, or brandy. Old recipes call for whipping the eggs to create a frothier drink.

ENGLISH MUFFIN: A yeasted roll cooked on a griddle, usually in a ring mold. English muffins are filled with airholes that serve as pockets for catching butter after the muffins are split and toasted.

FINANCIER: A moist French sponge cake made rich with ground almonds and delicate with beaten egg whites. The cake may be served on its own or used to make petit fours.

FLAN: See Crème caramel.

FLOATING ISLAND: A dessert of sweetened, whipped egg whites poached in milk and served over crème Anglaise; it may be any flavor, such as vanilla, chocolate, pistachio, caramel, or espresso.

FLUMMERY: A modern flummery is a cornstarch or gelatin-thickened fruit pudding. Older flummeries were sweet porridges of any flavor, usually thickened with oats.

FOOL: A dessert of mashed fruit, whether raw, cooked, or sweetened, partially folded into whipped cream. Tart berries are most frequently used.

FRIED PIES: Miniature pies, deep-fried rather than baked. Discs of flaky pie dough are filled with fruit filling, folded in half, crimped, and fried. Once cool, they may be dusted with confectioners' sugar or drizzled with confectioners' sugar glaze.

FRITTER: Food, such as chopped apples, mixed with a batter and deep-fried. Fritters have a cake-like texture.

GALETTE: A rustic pie or tart, usually baked free-form.

GIANDUJA: A thick, very smooth mixture of ground toasted nuts, sugar, and chocolate, eaten on its own as a treat or used to flavor other desserts.

GRASSHOPPER PIE: Flavored with crème de menthe and crème de cacao, this creamy chiffon pie is made in a crumb crust. Some versions are merely mint-flavored and lack the liqueurs, as the name is now associated with mint rather than the drink for which the pie was named.

GRUNT: See Slump.

HAMANTASCHEN: These cookies, served during Purim, the Jewish holiday, are composed of rounds of sweet dough folded into a triangular shape and filled with poppy seed, prune, or apricot filling. They are named after the biblical figure Haman, whose plot to exterminate the Jews was thwarted.

HONEY CAKE: A traditional cake made for Rosh Hashanah, the Jewish New Year. It can be round or loaf-shaped and may contain apples. Both honey and apples represent good luck for the next year.

INDIAN PUDDING: Pudding made with cornmeal and molasses.

JOCONDE: A biscuit (sponge cake) named after the Mona Lisa, La Joconda in French. It contains ground almonds. Its unique method calls for beating whole eggs and egg whites separately and then folding them together. In addition to being used as the base for gateaux, joconde may be sliced and used to line charlotte molds.

JALOUSIE: Strips of puff pastry filled with marzipan or fruit preserves. The top strip is "latticed," so that the finished pastry resembles a Venetian blind. (*Jalousie* is French for Venetian blind.)

KAISER ROLL: Topped with poppy seeds, this light yeasted roll is split to hold a hamburger or other sandwich filling. Some chefs use stamps to give the rolls their characteristic pinwheel pattern on top, others simply incise lines from the top center like spokes on a wheel. The most traditional method, however, uses a specific knotting technique to create the pattern.

KOLACHY: An Eastern European sweet bun, leavened with yeast or baking powder, that is stuffed with fruit or a poppy seed filling.

KUCHEN: Fruit- or cheese-filled cake, much like a coffee cake. Old recipes were yeasted, but most modern ones call for baking powder.

KUGELHOPF: A rich, buttery, slightly sweet yeasted bread, much like brioche, baked in a tall round fluted tube pan that has been buttered and dusted with sliced almonds. Kugelhopf may be lemon-flavored. It is sprinkled with confectioners' sugar after cooling.

LADY BALTIMORE CAKE: White layer cake, usually three layers high, filled with chopped nuts and dried fruit, usually raisins and figs. The cake is iced with seven-minute (boiled) frosting, some of which is mixed with the filling to help bind it together.

LANE CAKE: Yellow or white layer cake filled with chopped nuts, coconut, and dried fruit. The cake is iced with seven-minute (boiled) frosting, some of which is mixed with the filling to help bind it together.

LEBKUCHEN: A centuries-old cake-like cookie flavored with honey and spices. It is popular at Christmas, and keeps well. Confectioners' sugar icing and candied fruit or nuts are used to garnish lebkuchen.

LORD BALTIMORE CAKE: Yellow layer cake, usually three layers high, filled with chopped nuts, crushed coconut macaroons, and maraschino cherries. The cake is iced with seven-minute (boiled) frosting, some of which is mixed with the filling to help bind it together.

MARJOLAINE: A rectangular cake composed of nut meringue layers (called dacquoise) filled and frosted with buttercream. Marjolaines can have more than one flavor of buttercream and are usually glazed with ganache.

MAYONNAISE CAKE: This recipe calls for mayonnaise in place of fat and eggs and produces an exceptionally moist cake. Mayonnaise cakes are almost always chocolate, though there are recipes for carrot and other flavors.

MELBA SAUCE: Dessert sauce made from pureed raspberries (strained to remove seeds), red currant jelly, sugar, and cornstarch, if needed.

MEXICAN WEDDING CAKES: Crescent- or ball-shaped cookies made with butter, confectioners' sugar, ground toasted nuts, and flour. The cookies are very tender and crumbly, and they are usually dusted with confectioners' sugar.

MONT BLANC: A dessert of mounded sweetened chestnut puree topped with whipped cream.

NESSELRODE: Named for Count Nesselrode, the word refers to any chestnut custard–based dessert (pastry, pie, pudding, or bombe) that includes candied fruits and dried raisins or currants. Cherry liqueur is a common ingredient.

OEUFS À LA NEIGE: See Floating island.

PANDOWDY: A cooked fruit dessert similar to a cobbler, but with a pastry top that is rolled thin and covers the fruit entirely. During baking, the top crust is sliced into squares and pressed gently into the bubbling juices.

PARKER HOUSE ROLL: Named for the hotel in which it was created, this yeasted roll gets its characteristic off-center crease from folding a round of soft, rich dough almost in half before baking.

PARFAIT: An ice cream or custard dessert served in a tall glass with a foot (known as a parfait glass). Whipped cream and flavored sauces intersperse the layers of ice cream or custard and are used to garnish the top of the parfait.

PARIS-BREST: A ring of choux paste baked, split in half, and filled with praline mousseline cream (buttercream lightened with Italian meringue). It is garnished with confectioners' sugar and toasted sliced almonds.

PEACH MELBA: This dessert, named for an opera star, consists of poached peach halves served over vanilla ice cream with raspberry sauce. See also Melba sauce.

PEANUT BRITTLE: Similar to praline, but usually a lighter caramel, peanut brittle is sugar syrup cooked to the hard crack stage, with peanuts. Often baking soda and cream of tartar are included in the recipe (the baking soda is added at the very end); this makes the mixture foam with carbon dioxide bubbles, creating a flaky texture in the cooled candy.

PFEFFERNUESSE: Literally "pepper nuts" in English, these German Christmas cookies are fragrant with spices, including black pepper. Pfeffernuesse are made well ahead of the holidays to allow the flavors to meld.

PITHIVIERS: Classic French treat of frangipane-filled puff pastry, usually baked as large or small rounds. The tops of pithiviers are incised with the tip of a knife before baking to create beautiful, intricate designs.

POIRE HÉLÈNE: See Belle Hélène.

POPOVER: Made from a thin batter rich in eggs, popovers are baked in special pans that resemble deep muffin tins. The batter puffs and "pops over" the edges of the pan during baking.

PULLMAN LOAVES: Sandwich bread, named for the long straight-sided loaf pans with covers used for making it.

RICE IMPÉRATRICE: This molded cold dessert starts with rice cooked in milk. The rice is folded into a gelatin-stabilized custard (a Bavarian) to which whipped cream has been added. Candied fruits, such as cherries, are the usual flavorings.

RUSSIAN TEA CAKES: See Mexican wedding cakes.

SABAYON: French word for zabaglione.

SABLÉS: French butter cookies with a sandy texture (*sablé* means "sandy").

SAINT-HONORÉ: Named for the patron saint of bakers, this dessert begins with a pâte brisée crust, onto which creampuffs are piped and then baked. The puffs are sliced open and filled with chiboust cream.

SALLY LUNN: Lighter than even brioche, Sally Lunn is a sweet yeast bread hailing from England that comes close to resembling sponge cake.

SAVARIN: A rich sweetened yeasted cake, much like brioche, baked in a ring mold, brushed with rum syrup, and filled with whipped or pastry cream.

SCRIPTURE CAKE: A spice cake whose ingredients (except for modern-day baking powder) can be found in different verses of the Old Testament.

SEMIFREDDO: Italian for "half-frozen," this term refers to any frozen dessert composed of cake, custard, and whipped cream, in any combination.

SHAKER LEMON PIE: This frugal pie uses whole lemons, rind and all. Lemon slices are combined with sugar for 24 hours before the pie is baked, which changes their texture. Eggs are used in the pie to create a custard-like texture.

SHERBET: A sweet, frozen dessert similar to sorbet except that it may contain milk.

SHOO-FLY PIE: Pennsylvania Dutch pie with a sweet, buttery molasses custard filling.

SLUMP: In this stove-top version of fruit cobbler, cooked in a covered saucepan or skillet, the dough is steamed and thus resembles dumplings more than biscuits. Also called a grunt.

SORBET: A frozen dessert, a sweet sorbet can be any flavor, but it never contains milk. Sorbets are usually smoother than ices.

SNICKERDOODLES: Nutmeg- or cinnamon-scented sugar cookies with a cracked or bumpy top. Usually the cookies are sprinkled or rolled in cinnamon sugar before being baked.

STEAMED PUDDING: Steamed puddings are cooked in decorative molds, set on a rack over simmering water in a large, covered stockpot. They must be firmly set, or they will not hold their decorative shape when unmolded. They are usually served with a sauce. Plum pudding is the most well known steamed pudding.

STRUDEL: The dough for strudels is rolled and stretched paper-thin, much like phyllo. Sweetened and spiced fruit, such as apples, is used to fill the dough, which is then rolled up into a long tube and baked.

SUMMER PUDDING: A refreshing dessert of sweetened summer berries that are briefly cooked on the stove top and then layered with bread slices in a mold. The pudding is weighted and refrigerated until cold and set, then unmolded. Summer pudding is served with whipped cream.

SWEDISH LIMPA RYE: A moist rye bread flavored with a combination of anise seed, fennel seed, cumin seed, and orange zest.

SWISS ROLL: The English version of a jelly roll, a sponge cake spread with jam and rolled up, then sliced into spirals. In the United States, the term "Swiss roll" is also used to describe a chocolate sponge cake rolled with a cream filling.

SYLLABUB: A frothy English dessert sauce made by whipping sweetened and spiced wine with milk or cream. Egg whites are sometimes used to make a lighter, more stable foam.

TRIFLE: A rich dessert of English origin made by layering sherry-drizzled sponge cake, custard, fruit, and whipped cream in a straight-sided decorative glass dish.

UPSIDE-DOWN CAKE: Also called skillet cake, this dessert begins with melting butter and brown sugar in a pan and spreading sliced fruit over it; the fruit is usually pineapple, plum, peach, or apricot. Cake batter is spread over the fruit and the pan is transferred to the oven. After baking, the cake is cooled slightly and then inverted to reveal the shiny, caramelized fruit.

APPENDIX

METRIC CONVERSIONS AND OTHER HELPFUL INFORMATION

FRACTIONS AND THEIR DECIMAL EQUIVALENTS

$1/25 = .04$	$1/8 = .125$	$1/2 = .5$	$4/5 = .8$
$1/20 = .05$	$1/6 = .167$	$3/5 = .6$	$5/6 = .833$
$1/16 = .063$	$1/5 = .2$	$5/8 = .625$	$7/8 = .875$
$1/12 = .083$	$1/4 = .25$	$2/3 = .667$	
$1/10 = .1$	$1/3 = .333$	$3/4 = .75$	

DECIMAL EQUIVALENTS FOR OUNCES

1 ounce = .0625	5 ounces = .3125	9 ounces = .5625	13 ounces = .8125
2 ounces = .125	6 ounces = .375	10 ounces = .625	14 ounces = .875
3 ounces = .1875	7 ounces = .4375	11 ounces = .6875	15 ounces = .9375
4 ounces = .25	8 ounces = .5	12 ounces = .75	1 pound = 1.0

FAHRENHEIT TO CELSIUS

32°F = 0°C	110°F = 43°C	210°F = 99°C	290°F = 143°C
40°F = 4°C	120°F = 49°C	212°F = 100°C	300°F = 149°C
50°F = 10°C	130°F = 54°C	220°F = 104°C	325°F = 163°C
60°F = 16°C	140°F = 60°C	230°F = 110°C	350°F = 177°C
70°F = 21°C	150°F = 65°C	235°F = 113°C	375°F = 190°C
80°F = 26°C	160°F = 71°C	240°F = 115°C	400°F = 205°C
85°F = 29°C	170°F = 77°C	250°F = 121°C	425°F = 220°C
90°F = 32°C	180°F = 82°C	260°F = 127°C	450°F = 233°C
95°F = 34°C	190°F = 88°C	270°F = 132°C	475°F = 246°C
100°F = 38°C	200°F = 94°C	280°F = 138°C	500°F = 260°C

USEFUL METRIC CONVERSIONS

- Ounces to grams: multiply by 28.35
- Pounds to kilograms: multiply by .454
- Fluid ounces to milliliters: multiply by 29.57
- Quarts to liters: multiply by .946

Note: To convert from metric, simply divide by the same number.

WEIGHT-VOLUME EQUIVALENTS FOR COMMON INGREDIENTS	
Food	Volume Conversion
Grains/Crumbs	Ounces in 1 cup
All-purpose flour	4.25
Cake flour	4
Bread flour (organic)	4.75 (4.6)
Whole wheat flour	4.5
Rye flour	4
Pumpernickel flour	4
High-gluten flour	4.75
Fine cornmeal	5
Coarse cornmeal	6
Rolled oats	3.5
Bran cereal	2.25
Bran flakes	2
Wheat germ	4
Graham cracker crumbs	4
Chocolate cookie crumbs	4

Note: The dry ingredients were measured by the spoon-and-sweep method, meaning that the flour was lightly spooned into the measuring cup and swept with the edge of a knife to level. Other chefs prefer dipping the measuring cup directly into the bin of flour, which yields a higher weight by compacting the flour into the cup. Liquid measures were used for liquids, dry measuring cups for the dry ingredients.

WEIGHT-VOLUME EQUIVALENTS FOR COMMON INGREDIENTS (Continued)

Food	Volume Conversion
Starches	**Ounces/Volume**
Cornstarch	1 oz = 3 Tbs
Tapioca	.5 oz (.43) = 1 Tbs
Potato starch	.37 oz = 1 Tbs
Gelatin	.25 oz = 2^1/$_4$ tsp
Sugars/Syrups	**Ounces in 1 cup**
Granulated	7
Confectioners'	4
Dark/light brown	8
Superfine	7.33
Dark corn syrup	12
Light corn syrup	12
Molasses	11
Honey	12
Dark honey	12
Malt syrup	12
Maple syrup	12
Leavenings/Salt	**Ounces/Volume**
Cream of tartar	.33 oz = 1 Tbs
Baking powder	.50 oz (.45) = 1 Tbs
Baking soda	.50 oz (.57) = 1 Tbs

WEIGHT-VOLUME EQUIVALENTS FOR COMMON INGREDIENTS (Continued)	
Food	Volume Conversion
Leavenings/Salt	Ounces/Volume
Fresh yeast	.66 oz = 2 Tbs crumbled
Active dry yeast	.11 oz = 1 tsp
Instant active dry yeast	.11 oz = 1 tsp
Gold Saf Yeast, osmotolerant	.11 oz = 1 tsp
Diastatic malt powder	.3 oz = 1 Tbs
Salt (granular/kosher)	.50 oz = 1 Tbs; .33 oz = 1 Tbs
Chocolate	Ounces in 1 cup
Chocolate chips (regular)	6
Chocolate chips (mini)	6
Cocoa powder (Dutch-processed)	3.75
Nuts	Ounces in 1 cup
Natural whole almond	5
Natural sliced almonds	3
Blanched slivered almonds	4.5
Walnut pieces	4
Pecan pieces	3.75
Pecan halves	4
Hazelnuts, whole, unblanched	4.75
Macadamia nuts	4.75
Peanuts	4.75

WEIGHT-VOLUME EQUIVALENTS FOR COMMON INGREDIENTS (Continued)	
Food	**Volume Conversion**
Nuts	**Ounces in 1 cup**
Almond paste	9.5
Peanut butter	8
Sweetened flake coconut	3
Unsweetened coconut	2.75
Flavorings	**Equivalents**
Vanilla extract	.5 oz = 1 Tbs
Vanilla beans	4 beans = 1 oz
Espresso powder	4 oz = 1 cup/25 oz = 1 Tbs
Malted milk powder	4 oz = 1 cup
Spices	**Equivalents**
Poppy seeds	.65 oz = 1 Tbs
Ground spices	.25 oz = 1 Tbs
Dried Fruit	**Ounces in 1 cup**
Chopped candied fruit	5.5
Figs and prunes	6
Dried apricots	4.5
Raisins	6
Tart cherries	5
Jams/Glazes	**Ounces in 1 cup**
Apricot jam	12
Gelstar apricot glaze	12

Food	Volume Conversion
Jams/Glazes	Ounces in 1 cup
Raspberry preserves	12
Fruit coulis	9
Dairy	Ounces in 1 cup
Milk	8.5
Half-and-half	8.5
Heavy cream	8.5
Sour cream	8.5
Baker's dry milk powder	4.75
Eggs	**Equivalents**
Fresh-large	1 egg (no shell) = 1.70 oz 5 eggs (1 cup + 2 Tbs) = 8.75 oz
Frozen yolks, sugared	1 yolk = .55 oz
Frozen whites, pasteurized	1 white = 1.15 oz
Meringue powder	.25 oz = 1 Tbs
Canned Goods	Ounces in 1 cup
Pineapple, crushed	8
Pumpkin	8.57
Cream of coconut	10
Coconut milk	8.5
Evaporated milk	9
Sweetened condensed milk	11
Fats/Oils	Ounces in 1 cup
Vegetable shortening	5.75
Vegetable oil	8
Butter	8

This chart of baking pan volumes will help you find pan substitutions when you want to bake a recipe in a different pan than called for in the recipe. All the pans are metal, not Pyrex. Remember that baking a cake batter in a radically different shaped pan may require recipe adjustments. Pans are measured inside edge to inside edge. If the sides of the pan are at an angle, the measurement is averaged.

$3^1/_2$ by $5^3/_4$ by 2-inch mini-loaf pan	2 cups
$8^1/_2$ by $4^1/_2$ by $2^1/_2$-inch loaf pan	6 cups
9 by 5 by 3-inch loaf pan	8 cups
8 by $1^1/_4$-inch pie plate	Scant 4 cups
9 by $1^1/_4$-inch pie plate	5 cups
6 by 2-inch round cake pan	Generous 4 cups
8 by $1^1/_2$-inch round cake pan	5 cups
9 by $1^1/_2$-inch round cake pan	6 cups
8 by 2-inch round cake pan	Scant 7 cups
9 by $1^3/_4$-inch round cake pan	8 cups
9 by 2-inch round cake pan	Scant 9 cups

VOLUME OF BAKING PANS (Continued)	
8 by 3-inch round cake pan	10 cups
10 by 2-inch round cake pan	11 cups
8 by 8 by 2-inch square pan	8 cups
8¾ by 1¾-inch square pan	10 cups
13 by 9 by 2-inch rectangle	16 cups
10½ by 15½ by 1-inch jelly roll	10 cups
8¾ by 12 by 1-inch quarter sheet pan	8 cups
12 by 17 by 1-inch half sheet pan	14 cups
17 by 25 by 1-inch (full) sheet pan	Generous 28 cups
8 by 3-inch (small) Bundt pan	6 cups
10 by 3½-inch Bundt pan	12 cups
6½ by 3½-inch kugelhopf	5 cups
8½ by 4-inch kugelhopf	10 cups
9½ by 4⅛-inch tube pan (10 by 4-inch)	16 cups

HIGH-ALTITUDE BAKING

As altitude increases, atmospheric pressure decreases. With less atmospheric pressure, it takes less energy to convert water to steam—water evaporates more readily. This is exemplified by the change of temperature at which water boils, which becomes steadily lower as the altitude increases. At sea level, water boils at 212°F, but at 10,000 feet, it boils at 194°F. Naturally, the temperature chart for candymaking and cooking sugar syrups will be off slightly.

Stove-top adjustments are more straightforward than changes for baked goods. The following is a list of possible recipe adjustments for high-altitude pastry work. They are not hard-and-fast rules. Generally, each recipe may need to be tested as written for sea level to assess the extent of changes necessary.

BUTTER AND SHORTENING-BASED CAKES AND QUICKBREADS

- Reduce leavening slightly because gas bubbles rise more easily and pop with less atmospheric pressure. The danger is that a cake may fall because it will rise faster than it can set.

- Reduce fat and sugar slightly, which lowers the temperature at which the cake will set. (Remember, sugar competes with starch for moisture, and it raises the temperature of starch gelatinization.) Decreasing the baking time prevents the cake from drying out before it is set. *Or* increase flour (the protein structure from gluten) to set the batter faster.

- Increase oven temperature by 25°F to promote faster setting of cake structure, which will help trap bubbles and retain moisture.

- Increase eggs to provide more structure. Eggs, especially the yolks, provide additional moisture for longer shelf life. Dryness is associated with high-altitude air, which shortens the shelf life of baked goods.

- Grease pans well and turn out cooled cakes promptly, as baked goods have a greater tendency to stick at higher altitudes.

SPONGE CAKES

- Decrease sugar slightly to allow faster coagulation of eggs. This will prevent moisture loss.

- Increase oven temperature by 25°F. Cooking the cake faster lets the structure set before the cake becomes dry.

YEASTED BREADS

- Decrease amount of yeast, since less gas is needed to raise the dough.

- Be careful of overproofing. Since gas bubbles will rise and expand more readily, proof time may shorten.

- Flour is likely to be dryer at high altitudes, so more liquid may be needed to achieve the same moisture as the same dough at sea level.

- Reduce sugar in sweet doughs to promote faster gelatinization of starch.

- Choose a flour with a higher protein content to create a stronger gluten network that will set faster and trap the rapidly expanding air bubbles.

- Increase oven temperature by 25°F to promote faster setting of bread, which will help trap bubbles and retain moisture.

BIBLIOGRAPHY

Albright, Barbara, and Leslie Weiner. *Simply Scones*. New York: St. Martin's, 1994.

Alburey, Pat. *The Book of Cookies*. Los Angeles, CA: HP Books, 1988.

Alford, Jeffery, and Naomi Duguid. *Flatbreads & Flavors*. New York: William Morrow, 1995.

Alston, Elizabeth. *Muffins: Sixty Sweet and Savory Recipes From Old Favorites to New*. New York: Clarkson Potter, 1985.

American Egg Board. *Egg Handling & Care Guide*, 2nd ed. Park Ridge, IL: American Egg Board, 2000.

Anderson, Jean. *The American Century Cookbook: The Most Popular Recipes of the 20th Century*. New York: Clarkson Potter, 1997.

Bagget, Nancy. *The All-American Cookie Book*. New York: Houghton Mifflin, 2001.

———. *The International Cookie Book*. New York: Stewart, Tabori & Chang, 1988.

Bau, Frederic. *Au Couer Des Saveurs*. Spain: Montagud Editores, 1998.

Beard, James. *James Beard's American Cookery*. Boston: Little, Brown, 1972.

Benning, Lee Edwards. *Oh, fudge! A Celebration of America's Favorite Candy*. New York: Henry Holt, 1990.

Beranbaum, Rose Levy. *The Pie and Pastry Bible*. New York: Scribners, 1998.

———. *The Cake Bible*. New York: William Morrow, 1988.

Beranbuam, Rose Levy, trans., and Maurice and Jean-Jacques Bernachon. *A Passion for Chocolate*. New York: William Morrow, 1989.

Bilheux, Roland, and Alain Escoffier. *Doughs, Batters and Meringues*. From the French Professional Pastry Series. New York: Van Nostrand Reinhold, 1988.

———. *Creams, Confections and Finished Desserts*. From the French Professional Pastry Series. New York: Van Nostrand Reinhold, 1988.

Boyle, Tish. *Diner Desserts*. San Francisco: Chronicle Books, 2000.

Boyle, Tish, and Timothy Moriarty. *Chocolate Passion: Recipes and Inspiration from the Kitchens of Chocoaltier Magazine*. New York: John Wiley, 2000.

Braker, Flo. *The Simple Art of Perfect Baking*. New York: William Morrow, 1985.

Clayton, Bernard, Jr. *The Complete Book of Pastry, Sweet and Savory*. New York: Simon and Schuster, 1981.

Corriher, Shirley O. *Cookwise: The How's and Why's of Successful Cooking*. New York: William Morrow, 1997.

Cunningham, Marion. *The Fannie Farmer Baking Book.* Avenel, NJ: Wings Books, 1996.

David, Elizabeth. *English Bread and Yeast Cookery.* Newton, MA: Biscuit Books, 1994.

Davidson, Alan. *The Oxford Companion to Food.* Oxford University Press, 1999.

Dodge, Jim, and Elaine Ratner. *The American Baker.* New York: Simon & Schuster, 1987.

Field, Carol. *The Italian Baker.* New York: HarperCollins, 1985.

Fobel, Jim. *Jim Fobel's Old-Fashioned Baking Book: Recipes from an American Childhood.* New York: Lake Isle Press, 1987.

Fortin, Francois, and Les Editions Quebec/Amerique Inc. *The Visual Food Encyclopedia.* New York: Macmillan, 1996.

Friberg, Bo. *The Professional Pastry Chef*, 3rd ed. New York: Van Nostrand Reinhold, 1996.

Fryatt, Evelyn Howe. *Candymaking for Beginners.* New York: Sterling, 1996.

General Mills. *Betty Crocker's Best of Baking.* New York: Macmillan, 1997.

Gisslen, Wayne. *Professional Baking,* 2nd ed. New York: John Wiley, 1994.

Glezer, Maggie. *Artisan Baking Across America.* New York: Artisan, 2000.

Gonzalez, Elaine. *The Art of Chocolate.* San Francisco: Chronicle Books, 1998.

Good Housekeeping. *Good Housekeeping Baking.* New York: Hearst Communications, 1999.

Greenspan, Dorie. *Baking with Julia: Based on the PBS series hosted by Julia Child.* New York: William Morrow, 1996.

———. *Desserts by Pierre Herme.* New York: Little, Brown, 1998.

Healy, Bruce, and Paul Bugat. *Mastering the Art of French Pastry.* Woodbury, NY: Barron's Educational Series, 1984.

———. *The French Cookie Book.* New York: William Morrow, 1999.

———. *The Art of the Cake: Modern French Baking and Decorating.* New York: William Morrow, 1994.

Heatter, Maida. *Maida Heatter's Cakes.* New York: Cader Books, 1997.

———. *Maida Heatter's Cookies.* New York: Cader Books, 1997.

———. *Maida Heatter's Pies & Tarts.* New York: Cader Books, 1997.

Herbst, Sharon Tyler. *The New Food Lover's Companion: Comprehensive Definitions of over 4000 Food, Wine and Culinary Terms*, 2nd ed. New York: Barron's Educational Series, 1995.

Hyman, Philip and Mary. *LeNotre's Desserts and Pastries*. New York: Barron's Educational Series, 1977.

Jacob, H. E. *Six Thousand Years of Bread*. New York: Lyons & Burford, 1997.

Kamman, Madeleine. *The New Making of a Cook*. New York: William Morrow, 1997.

Kimball, Christopher. *The Cook's Bible: The Best of American Home Cooking*. Little, Brown, 1996.

Kiple, Kenneth, and Kriemhild Conee Ornelas, eds. *The Cambridge World History of Food*. UK: Cambridge University Press, 2000.

Lang, Jenifer Harvey, ed. *Larousse Gastronomique: The New American Edition of the World's Greatest Culinary Encyclopedia*. New York: Crown, 1988.

London, Sheryl and Mel. *Fresh Fruit Desserts, Classic and Contemporary*. New York: Prentice-Hall, 1990.

Luchetti, Emily. *Stars Desserts*. New York: Harper Perennial, 1993.

———. *Four Star Desserts*. New York: HarperCollins, 1996.

Malgieri, Nick. *How to Bake*. New York: HarperCollins, 1995.

McGee, Harold. *On Food and Cooking: The Science and Lore of the Kitchen*. New York: Scribner's, 1984.

McNair, James. *James McNair's Cakes*. San Francisco: Chronicle Books, 1999.

Medrich, Alice. *Alice Medrich's Cookies and Brownies*. New York: Warner Books, 1999.

———. *Cocolat: Extraordinary Chocolate Desserts*. New York: Warner Books, 1990.

Moore, Marylin M. *The Wooden Spoon Bread Book*. New York: Atlantic Monthly Press, 1987.

Nathan, Joan. *The Jewish Holiday Baker*. New York: Schocken Books, 1997.

Parker, Dorian Leigh. *Doughnuts: Over 3 Dozen Crullers, Fritters and Other Treats*. New York: Clarkson Potter, 1994.

Pepin, Jacques. *Sweet Simplicity: Jacques Pepin's Fruit Desserts*. San Francisco: Bay Books, 1999.

Pillsbury Company. *The Complete Book of Baking*. New York: Viking Penguin, 1993.

Pyler, E. J. *Baking Science & Technology*, 2 vols., 3rd ed. Kansas City, MO: Sosland Publishing, 1988.

Regan, Mardee Haidin, ed. *Food & Wine Great Desserts*. New York: Stewart, Tabori & Chang, 1989.

Reinhart, Peter. *Crust and Crumb: Master Formulas for Serious Bread Bakers.* Berkeley, CA: Ten Speed Press, 1998.

Rombauer, Irma S., Marion Rombauer Becker, and Ethan Becker. *Joy of Cooking Christmas Cookies.* New York: Scribner, 1996.

——. *The All New Joy of Cooking.* New York: Scribners, 1997.

Rombauer, Irma S., and Marion Rombauer Becker. *Joy of Cooking.* New York: Plume, 1973.

Rosenberg, Judy. *Rosie's Bakery All-Butter Fresh Cream Sugar-Packed No-Holds-Barred Baking Book.* New York: Workman, 1991.

——. *Rosie's Bakery Chocolate-Packed Jam Filled Butter-Rich No-Holds-Barred Cookie Book.* New York: Workman, 1996.

Sands, Brinna B. *The King Arthur Flour 200th Anniversary Cookbook.* Woodstock, VT: Countryman Press, 1991.

Sax, Richard. *Classic Home Desserts: A Treasury of Heirloom and Contemporary Recipes from Around the World.* Shelburne, VT: Chapters Publishing, 1994.

Sherber, Amy, and Toy Kim Dupree. *Amy's Bread.* New York: William Morrow, 1996.

Silverton, Nancy. *Desserts by Nancy Silverton.* New York: Harper & Row, 1986.

Sizer, Frances, and Eleanor Whitney. *Nutrition: Concepts and Controversies,* 8th ed. Belmont, CA: Wadsworth Thomson Learning, 2000.

Steingarten, Jeffery. *The Man Who Ate Everything And Other Gastronomic Feats, Disputes, and Pleasurable Pursuits.* New York: Alfred A. Knopf, 1997.

Time-Life Books. *Cakes.* From The Good Cook/Techniques & Recipes Series. Alexandria, VA: Time-Life Books, 1981.

——. *Cookies & Crackers.* From The Good Cook/Techniques & Recipes Series. Alexandria, VA: Time-Life Books, 1982.

Teubner, Christian. *The Chocolate Bible.* New York: Penguin Studio, 1997.

Walter, Carol. *Great Cakes.* New York: Clarkson Potter, 1998.

——. *Great Pies and Tarts.* New York: Clarkson Potter, 1998.

Wells, Patricia, and Joel Robuchon. *Simply French: Patricia Wells Presents the Cuisine of Joel Robuchon.* New York: Hearst Books, 1991.

Wing, Daniel, and Alan Scott. *The Bread Builders: Hearth Loaves and Masonry Ovens.* White River Junction, VT: Chelsea Green, 1998.

Wilson, Dede. *Bake It to the Limit.* New York: William Morrow, 1999.

INDEX

ABOUT THE AUTHOR

To the surprise and dismay of her family, Nicole was born with a persistent sweet tooth. By the age of nine she was using her mother's copy of *Joy of Cooking* as the foundation for creating strange new dishes, usually cakes and cookies. Driven by the desire to understand the hows and whys behind cooking, and various hunger cravings, she took this hobby to a legitimate profession when she began catering and recipe development. Nicole has served as associate food editor, test kitchen director, and writer/contributor for several magazines, among them *Woman's World*, *Chocolatier*, and *Pastry Art & Design*. She is a member of IACP and contributes her spare time to anti-hunger efforts such as Share our Strength. Recently, she moved from New Jersey to Portland, Oregon, where she continues to bake every day.